THE
EVERYTHING

MICR
W   00

All you   orld's
most pop   letters,
gr   re

Adams Media Corporation
Holbrook, Massachusetts

An Everything Series Book.
"Everything" is a trademark of Adams Media Corporation.

Published by Adams Media Corporation
260 Center Street, Holbrook, MA 02343. U.S.A.

ISBN: 1-58062-306-9

Printed in the United States of America.

J I H G F E D C B

Library of Congress Cataloging-in-Publication Data
Walters, John K. (John Kevin)
The everything Microsoft Word 2000 book / John K. Waters
p.   cm.
ISBN 1-58062-306-9
I. Microsoft Word. 2. Word processing. I. Title
Z52.5.M52 W38 2000
652.5'5369—dc21   99-088054

This publication is designed to provide accurate and authoritative information with regard to the subject matter covered. It is sold with the understanding that the publisher is not engaged in rendering legal, accounting, or other professional advice. If legal advice or other expert assistance is required, the services of a competent professional person should be sought.
- From a *Declaration of Principles* jointly adopted by a Committee of the American Bar Association and a Committee of Publishers and Associations

Microsoft® Word 2000 is a trademark of the Microsoft Corporation. Neither Adams Media Corporation nor the author is associated with Microsoft or with any product or company mentioned in the book. The Microsoft Corporation does not endorse or sponsor this book.

Many of the designations used by manufacturers and sellers to distinguish their products are claimed as trademarks. Where those designations appear in this book and Adams Media Corporation was aware of a trademark claim, the designations have been printed in capital letters.

Book design by Barb Karg.
Illustrations by Barry Littmann.

This book is available at quantity discounts for bulk purchases.
For information, call 1-800-872-5627.

Visit our home page at http://www.adamsmedia.com

Contents

Acknowledgments

All writers work alone, staring at that blank screen, their fingers poised over keyboards, tiny beads of panic sweat anointing their stricken faces. But darned few manage to turn the resulting moist prose into a publishable book without an awful lot of help.

To say that I had a lot of help with this book would be the understatement of the new millennium. Many people worked long and hard to keep me from looking like an idiot in these pages, and I would like to extend my heartfelt thanks to one and all:

To the folks at Adams Media Corporation for their decision to publish the book, and for their support and patience throughout the process of creating it.

To the book's chief tech editor, Colleen Sell, whose experienced eye and ruthless dedication to making sure that my directions led readers where I said they would will keep a lot of people out of the woods.

To designer Barb Karg, who slogged her way through all my tips and sidebars to produce a visually welcoming book that readers can actually use.

To production mavens Chris Ciaschini and Susan Beale who brought the book's visual elements together.

To Catherine Morris, production editor, for her seemingly endless patience.

To managing editor Linda Spencer and the Adams copy editing pros who kept me from dangling my participles in public.

And special thanks to senior editor Paula Munier Lee for keeping me on track and (almost) on time, and for her support and encouragement over more than a decade of collaboration and friendship.

1

Word Up!
Introduction

Welcome to Word World!

Welcome to the twenty-first century, where advanced computer technology has transformed word processing into a simple and painless task, where editing and formatting is a snap, printing is trouble free, and the creation of sophisticated, graphics-rich documents is shear child's play.

Yeah, right.

Without a doubt, desktop computers have changed forever the way we create, edit, manage, and interact with documents. With the advent of the World Wide Web and collaborative workflow features, software developers are changing the very definition of "document." The things we can do today with letters, memos, reports, flyers, manuscripts, greeting cards, and newsletters is nothing short of amazing.

But simple? Trouble-free? Hardly!

Even established, enormously popular programs like Microsoft® Word can be both empowering and intimidating. Word is the best-selling word processing program on the planet. It's not exactly ubiquitous, but if you use a word processor at work or at home, chances are you're using Word. Even those who don't use it probably find themselves dealing with Word documents on a fairly regular basis. Word has been around for years, millions use it, and it's a genuinely terrific program—and it can be a real pain in the hard drive! I've been using the program myself for most of my professional life—I'm writing this manuscript with it right now—and sometimes it even vexes me. Let's face it: Word is bulky and complicated, and the latest version is positively groaning with new features and enhanced functions.

Which is probably why you picked up this book.

In The *Everything Microsoft® Word 2000 Book*, you'll find well . . . everything you need to know to tame this powerful program. New users will find everything they need to get up and running quickly; veteran Word warriors will find everything they need to refine and enhance their skills.

The truth is, you don't need to know *everything* about Microsoft® Word 2000 to use the program, or even to get a lot out of it. But since I couldn't know which of Word's many features and functions you do need, I've done my best to include them all in this book.

How to Use This Book

The *Everything Microsoft® Word 2000 Book* is organized with an eye toward easy information access and quick answers to common questions about the functions and features of Word 2000. If you're a Word neophyte, you should probably start with "The Basics." But if you've already mastered the fundamentals of the program, you can use this book in a number of ways:

- **Use the Table of Contents to find subject headings that interests you.**
- **Use the Index to pinpoint specific actions or functions.**
- **Thumb through the book, picking up tips and tricks at random.**

In other words, this isn't a step-by-step sort of book. The information is here, laid out in what I hope is a logical order, but succeeding chapters don't depend on preceding chapters. Feel free to access the information contained herein any way you like and in whatever order fits your personal learning style.

Once you've gained sufficient mastery of the program to suit your needs, keep this book on a shelf near your computer for easy reference. Grab it when you forget a keyboard shortcut, or when your needs change and you suddenly find yourself building a Web page or starting up a mail merge.

Conventions

I've employed certain conventions in this book to explain and describe the various Word tasks. I've tried to keep the explanations simple and bite-sized, and I've loaded the book with screenshots, bulleted lists, tips, and sidebars. For every task, there's a step-by-step "walk through" that shows you exactly what you need to do and what should happen when you do it. For example, here's how I describe the procedure for turning off Word 2000's intuitive menus:

- **Go to the Menu Bar.**
- **Open View.**
- **Select Toolbars.**
- **Click on Customize to open the Customize dialog box.**
- **Click on the Options tab.**
- **Click in the "Menus show recently used commands first" check box to unselect it.**

- **Click on the Close button.**
- **You will now see complete menus the instant you open them.**

Here's what all that means:

Go to the Menu Bar. . . .

Obviously, you can't "go" to the Menu Bar. But rather than write, "Position your mouse pointer over the menu bar," or "Turn your attention to the Menu Bar," or something equally clunky, I just say "go."

Open View. . . .

By the time you start reading these explanations, I will have described several different ways to open a menu from the Menu Bar. Rather than write, "Click on the View heading," or "Hit the Alt key," I just say *open*, and leave it to you to decide how you want to get it done.

Select Toolbars. . . .

"Select" basically means "highlight." Again, there are at least a couple of ways to select a menu listing. Once I've explained it, I leave the selection method to you.

Click on Customize . . .

As you will learn shortly, some of Word 2000's menu listings have little arrows next to them that lead to other menus (called submenus). In this action, you select the Toolbars command in the main View menu, then open the submenu and select the Customize command.

to open the Customize dialog box. . . .

Most of the time I like to describe where you should end up after you select a menu command. Most of the time, you end up at a dialog box. The dialog box in this example is entitled "Customize."

Click on the Options tab. . . .

"Click" means hit the left button on your mouse. "Click on" means position your mouse pointer over the thing (in this case, the Options tab) and then click. "Double-click" means hit the left mouse button twice in rapid succession; "right-click" means hit the right mouse button once.

Click in the "Menus show . . .

"Click on" is for positive space (a tab, a button), "click in" is for negative space, in this case, a checkbox.

the "Menus show recently used commands first" check box . . .

I've thrown quotation marks around checkbox and textbox labels, just for clarity.

to unselect it. . . .

As English, this ain't so good, but it is succinct, and it's a common convention in computer books. In this example, clicking in the checkbox removes the checkmark and turns off the feature. I use "unselect" to describe all this (which should make sense to most readers) instead of "deselect" (which looks like the name of a fungus powder).

Click on the Close button. . . .

Put your mouse pointer over the button and yadda-yadda-yadda . . . I know, you *get* it.

You will now see complete menus the instant you open them.

Where it's appropriate, I've tried to add a concluding line to let you know what things should have been changed by your actions—basically, what should happen or be happening now.

Plain English

For the most part, this book is written in plain English, and I've used as few acronyms as I could manage. But some tech talk was unavoidable; the Geekspeak-to-English dictionary at the back of the book provides translations.

Still, some of the plain English I use to describe commands could use some clarifying:

- **Enter: I've really tried not to use it, but here and there, I couldn't help it. When you "enter" something, you just type it in.**

- **Hit: Refers to something you do to a keyboard key. I could have said "press," I suppose, but hit is shorter, and to tell you the truth, it more accurately describes the way I type.**

- **Hover: Means to position your mouse pointer over something—a button usually—without clicking.**

- **Command: Refers to a menu listing. In this example, "Toolbars" and "Customize" are commands.**

Keystroke Commands

I'm big on keyboard shortcuts, and I've included them wherever possible. Here's how I spell them out in this book:

- **I've capitalized the letter keys in the keystroke combinations described (for example, Ctrl + N), because that's the way they appear on your keyboard. You don't have to use caps when executing the keystroke combo.**

- **All combinations of keystrokes are written with + signs between the various keys. For example: Ctrl + N.**

- **When the Ctrl key is the first in a two-keystroke combination, you must hold it down while you're hitting the second key.**

- **When Ctrl and Shift are used together (for example, Ctrl + Shift + A), hit Ctrl, hold it down while you hit Shift, and then hold them both down as you hit the third button.**

- **Key combinations utilizing the Alt key are executed a little differently: You don't have to hold down any of the keys. The command Alt + F + C, for example, goes like this:**
  - **Hit the Alt key, which activates the Menu Bar.**
  - **Hit the F key, which pulls down the menu.**
  - **Hit the C key to select the Close command.**

Using an F-key command (one that includes a key from the very top row of your keyboard) works the same way. For example, one of the Save shortcuts goes like this:

- **Hit the F12 key, which opens the Save As dialog box.**
- **Hit the Enter key.**

I want to encourage keyboard mastery, but sometimes it's more of a pain than it's worth. Sometimes it's just easier to click your way through a task. In those instances—say you'd have to use the Tab and Arrow keys to navigate a complicated dialog box—I leave determined keyboarders to find their own way. In fact, you'll probably end up using a combination of both, say, hitting the Alt + F + N keys to get to the Bullets and Numbering dialog box, and then clicking on two buttons to select and apply the bullets you want. So, do what works for you.

Good luck!

2

All This Thing Needs Is Fins
What's New In Word 2000

In This Chapter
- 🖱 Faster Installation
- 🖱 Intuitive Menus and Toolbars
- 🖱 Beefier Spellcheck and Thesaurus, and Smarter Grammar Checkers
- 🖱 Improved Clip Art Gallery
- 🖱 Flexible Tables and Cool Tools
- 🖱 Web Stuff

Microsoft® Word 2000 is a collection of powerful editing and publishing tools that together constitute what is probably the most feature-rich word processing program available today. This thing is loaded with hundreds of ways to create, modify, enhance, store, and publish documents. In this version, Microsoft has refined and enhanced many of the program's existing features and added a bunch of brand new ones, all of which make it more powerful, and in many cases easier to use.

Faster Installation

Word 2000's new installation features get users up and running faster than ever before. Intelligent Install checks which programs you have currently installed on your machine (primarily other Office 2000 programs), and determines the best installation profile for your computer. The Install On Demand features keep the program's footprint small by installing a basic version; when you try to use a file not installed initially—say, a template or theme—Word offers to install it then.

Click and Type

This feature simplifies document layout. You just position your insertion-point cursor where you want your text to start on the page, double-click, and begin typing. Word 2000 automatically fills in the extra lines, tabs and text alignment. (You must be in Print Layout or Web Layout View to use this feature.)

Print Zoom

This is a cool feature that allows you to size your on-screen pages when you print them, so that you can fit your document onto odd sized sheets, or fit more than one page of your document onto a single sheet.

Collect and Paste

Another very cool new feature, Collect and Paste lets you gather up as many as twelve items (lines of text, graphics, sound clips) from different sources (documents, galleries) onto the Clipboard, and then paste them individually or as a group into your document. This one is a real productivity booster!

Intuitive Menus and Toolbars

When you first open Word 2000's pull–down menus, they display a short list of the commands you used frequently or most recently. Word automatically "promotes" the commands you use the most and suppresses the ones you use the least. The result is a cleaner and simpler interface. (A click on the down-arrow button at the bottom of each open menu expands it to reveal all available commands.)

New Open and Save As Dialog Boxes

Word 2000's new Open and Save dialog boxes display 50 percent more files than previous versions of the program. They also include the new Places Bar, which provides one-click shortcuts to History, Desktop, Favorites, and Web Folders. (More on these later in the book.)

Docs in the Taskbar

The Word 2000 taskbar now displays a button for each document you have open. You no longer have to go to the Window menu to switch between documents. (You can if you want to.)

More Viewing Options

Word 2000 gives you even more on-screen configurations, or "views," of a document. These include Print View, Web Layout View (an improved version of the Word 97 Online View), and Outline View for longer, structured documents.

Beefier Spellcheck and Thesaurus, and Smarter Grammar Checkers

Word 2000 has a bigger dictionary and a grammar checker that actually helps you write better sentences without throwing up red flags at every use of a semicolon.

Advanced AutoCorrect

If you like having your spelling fixed on the fly, you'll love the improved AutoCorrect feature. The bigger dictionary was a big help here.

Improved Clip Art Gallery

The new Word 2000 Clip Art Gallery is an awesome feature. It now has a browser-like interface, and it includes lots of new artwork, sounds, and animated graphics. You can leave the gallery open on the screen while you're working on a document and then simply drag and drop objects onto the page. The new gallery also includes some advanced search tools that allow you to search for, say, images related to Christmas, work, or music. It also allows you to create your own customized galleries.

Flexible Tables and Cool Table Tools

Word 2000 offers new table options that are a godsend to anyone who spends much time dealing with tables in their Word documents. The new options include nested tables, floating tables, side-by-side tables, and easy table movement. The new and improved Table Tool allows you to draw on text, draw cells one at a time, create diagonal cell borders, and erase several lines at once. And graphics now behave the same inside a table cell and out. You can, for example, put a picture inside a cell and still wrap text around it.

Better Graphics Handling

Working with graphics in general has become easier in Word 2000. The new version makes it easier to insert objects, change between floating and inline pictures, turn text wrapping on and off, and position or align graphics. It's easier to align WordArt objects next to text, because Word 2000 automatically inserts them in the line. Word 2000 also offers picture bullets and makes it easy to copy and paste graphical bullets from other documents.

Improved Office Assistant

If you're using Word 2000 in conjunction with Office 2000, you'll find the new improved Office Assistant. I've always found these animated gremlins to be more annoying than helpful, but scores of people love them. The new versions float free on the screen, are easier to hide and show, and (thank you Microsoft) easier to shut off completely.

Collaboration

Word 2000 gets the benefit of Microsoft's efforts to improve its Office collaboration features. You can now schedule and participate in NetMeetings while working in Word. And the program lets you establish threaded network discussions in Web documents.

Self-Diagnosis and Repair

Word 2000 now automatically scans its own files for problems and then repairs them itself. When installed as part of the Microsoft Office suite, Word uses the Office Tune-Up Wizard to track down and fix corrupted file or registry information, missing program files, and similar problems. The Office Clean-Up Wizard detects previous versions of Office and offers to remove them. Detect and Repair is a new command on the Word 2000 Help menu. Select it, and Word locates and fixes problems with its noncritical files. And the program's improved virus checking system allows macro creators to add digital signatures that keep Word's macro virus alert from popping up every time one of their documents is opened.

Web Stuff

This version of Word includes some significantly expanded HTML features, which make it possible to save any document as a Web page, publish it on a server, and create a folder for all of its supporting files. Word 2000 lets you use themes to design a Web page, insert and manage hyperlinks, preview the document in a browser before you save it, and use HTML scripts.

3

A Better Mouse Trap

The 22 Keyboard Shortcuts
Every Word User Should Know

Word 2000 provides you with many toolbar icons and pull-down menus, so you could probably mouse-click your way through all your Word work without ever learning any of these keyboard shortcuts. But taking your hands off the keyboard to grab the mouse every time you want to move the cursor around the page, search for a phrase, cut and copy text, or change a formatting option does slows down the process. A lot. To get a real grip on this program, you'll want to learn at least a few keyboard shortcuts.

The 22 Essential Keystroke Commands

Sometimes more than one keystroke combination will do the same thing. Here, I've listed only the simplest ones. (There's no point hitting three keys when you can get the job done with two.) You'll find a complete listing of all keyboard shortcuts in Word's Help files, and a nearly complete listing in the back of this book.

There are many more keyboard shortcuts, but in my opinion, these 22 are as essential as the space bar or the Tab key to your mastery of Word:

Open an Existing Document	**Ctrl + O**
Open a New Document	**Ctrl +N**
Close Document	**Ctrl + W**
Save	**Ctrl + S or Shift + F12**
Save As	**F12**
Copy	**Ctrl + C or Ctrl + Insert**
Cut	**Ctrl + X or Shift + Delete**
Paste	**Ctrl + V**
Jump to the Beginning of a Word	**Ctrl + right Arrow**
Jump to the End of a Word	**Ctrl + left Arrow**
Jump to the Beginning of a Line	**Home**
Jump to the End of a Line	**End**
Jump to the Beginning of a Document	**Ctrl + Home**
Jump to the End of a Document	**Ctrl + End**

In most cases, the same keystroke combination reverses the action. For example, use Ctrl + B to "bold" the selected text, and then use Ctrl + B to "unbold" it.

TIP

Bold	**Ctrl + B**
Italics	**Ctrl + I**
Underline	**Ctrl + U**
Spellcheck	**F7**
Thesaurus	**Shift + F7**
Print	**Ctrl + P**
Redo	**Ctrl + Y**
Undo	**Ctrl + Z or Alt + Backspace**

To create a nice Em Dash, hit Ctrl + Alt + the minus key on the number pad. You can also set up your program to change a double dash (—) to an Em Dash (—) automatically.

TIP

22 More Keystrokes
It Wouldn't Kill You to Learn

The 22 keyboard shortcuts in the previous list are essential to any Word user; learn the following 22, and you're on your way to becoming a true power user.

Change Case (all caps, all lower case, title)	**Shift + F3**
Delete a word	**Ctrl + Delete**
Date Field (inserts today's date, e.g. 9/9/99)	**Alt + Shift + D**
Double Underline	**Ctrl + Shift + D**
Open Font Dialog Box	**Ctrl + D**
Mark Index Entry	**Alt + Shift + X**
Insert Hyperlink	**Ctrl + K**
Next Window	**Alt + F6 or Ctrl + F6**
Normal Style (imposes your normal style)	**Ctrl + Shift + N**
Outline	**Alt + Ctrl + O**
Page Break	**Ctrl + Enter**
Page Numbers (inserts at the cursor)	**Alt + Shift + P**
Print Preview	**Ctrl + F**
Select Entire Document	**Ctrl + A**
Select to End of Line	**Shift + End**

Select to Beginning of Line	**Shift + Home**
Show All Formatting Characters	**Ctrl + Shift + 8**
Subscript	**Ctrl + =**
Superscript	**Ctrl + Shift + =**
Shrink Font Size One Point	**Ctrl + [**
Increase Font Size One Point	**Ctrl +]**

4

Even the Journey of a Thousand Miles . . .

Word Basics

f you've never worked with Word before, this is where you'll want to begin. But even if you've been using the program for years, you're bound to find at least a few things in this chapter you didn't know (even if it's just that the blue strip across the top of the program window is called the Title Bar).

Starting Word 2000

I'm assuming your computer is turned on and running Windows 95/98 or Windows NT/2000 and Word 2000 is installed on your machine. (Hey, Microsoft should have gotten you at least that far.) Starting the program is simple as . . . um . . . one, two, three:

- **Go to the Task Bar.**
- **Click on the Start button.**
- **Select Programs/Microsoft® Word.**

Word 2000 launches and presents you with the Program Window and a new, blank Document Window. (See Figure 4-1.)

The Word Shortcut Icon

Another way to launch Word 2000 is by clicking on a shortcut icon on your desktop. That's how I do it. But you've got to create this shortcut yourself; it's not automatic with the program's installation. (If you are installing Word 2000 as an upgrade and you already have the Word shortcut icon on your desktop from a previous version, the new Word shortcut icon will replace the old one automatically.)

There are two ways to create a Word launch shortcut:

Option One:
- **Go to your Windows desktop.**
- **Right-click on an empty area to open the Desktop Options menu.**
- **Select News to open a submenu.**
- **Click Shortcut to open the Create Shortcut dialog box.**
- **Click on the Browse button to open the Browse dialog box.**
- **Double-click on the Program Files folder.**
- **Double-click on the Microsoft Office folder.**

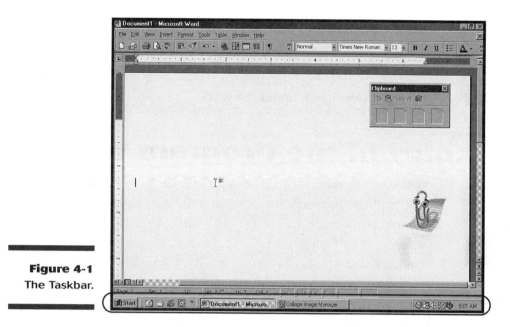

Figure 4-1
The Taskbar.

- Double-click on the Office folder.
- Double-click on the Winword.exe icon (it's a blue W).
- Back in the Create Shortcut dialog box, click on the Next button.
- Type a shortcut name in the text box. (I use "Word;" a friend of mine uses "Word 2000.")
- Click on the Finish button.
- The renamed Word 2000 shortcut icon appears on your desktop.

Option Two:
- Go to your Windows desktop.
- Double-click on the My Computer icon.
- Double-click on the C drive icon.
- Double-click on the Program Files folder.
- Double-click on the Microsoft Office folder.
- Double-click on the Office folder.
- Double-click on the Winword.exe icon.
- Close or move any open program windows to clear a space on the desktop.

- **Click on the Word icon and drag it onto the desktop.**
- **Right-click the Winword.exe shortcut icon to open the Options menu.**
- **Select Rename.**
- **Type a new name under the icon.**

Anatomy of the Program Window

When Word opens, your screen should be filled with the Document Window. If it's not, and you're instead looking at a smaller window floating in the center of your screen, you'll need to click on the Restore button (see illustration) to resize the window. (See Figure 4-2.)

Figure 4-2 shows the Windows 2000 Program Window and a blank Document Window in Print Layout View. For the purposes of illustration, I've opened the Standard Tool Bar, the Formatting Toolbar, the Ruler, and the Office Assistant. I've also activated a pull-down menu and submenu, and shown two mouse pointer forms. (If you actually ever see two mouse pointers on your screen, call for help!) Unless you have a huge monitor, chances are, you won't have all of this clickable firepower open at the same time. There's no reason to if you've learned your keyboard shortcuts, and all this stuff can really cramp the document area. If you are working with a large screen, you might

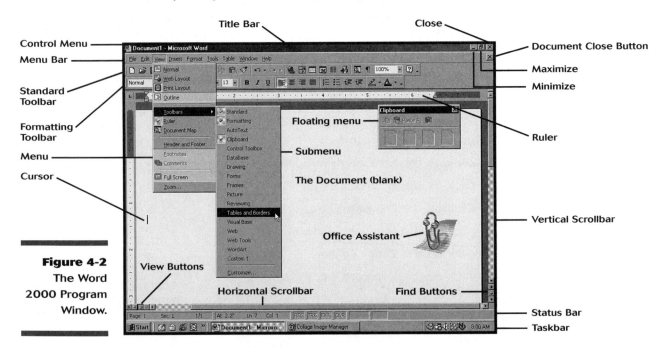

Figure 4-2
The Word
2000 Program
Window.

like it this way. My admonitions to learn the keyboard shortcuts notwithstanding, I know several people who work this way, happily. But if your screen is small—say, you're working on a laptop—you might even want to get rid of all of them.

Title Bar

The Title Bar is the colored strip (probably blue) at the very top of your screen. It identifies both the program and the document you are currently viewing. in this example, "Document 1–Microsoft® Word." Once you save the document and give it a name, "Document 1" is replaced by that name.

The Title Bar is also home to several buttons:

- **Application Control Menu: commands for resizing and moving the window, and for closing the program.**
- **Minimize: Reduces the Program Window to a button on the Taskbar.**
- **Restore/Maximize: if the Program Window is opened to its full size, this button reduces it; if the window is smaller than full size, this button restores it to full size.**
- **Close Button: closes the document; prompts you to save changes.**

Menu Bar

All of Word's functions are accessible through the pull-down menus that live on the Menu Bar. In Word 2000, all of these menus are "intuitive" (Microsoft calls them "personalized). Designed to reduce screen clutter, they open initially with only the functions you use most often. You can click on the button at the bottom of each menu to reveal the entire list, or you can set them up so they open fully after a few seconds.

To access a pull-down menu from the Menu Bar, just click on the heading you want and the menu will drop down. Once you activate the Menu Bar, you can move your mouse pointer back and forth over any heading and the appropriate menu will drop.

Word's Personalized Menus

Under the headings in Word 2000's Menu Bar you'll find lists of commands that lead you to every feature and function of the program. Every shortcut button and combination of keystrokes is just another way of accessing all the stuff in those menus. To tell you the truth, you could probably learn everything you need to know about this program by playing around with the Menu Bar.

The menus in Word 2000 work differently from menus in any other version of this program. Described variously as "adaptive," "intuitive," and "personalized," they have the ability to react to your habits. Rather than displaying the entire list of controls available in each menu, Word 2000 menus are initially truncated, a list of only the commands you choose most often. After they're open for a few seconds they expand to show the full list, or you can click on the button at the end of the menu to open it fully. The previously hidden commands are displayed in lighter gray.

If you'd rather see complete menus every time you click on a category name, you can turn off this feature. Here's how:

- **Go to the Menu Bar.**
- **Open View.**
- **Select Toolbars/Customize to open the Customize dialog box.**
- **Click the Options tab.**
- **Click in the "Menus show recently used commands first" checkbox to unselect.**
- **Click the Close button.**
- **You will now see complete menus the instant you open them.**

A quicker way to access the Menu Bar is to use the Alt and the Arrow keys. Here's how you do it:

- **To activate the Menu Bar, hit the Alt key. (Notice that the mouse pointer stops blinking and the state of the File button changes—it suddenly looks like a button.)**
- **To move from menu to menu, hit the right and left Arrow keys.**
- **To open the pull-down menus, hit the down Arrow key.**
- **Or, hit the key of the letter underlined in the menu heading. (V for View; O for Format, etc.)**
- **To close a pull-down menu, hit Esc.**
- **To highlight controls listed in the menu, use the up and down Arrow Keys.**
- **To select a highlighted heading, hit the Enter key.**
- **To deactivate the Menu Bar at any time, hit the Alt key or hit Esc.**

Submenus

Where there are menus, there are submenus—at least in Word 2000. Submenus are just menus within a menu. You might have noticed that some of the menu listings

SHORTCUT MENUS

Right-click on just about anything in Word, and you'll invoke a shortcut menu. Shortcut menus are "floating" menus—gray boxes not attached to the edges of the Program Window. Shortcut menus hold lists of commands that seem appropriate to whatever you clicked on. You can display a shortcut menu for text, tables, words flagged by the spellchecker, and graphics. Right-click on any toolbar to invoke the Toolbar Submenu—the same submenu you get by opening View and selecting Toolbars. Right-click on the Office Assistant, and you get shortcuts to tools for modifying or changing your Assistant. Right-click on the Title Bar, and you get the same menu as when you click on the Control Menu icon. (You also get that same menu when you right-click on a minimized document button in the Windows Task Bar.)

have little arrows next to them. When you move your mouse pointer over those arrows, you open the submenu for that menu item.

Toolbars

Word 2000's Toolbars are designed to make life easier for Word users by providing shortcuts to many of the program's commands. Instead of opening a menu category and clicking through a bunch of dialog boxes, Word lets you execute common commands with a mouse click on a toolbar shortcut button.

Docked and Floating Toolbars

A toolbar is "docked" when it is attached to one edge of the Program Window. You can dock a toolbar at any edge of the window. Floating toolbars are undocked toolbars that "float" in the Document Window. The Clipboard is a good example of a floating toolbar. (See Figure 4.3.)

Position your mouse pointer over a toolbar button for a few seconds and a ScreenTip box appears with the name of the shortcut

TIP

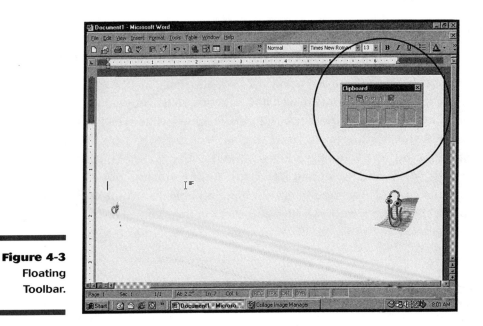

Figure 4-3
Floating
Toolbar.

Missing Toolbars

If any toolbars seem to be missing from your Program Window, here's how to get them back:

- **Go to the Menu Bar.**
- **Open View.**
- **Select Toolbars.**
- **Open the Toolbars submenu.**
- **Select the missing toolbar commands.**
- **The missing toolbars appear at the top of your Program Window.**

You'll have to repeat these steps to recover each missing toolbar. To make a toolbar go away, do the same thing.

> **To use a toolbar button, just position your mouse pointer over it and click.**
>
> **TIP**

Rulers

For those who create newsletters and documents with graphics and tables in them, Word's rulers come in handy. And they make setting tabs fast and easy. The horizontal ruler shows you the width of your text, indents, and tabs. The vertical ruler (only viewable in Print Layout view) gives you the same information going the other way.

If you don't see the horizontal Ruler on your screen, you can summon it like this:

📂 **Go to the Menu Bar.**
📂 **Open View.**
📂 **Click on Ruler to select it.**
📂 **The Ruler now appears at the top of the Document Window.**
📂 **To make it go away, go back to the View menu and click on Ruler to select it.**

TIP

Scrollbars

The scrollbars allow you to use your mouse to move to different parts of your document. You can click on the arrows at the ends of each scroll bar, or use the "drag box" to rocket to different parts of the document. The three buttons at the lower end of the vertical scroll bar provide quick access to various "find" and "browse" functions (see "Getting Around" in this chapter); the four buttons at the left end of the horizontal scroll bar allow you to switch between document "views."

Use the "drag" button on the scrollbars when you want to move through the pages of your document fast.

Status Bar

Located just beneath the Horizontal Scroll Bar at the bottom of your screen, the Status Bar contains information about the document you're viewing, the location of your mouse pointer in it, and the operations your are performing. (See Figure 4-4.)

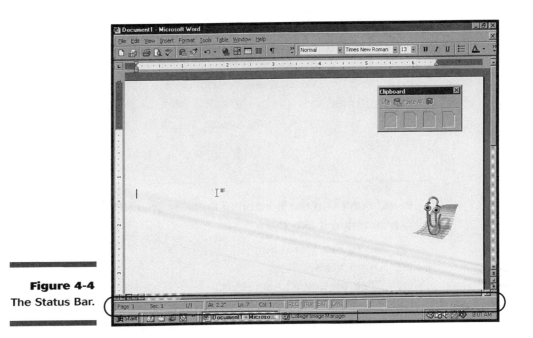

Figure 4-4
The Status Bar.

The document information may be found in the two long boxes on the left. In Figure 4-4, you can see that you are looking at page 1, Section 1 of a one-page document. Your mouse pointer is located one inch into the document on line 1 of the column 1.

Next, you'll find four toggle switches for four options: recording a macro, tracking changes, extended selections, and overtype.

If you are spell- and/or grammar-checking as you work, the next box will contain an animated book-and-pencil icon. When you save the document manually or use the Auto Save feature, a floppy disk icon appears in the next box.

Task Bar

Located at the very bottom of your screen is the Windows Task Bar, which includes the Windows Start button, buttons for some Windows control settings, and various program shortcut buttons. In Figure 4-4, you'll notice buttons on the left side to get you back to the Windows desktop, a file shortcut, a button to launch the Internet Explorer browser, and one for Outlook 2000; on the right you'll see shortcuts for the printer, the volume control, utilities, and several browser plug-ins. When you minimize a document or when you have more than one document open at the

If either your status bar or your scrollbars seem to be missing from your Program Window, here's how you get them back:

📂 **Go to the Menu Bar.**
📂 **Open Tools.**
📂 **Select Options.**
📂 **Click on the View tab.**
📂 **In the "Show" section, click in the "Status Bar," "Horizontal Scrollbar," and "Vertical Scrollbar"**
📂 **checkboxes.**
📂 **Click OK.**
📂 **All the bars appear in their proper places.**

TIP

same time, buttons for these documents appear in the Task Bar; clicking on a different button restores the minimized document to full size or opens a different document in the Document Window.

The Windows Task Bar also holds buttons to restore those documents to the screen. In Figure 4-4 you'll notice a second Word document called Document 2 is open "behind" Document 1.

You might have noticed the little nub or lip at the end of the toolbars that looks sort of like a handhold. The task bar at the bottom of your screen has them, too. These nubs are Move Handles. You use them to move your toolbars and task bars around. Here's how:

- **Position your mouse pointer over the Move Handle.**
- **The mouse pointer changes as in the example to look like a double line and two up-down arrows.**
- **Click and drag your toolbars to different lines, or expand or contract them.**

When you have two toolbars sharing a line (which is the Word 2000 default setting for the Standard and Formatting toolbars), you'll use the Move Handles to slide one toolbar back so that you can access more shortcuts.

View Buttons

These buttons, located in the lower left corner of the Program Window between the Status Bar and the Taskbar, control how the document is displayed. Your options are Normal, Web Layout, Print Layout, and Outline. All of these options are available in the View pull-down menu.

Mouse Pointer Types

The standard Word 2000 mouse pointer looks like a slightly thickened, blinking vertical line. Sometimes called the insertion mouse pointer, this is the one you move around your document using your keyboard, and use to mark the spot where you intend to type or insert copied text or to insert graphics or other elements. The mouse pointer with the horizontal lines next to it is only visible in Print Layout view. When you see this mouse pointer, you'll know that Word 2000's click-and-type feature is activated.

Office Assistant

That cute and (for some of us at least) *annoying* little character sitting in the middle of the Document Window in Figure 4-5 is an animated paper clip known as the Office Assistant. (More on the Office Assistant in the next chapter.)

The Birth of a New Document

A "document" in Word 2000 is that thing you're working on in the white space in the middle of your screen. It can be a memo, a letter, a chapter of a book, a newsletter, a flyer—whatever. Word documents can be of virtually any length (number of pages). One document might be a two-page, text-only family Christmas letter; another might be a four-page newsletter complete with graphics. A document could be a 10-page chapter of your novel or your entire 300-page book. (See Figure 4-6.)

Notice that your mouse pointer looks like the letter "I" when you move it into the typing area (basically, all of the Document Window). The so-called I-beam pointer allows you to position the mouse pointer with a mouse click.

TIP

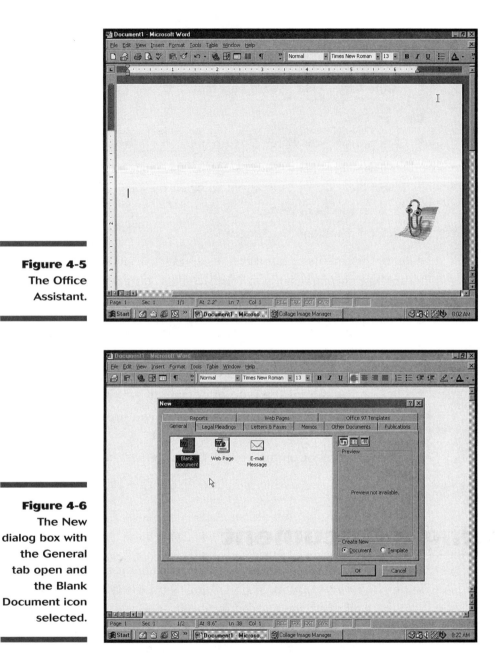

Figure 4-5
The Office
Assistant.

Figure 4-6
The New
dialog box with
the General
tab open and
the Blank
Document icon
selected.

When first launched, Word 2000 automatically gives you a new, blank document. The document margins and layout are based on your default Normal Page Setup settings. (You'll find more on margins and layouts in Chapter 13, Start the Presses: Printing Documents Created in Word.)

You can create additional new documents in three ways. The two easiest ways are:

Option One:

- Hit the Ctrl + N keyboard shortcut.

Option Two:

- Click on the New Blank Document icon on the Standard Toolbar.
- Click on the Start button in the Windows Task Bar
- Select New Office Document to open the New Document dialog box.
- Click on the General tab.
- Click on the Blank Document icon.

New documents created in these ways will be set up according to your Normal template parameters. If you want to use a different template—say a memo or fax cover sheet—here's how to do it:

- Go to the Menu Bar.
- Open File.
- Select New to open the New Document dialog box.
- Click on the tab for the type of document you want to create.
- Double-click on the template icon. (You can preview the template by clicking its icon and looking in the Preview area.)
- A new document opens in your Document Window based on that template.

You'll find more on using templates in Chapter 15, Word Magic: Working with Styles.

Saving a Document

Word 2000 documents are saved as individual files by default in the My Documents folder. It's a very good idea to save your work often. You can set the program to save automatically, but the Ctrl + S keyboard shortcut makes it easy to save manually too. (See Figure 4-7.)

The first time you save a document, you must designate where you want the file kept and give it a file name. You may also choose the file format. If, instead, you just hit Ctrl + S, Word will automatically save the document in the My Documents folder on your hard disk as a Word 2000 file with whatever numbered document name Word gave it when you first opened it. Once you've saved a file, you don't have to name it again or re-choose the file format.

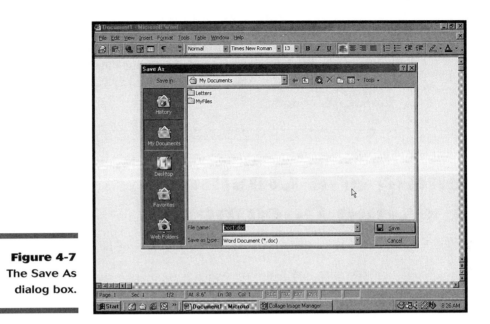

Figure 4-7
The Save As
dialog box.

To save a document for the first time:

- Go to the Menu Bar.
- Open File.
- Select Save As to open the Save As dialog box.
- Click on the My Documents folder. (You'll learn how to save in different folders in Chapter 6, You Put It Where? Using Word's File Management Tools.)
- Type a name in the File Name text box at the bottom of the dialog box.
- Click on the drop-down arrow in the "Save As Type" text box. For now, go with the default format.
- Click the Save button, at bottom right.

Once you've saved the document, you'll be sent back to the Document Window, where you'll notice that the new file name now appears in the Title Bar. Don't forget that hitting the F12 key takes your right to the Save As dialog box.

To save an existing file under a new name, save it using the same steps you used to save a new file, but type something different in the File Name text box before you click Save. A file with the old name will still exist in the form in which it was last saved.

Opening and Closing an Existing Document

Once you have saved your document, you can close it in one of three ways:

1. Hit the Ctrl + W shortcut key.

2. Click on the Close button on the Title Bar.

3. Click File on the Menu Bar and highlight and click Close.

To open a file you have saved and closed:

- **Go to the Menu Bar.**
- **Open File.**
- **Select Open to open the Open dialog box.**
- **Double-click on the folder in which you saved the file (probably My Documents).**
- **Click on the file icon.**
- **Your document appears in the Document Window.**

Getting Around in a Document

When you first open a document in Word, the cursor appears automatically in the upper left corner, marking the place where you can begin entering text. This is true of both new, blank documents, and existing documents that are full of text and graphics. The upper-left corner may be a fine place to start when the Document Window is empty, but when you're working on a big, fat, full document, chances are you're going to want to move around a little—or a lot.

Word gives you several tools to help you navigate the Document Window: mouse, scrollbars, Go To, Page Up and Page Down keys, Home and End keys, and the four Arrow keys.

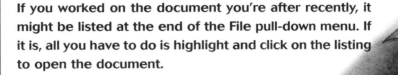

If you worked on the document you're after recently, it might be listed at the end of the File pull-down menu. If it is, all you have to do is highlight and click on the listing to open the document.

Mouse

As I mentioned in the Chapter 3, I'm a big fan of keyboard shortcuts, especially when it comes to working in Word. But even though I've memorized and internalized each and every one of those 44 key combinations, I still use my mouse quite a bit.

In Word, the mouse is all-powerful. It can go anywhere and touch anything. There is literally no spot on your screen you can't get to with a mouse, and that makes it a useful tool for navigating the Document Window.

Use your mouse to move your I-beam mouse pointer to any spot in your document and click to reposition the blinking mouse pointer. This creates a new insertion point for additional text, graphics, or other elements.

Scrollbars

The scrollbars bring parts of your document not currently displayed into the Document Window. As described earlier in this chapter, you need your mouse to make the scrollbars work. You can click on the arrow buttons at the ends of each bar to move up and down, or right and left. Click on an arrow button and your document scrolls by, slowly at first, faster after a few seconds. You can also grab the drag box and jam through the pages of your document much faster. If your document has more than one page, when you click on the drag box, a screen tip box appears next to it, giving you the page number. (See Figure 4-8.)

You can get to the Open dialog box quicker by using the Ctrl + O keyboard shortcut.

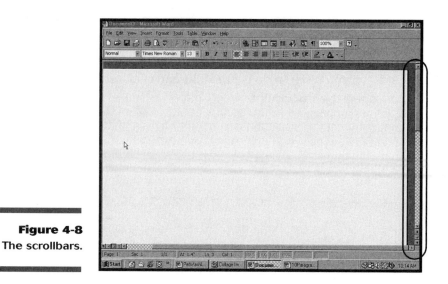

Figure 4-8
The scrollbars.

Go To

If you know the number of the page you want, you can use the Go To (Edit) feature to get there.

To go directly to a specific page:

- Go to the Menu Bar.
- Open Edit.
- Select Go To to open the Find and Replace dialog box.
- Click on the Go To tab.

This book is about Word, which is software, so I'm not sure it's the best place to talk about hardware, but I just have to mention one fairly recent innovation: the **scrolling mouse**. This is a type of mouse with a little wheel embedded between the right and left buttons. Rolling the wheel, which you do with a finger without changing your grip on the mouse, lets you scroll through your document very easily and with a lot of control. Microsoft's version is the IntelliMouse, but there are other brands on the market.

TIP

- Select Page in the "Go to what?" box.
- Type the page number in the "Enter section number" text box.
- Click on the Go To button.
- The Document Window now displays that page, and your cursor is positioned at the beginning of the first line.

The Go To dialog box also allows you to navigate through recent edits, doc headings, graphics, tables, fields, endnotes, footnotes, comments, and sections.

The tiny buttons at the lower end of the vertical scroll bar give you several navigation options. Depending on how you set it up, you can move forward or backward from page to page, edit to edit, heading to heading, graphic to graphic, table to table, field to field, endnote to endnote, footnote to footnote, comment to comment, or section to section. And you can activate the Find and Go To features.

To use this navigational feature to move from page to page:

- Click on the Select Browse Object button to open the little toolbar.
- Click on the Browse by Page icon in the lower right corner.
- Now, clicking the double arrow buttons on the scrollbar will move you forward or backward from wherever you happen to be in the document by one page.

Page Up and Page Down

The Page Up and Page Down buttons on your keyboard (usually found between the main keyboard and the number pad) work alone and in combination with other keys to move you around your document. Here's how to use them:

- Hit the Page Up key to move the cursor toward the beginning of your document by the length of one page.
- Hit the Page Down key to move the cursor toward the end of your document by the length of one page.
- Hit Ctrl + Page Up to move to the top of the previous page.
- Hit Ctrl + Page Down to move to the top of the next page.

Home and End

The Home and End buttons (usually found right next to the Page Up and Page Down keys) are indispensable keys for a number of common moves:

- Hit the Home key to move the cursor to the beginning of a line.
- Hit the End key to move the cursor to the end of a line.
- Hit Ctrl + Home to move the cursor to the first space of the first line of the beginning of your document.
- Hit Ctrl + End to move the cursor to the last space of the last line of the end of your document.

Arrow Keys

Another indispensable group of buttons, the Arrow keys, are also usually found between the main keyboard and the number pad, usually below the Page Up and Page Down and the Home and End keys). This is how they work:

- Click the up arrow to move the cursor up one line.
- Click the down arrow to move the cursor down one line.
- Click Ctrl + the up arrow to move the cursor up one paragraph.
- Click Ctrl + the down arrow to move the cursor down one paragraph.
- Click the left arrow to move the cursor left one character space.
- Click the right arrow to move the cursor right one character space.
- Click Ctrl + the left arrow to move the cursor left by one word.
- Click Ctrl + the right arrow to move the cursor right by one word.

Closing Word 2000

When you have finished your work, saved and closed your documents, and are ready for a round of Quake or a hot date with Laura Croft, you'll want to turn off Word 2000. There are five ways to close the program:

Option One:

- Go to the Menu Bar.
- Open File.
- Select Exit.

Option Two:

- Click on the Application Control icon in the Title Bar.
- Select Close.

Option Three:

- Click on the Close button in the upper right corner of the Program Window.

Option Four:

- Hit Alt + F + X.

Option Five:

- Hit Alt + F4.

5

You Are Not Alone
Getting Help in Word

Second only to the basic skills covered in Chapter 4, the ability to find quick answers to your questions while you work is essential. When you first begin using this program, you're probably going to have lots of questions, but no matter how good you get with this thing, you're going to find yourself scratching your head from time to time, and wondering, "How do you do that?"

Fortunately, Word 2000 includes a hefty Help feature that covers every feature of the program. It's keyword- and topic-searchable, it's animated, and it points you to help sites on the Web.

The Office Assistant

His name is Clippit, he's an animated paper clip, and he appears out of nowhere on the right side of your screen the first time you click on the Help button. You may like him, or you may hate him, but Microsoft's Office Assistant is at least an attempt to allow you to ask your questions in plain English. The program comes with a veritable horde of virtual critters, so if you don't get along with Clippit, you can call up another "personality." (See Figure 5-1.)

I'm not what you'd call a huge fan of the Office Assistant, but you should definitely give these little guys a try. They have a kind of intelligence and intuition, they jump

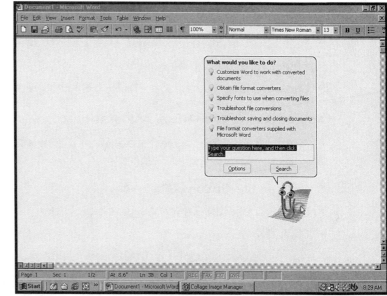

Figure 5-1
The Office Assistant with the dialog balloon open.

up to lend a hand at likely moments, they offer tips, they move out of your way, and for a lot of people, they add something to the overall experience of using Word 2000.

By default, the Office Assistant appears when you first open the program and whenever you enable a new feature. If the assistant isn't there, you can summon it by clicking on Help in the Menu Bar, and then highlighting and selecting Show the Office Assistant. You can move the little fella around the screen by dragging and dropping him with the mouse.

To ask your assistant for help:

- Click on the character to open the Office Assistant balloon.
- The balloon displays a number of options under the heading, "What would you like to do."
- If one of those options fits your need, click on it to a Help window on that subject.
- If you don't see what you need in the list, you can type your question in plain English in the text box.
- Click Search or hit Enter.
- A topic list relating to your question will appear in the balloon.
- Click on the topic that seems to address your question, or recast your question in the text box.
- Clicking on a topic in the balloon opens the Help window.

Of course, cute as they are, the animated desktop assistants aren't for everyone.

To boot the Office Assistant off your desktop:

- Right-click on the Help in the Menu Bar to open the menu.
- Select Hide the Office Assistant.
- The next time you click on Help, he'll reappear.

To deactivate the Office Assistant:

- Right-click on the character to open the menu.
- Select Options.
- Click on the Options tab.
- Uncheck Use the Office Assistant by clicking on the box.
- Click OK.

Now when you click Help in the Menu Bar and select Microsoft® Word Help, you will activate the Help Window, but not the assistant. To get him back, click Help in the Menu Bar, and then click Show the Office Assistant.

VIRTUAL CRITTERS

Clippit is the default Office Assistant, but Microsoft also included a veritable menagerie of virtual critters who can substitute for the bulgy–eyed paper clip. Each one is animated and engaging in it's own way.

The Office Assistant roster includes:

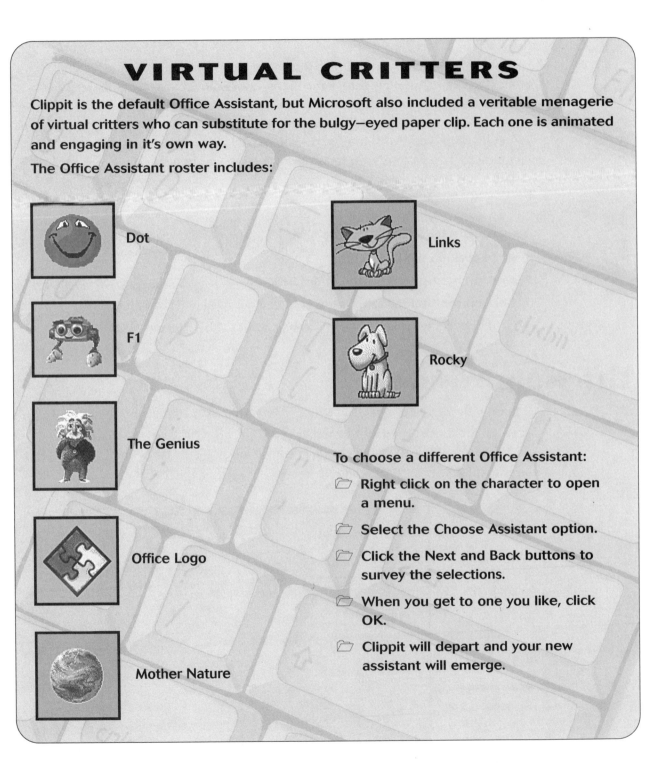

Dot

F1

The Genius

Office Logo

Mother Nature

Links

Rocky

To choose a different Office Assistant:

📁 Right click on the character to open a menu.

📁 Select the Choose Assistant option.

📁 Click the Next and Back buttons to survey the selections.

📁 When you get to one you like, click OK.

📁 Clippit will depart and your new assistant will emerge.

If you like to leave your Office Assistant open on your desktop, you'll notice that light bulbs appear over its head from time to time. Whenever this happens, click on the bulb, and the assistant will offer some advice that might help you with the work you're doing at that moment by pointing out a feature or function you might not know about.

TIP

To stop the Office Assistant's tips:

- Right-click on the character.
- Click on the Options button in the balloon.
- Click on the Options tab.
- Uncheck all the boxes under "Show tips about" by clicking on them.

The Help Window

Whether or not you use the Office Assistant, eventually you're going to find yourself looking at the Help window. The Help window gives you access to a huge database of Word 2000 help topics, and it allows you to search for answers in several different ways. (See Figure 5-2.)

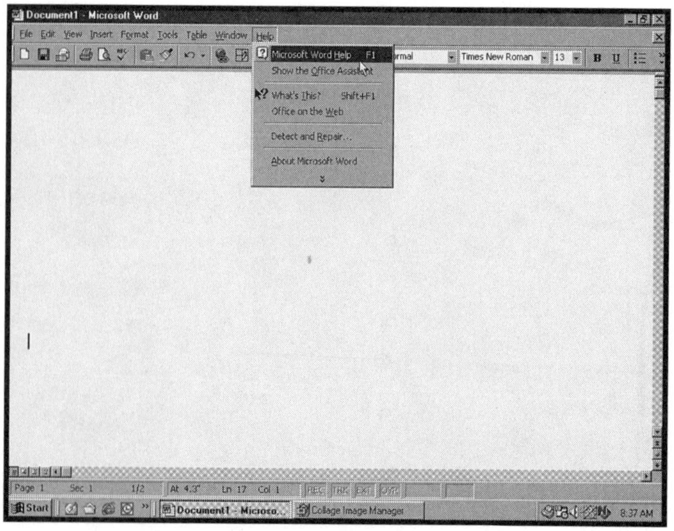

Figure 5-2
The Help
Menu.

If you've used the assistant to open the Help window (you asked a question and then clicked on the answer you liked best in the balloon), you'll see the main Help window with a list of topics that might answer your question. Double-click on any of these listings to access the article cited.

To expand the Help window from this point to its full size, click on the Show icon in the upper-left corner.

To open the Help window when the Office Assistant is disabled:

- Go to the Menu Bar.
- Open Help.
- Select Microsoft® Word Help.
- The Help window will open fully.

When the Help window is open fully, it includes a display window on the right, and a window on the left layered with three tabs. (See Figure 5-3.)

Here's how you use that left-hand window to search Help:

To get help using the Answer Wizard Tab:

- Click on the Answer Wizard tab to display two text boxes.
- In the smaller box under the question "What would you like to do?" type your question in plain English.
- Click Search or hit Enter.

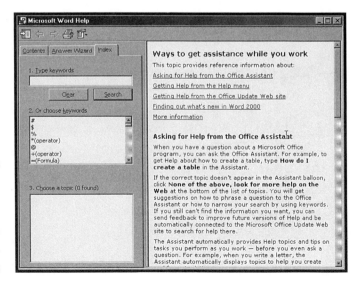

Figure 5-3
The Help dialog box with the Index tab selected.

- A list of topic headings appears in the larger box below.
- Click on a topic to display a list of entries under that heading in the left-hand window.
- Click on an entry listed to display it.

To get help using the Contents Tab:

- Click on the Contents Tab to display the entire Help table of contents (thirty-three categories, each marked by a book icon).
- Click on one of the boxes to the left of the books to open up a list of subcategories.
- Click on one of the boxes next to a subcategory to open a list of topic entries.
- Click on an entry to display it in the right-hand window, with links to related entries.

To get help using the Index Tab:

- Click on the Index Tab to display three new text boxes.
- In Box 1, type a keyword or words. (You won't be able to type words that aren't part of Help's list of search terms.)
- Click on Search or hit Enter.
- Box 2 displays an alphabetical listing of Help search terms, with the word closest to the one you typed highlighted.
- Alternatively, you could have scrolled through the list in Box 2 without typing in a keyword.
- Box 3 displays the related Help topics.
- Click on a topic to see its Help entries displayed in the right-hand screen.

What's This?

When Microsoft first introduced this feature, I couldn't stop using it. It's the most logical and intuitive way I can think of to find out what something on your screen *is*. Just like a child who points at a squirrel in the park and asks her mother, "What's that?" the What's This? feature lets you move your mouse pointer to anything displayed on your screen and ask the same question. (See Figure 5-4.)

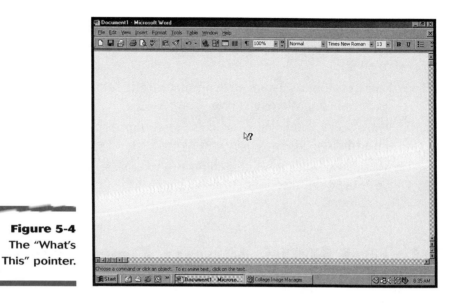

Figure 5-4
The "What's
This" pointer.

To activate What's This?:

- Go to the Menu Bar.
- Open Help.
- Select What's This?
- Your mouse pointer now has a question mark attached to it.
- While the question mark is there, click on any on-screen element.
- An information box appears with a description of the thing you clicked on.
- Click again anywhere on the screen or hit Esc to close What's This?

Help on the Web

If you can't find answers in the Word 2000 Help database on your computer, the program lets you reach out to the World Wide Web for more information. You must have an Internet dialup account and a Web browser installed on your computer to use this feature.

To get Word help from the World Wide Web:

- Go to the Menu Bar.
- Open Help.
- Select Office on the Web.

- Your computer will dial into your Internet service and launch your Web browser.
- Your browser will open the Word 2000 page of the Microsoft Office Update Web site.
- Click on the "Assistance" hyperlink on the left side of the page to open the Experiencing Microsoft® Word page.
- Here you'll find links to Articles, Tech Support, Tips and Tricks, developer information, Newsgroups, and even press releases; all about Word.
- When you're finished searching the Web site, click on the Close button to exit your browser, disconnect from your dialup service, and return to your Word document.

Additional Help Menu Commands

The Help Menu includes three more commands, which we might as well cover here.

Help for WordPerfect Users

This menu listing opens a special help window for WordPerfect users who are making the transition to Microsoft® Word. It's mainly a list of WordPerfect commands and their MS Word counterparts. If you weren't a WordPerfect user, chances are you didn't even install this option on your computer.

Detect and Repair

This is one of the new Word 2000 features. Detect and Repair uses the Windows installer to automatically search out and repair problems in Word (or whichever Office program you're running when you invoke it). It won't repair document files or worksheets.

To use Detect and Repair:

- Go to the Menu Bar.
- Open Help.
- Select Detect and Repair.
- (To restore program shortcuts to the Windows Start menu, click in the "Restore my shortcuts while repairing" check box.)
- Click the Start button.

About Microsoft® Word

This one simply opens a dialog box that tells you which version of the program you're using, who it's registered to, and your serial number—which you should write down somewhere, since you cannot get tech support without it.

The System Info button opens a dialog box that lists information about your computer hardware and software, which is good to know but doesn't really have anything to do with creating documents in Word 2000.

The Tech Support button opens the Help windows. Click OK to close.

6

You Put It WHERE?
Using Word's File Management Tools

C reating documents in Word is one thing; keeping track of them is another. Word lets you save your documents in different places, in different formats, and in different ways—which is great, but sooner or later you're probably going to want to open them up again. You might want to change them. You might want to call them something else. You might even want to put them someplace else. And when you're finished, you're probably going to want to be able to find them again and maybe change everything.

Word lets you do all this and more with a set of file management features that goes a long way toward dulling the pain of shuffling papers around the old file cabinet. But Word does have its own way of doing things—as always: its own filing hierarchy, with folders and directories and subdirectories; it's own file naming rules; it's own relationship to your data. But once your learn the rules, you'll find that you can organize your Word documents efficiently and effectively, and track down information quickly and in ways that must make the folks at Pendaflex green with envy.

File Formats

Word provides you with a bucket load of text-, paragraph-, and page-formatting tools, all of which you'll learn about in the next three chapters. But file formats, as they used to say on *Monty Python*, are something completely different.

Without getting excruciatingly technical, a file's *format* refers to the way information is stored in a file—basically, how your document was saved. A file's format tells a computer program what it needs to know to open the file so that it works.

You can identify a file's format by its three-letter *extension*—in Word it's *.doc*—attached to the filename. This chapter, for example, was saved on my hard drive as FileMngmnt.doc. Although documents created in Word 2000 and Word 97 have the same file formats, Word 95 documents have different formats—even though they carry that same *.doc* extension. (File that one under "things that make you go *aaaaaarrrrgggh!*").

New documents saved by Word 2000 are, by default, stored in the Word 2000 format, and carry the *.doc* file extension. But sometimes you need to share documents with people who don't use Word. There are other word processing programs out there; WordPerfect, for example, is still a popular program used by many people. Lots of people use Macintosh computers, which use a different version of Word. Even other Word users may find that their doc formats conflict with yours. (Let me say it again: *aaaaaarrrrgggh!*)

Format Types

By default, Word provides you with a selection of more than two dozen file formats. Many are self explanatory (for example: Word 5.1 for Macintosh and WordPerfect 5.1 for DOS). But two of the more commonly used formats could use a little explaining.

Text Only Format (.text): This file format is the barest of bare bones, consisting solely of ASCII characters (pronounced ASK-ee). ASCII stands for American Standard Code for Information Interchange, but believe me, you don't care. All you really need to know is that text-only files look crappy, but can be read by almost anything.

Rich Text Format (.rtf): Think of rich text files as ASCII plus. It's a basic document format that carries many of your text formatting instructions. Virtually all of the major word processing programs can read a rich text file, with the added advantage of also being able to read your text formatting.

Fortunately, Word lets you save files in a number of different formats. You can save a brand new document in a non-Word format the first time, and Word will remember to save it in that format until you tell it to do otherwise. And you can open an existing document and save in a different format. (See Figure 6-1.)

To save a Word document in a different file format using the Keyboard:

- Open the file to be saved.
- Hit F12 to open the Save As dialog box.
- Type in a new file name. The "File name" drop-down list is automatically selected when the Save As dialog box opens, so all you have to do is start typing. And don't worry about the file extension.
- Tab once and hit the Down Arrow key to open the "Save as type" drop-down list.
- Use the Down and Up Arrow keys to find a new file type.
- Hit Enter to select it.
- Hit Enter to save the document in the new file format.

To save a Word document in a different file format using the Menu Bar:

- Open the file to be saved.
- Go to the Menu Bar.
- Open File.
- Select Save As to open the Save As dialog box.
- The "File name" drop-down list is automatically selected.

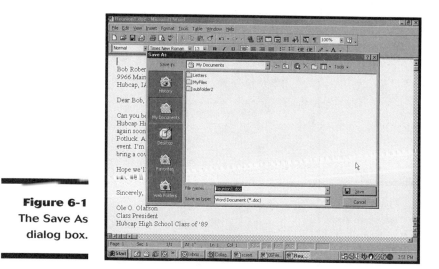

Figure 6-1
The Save As
dialog box.

- Type in a new file name.
- Click on the "Save as type" drop-down list.
- Scroll down the list to select a different file type.
- Click on the file type you want.
- Click on the Save button.
- Your file is saved in the new format.

Opening Files in Other Formats

Given how many people use computers nowadays, chances are good that you'll be given a file in a non-Word format that you want to open in Word. (See Figure 6-2.)

To open a non-Word file in Word:

- Go to the Open dialog box.
- Click on the arrow button next to the "Files of type list box."
- In the drop-down list, click on the file type that matches the document you wish to open.
- Locate the folder or drive containing the file you want to open.
- Select the file.
- Click the Open button.
- Word opens the file.

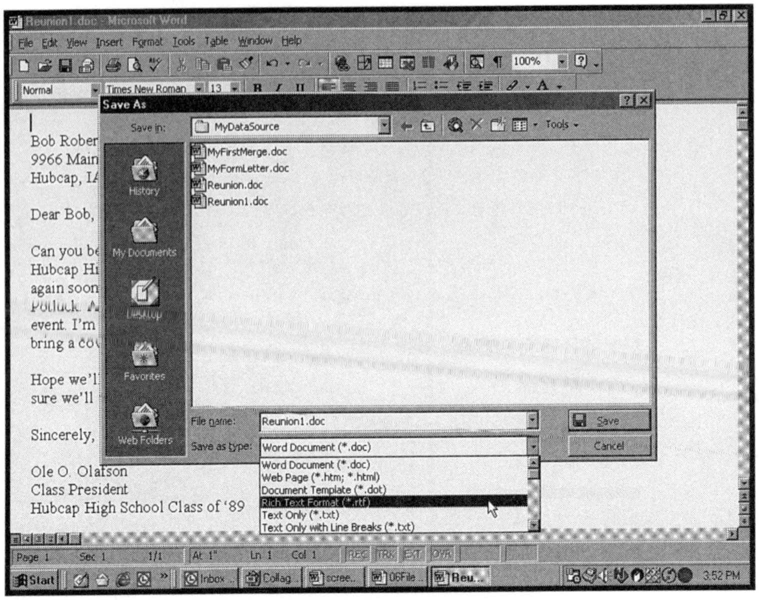

Figure 6-2
The Save As dialog box with the File Type drop down list open.

Filenames

All files created in Word have to have names. Word's file naming rules have changed over the years. Now they're very flexible, but you still have to follow them. Here's what you should know:

- **The bad old days of eight-character file names are long gone. Word 2000 lets you use up to 256 characters to name your files. Still, you should keep your file names short and descriptive—think compound words: grocerylist, xmaslet99, SmithFax, vacationpix, MyJournal.**

Word 2000 includes a number of file format converters. Most of them are put on your hard drive automatically with a typical install; some stay on the CD until you use them for the first time. (You'll be prompted to insert the CD, and then Word will install the converter.) If you can't find the converter you need in the drop-down list, go to the Microsoft Web site. There, you'll find format converters you can download and install to work with Word 2000.

TIP

- Word filenames may include all the alphanumeric characters on your keyboard: letters, numbers and spaces, but not punctuation marks. You can also use capitals. Periods, commas, hyphens, and so on mean something specific to Word. A period, for example, tells Word that a file extension is next.

- For the same reason, you can't use several other keyboard characters in your file names. These characters include: \?:*/<>|.

- You no longer have to type in the file extension (.doc, .rtf, .txt) as you did in early versions of Word. Just type in the name, select the file type, and Word adds the extension.

> Keep in mind that when you save existing files like this, you are creating a new file, but you're not getting rid of the old one. The file you originally opened still exists, with its old three-letter extension, right beside the new one.
>
> **TIP**

File Folders

Word uses a hierarchical file structure to organize your documents. You might hear terms like "directory" and "subdirectory" used here, but it can all be very confusing. For example: *a directory is a list of files, and a subdirectory is a list of files within that list of files, but because Windows is organized around a main or root directory, technically speaking, all directories in Windows and it's various programs are subdirectories.* So, enough of that!

As you begin to organize the documents you create in Word, just think in terms of folders and files: your *documents* are *files* stored in *folders*. Word lets you add depth to this hierarchy by putting subfolders inside folders, which is a great way to group and organize lots of documents.

It's a good idea to store all of your documents together in a main document folder, what Word calls a "working folder." Keeping your docs together makes it easy to keep track of them, save them, back them up, and move them to other folders or disks. But within that folder you have all the room you need to subdivide your documents into subfolders any way you want.

By default, Word provides the My Documents folder for this purpose, and the folks at Microsoft seem really anxious to have you save your documents there. The first time you save a document, Word sends you to the My Documents folder. My Documents is the default folder for each Office program you install on your

CHANGING THE DEFAULT FILE FORMAT

If you want to—and you should really give this some thought—you can change the default format in which you save documents. There might actually be a good reason to do this. Not that long ago, I was working for an editor who could only read Word for Mac files. Virtually all of the work I was doing for several months went to that person, and I got pretty sick of having to resave my documents in that format. So, for the duration of that project, I changed the default setting. When I was finished, I switched it back.

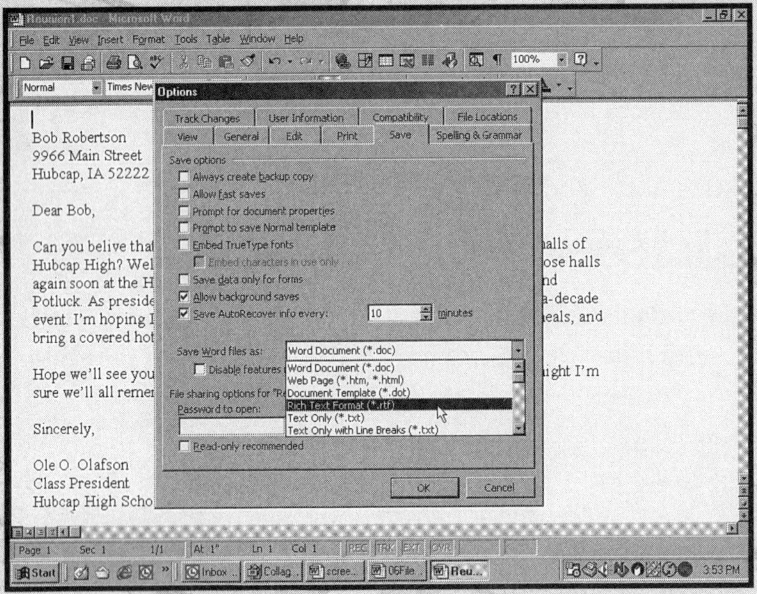

Figure 6-3
The Options dialog box, with the Save tab selected and the Word files as drop down list open.

To change Word's default file format:

📁 Go to the Menu Bar.

📁 Open Tools.

📁 Select Options to open the Options dialog box.

📁 Click on the Save tab.

📁 Click on the down arrow next to the "Save Word files as" drop-down list.

📁 Select the file format you want.

📁 Click OK.

📁 Now, when you save a new file, the first formatting option will be the one you chose.

machine. If you installed the Office Shortcut Bar, My Documents is the default folder that opens from the Open Office Document button on the Office Shortcut Bar. Word even puts a My Documents shortcut on your desktop when you install the program. (Like I said, they *really* want you to use this file.)

Word may want you to keep your documents in the My Documents folder, but it'll let you keep them anywhere. It'll even let you change the default working folder for your documents. For most people, My Documents is probably the best, and certainly the simplest, choice, but you might want to change It, to set up, say, a My Clients or a My Business working file that keeps you from having to dig down through layers of folders every time you want to save or open the files you use most.

When changing or creating a default folder, the action takes place in the Options dialog box. To open it, either hit Alt + T + O, or go to the Menu Bar, open Tools and select Options. (See Figure 6-4.)

To change the default working folder for your documents:

- **Click on the File Locations tab.**
- **In the "File types" window, you'll see a list of where, by default, certain documents are stored in Word.**
- **Select Documents.**

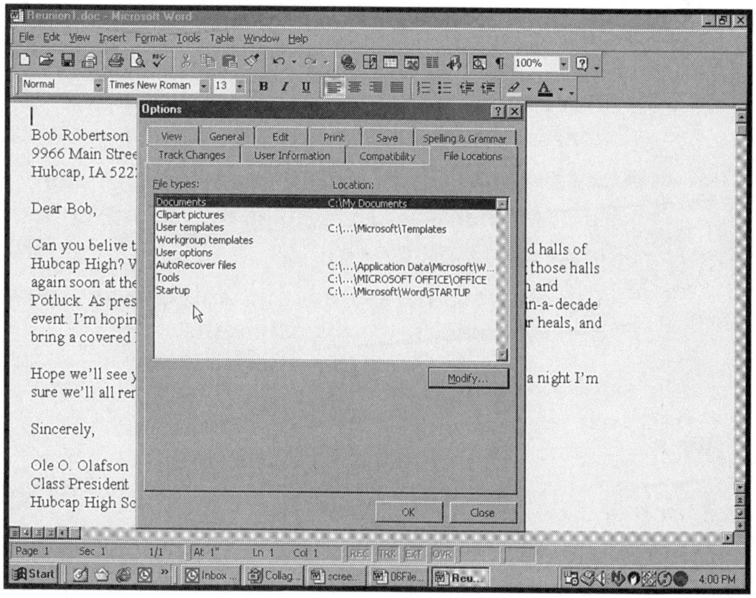

Figure 6-4
The Option dialog box with the File Locations tab selected.

- Click on the Modify button to open the Modify Location dialog box.
- Locate and click the folder you want in the folder list.

To create a new folder to display as the default working folder:

- Click on the Create New Folder icon to display as the default working folder.
- Type a name for the new folder in the "Name" box.
- Click OK.
- Now, when you begin to save a document for the first time, Word will take you to that folder in the Save dialog box.

The Places Bar

In certain Word 2000 dialog boxes, you might have noticed a bar along the left side with a column of big icons. This is the *Places Bar*. You'll see it when you open the Open, Save As, or Insert Picture dialog boxes. The Places Bar displays shortcuts to the History, My Documents, Desktop, Favorites, and Web Folders folders. To gain access to any of these folders from whichever dialog box you opened, just click on a shortcut.

- **The Desktop shortcut displays a list of desktop shortcuts, which I find very useful when I'm saving documents to floppy or zip disks, because I keep shortcuts to those drives on my desktop.**
- **The Favorites folder is supposed to show you, according to Word Help, "a list of shortcuts to files and folders you use often." All it shows me is my Web browser bookmarks.**
- **The History folder can be useful, because it gives you a list of shortcuts to the files and folders you most recently opened.**
- **Web Folders is where you might want to store your Internet and intranet files. These files live on a Web server and are available to others.**
- **The My Documents folder, as you already know, is Word's default home for your documents.**

Figure 6-5
The Places
Bar

Moving Files Between Folders

To really get control of your documents, you must be able to move them around from subfolder to subfolder, from "Current" to "Archive," from "momrecipes" to myrecipes." Shuffling files between folders is extremely simple in Word; you can do it with a few mouse clicks.

To change the location of an existing file:

- Go to the Menu Bar.
- Select File.
- Select Open to open the Open dialog box.
- Click through the folders to find your file.
- Right-click the file you want to move to open the shortcut menu.
- Click Cut.
- Open the folder into which you want to move the file.
- Right-click on an empty spot in the display window to open the shortcut menu. (make sure you don't accidentally select a file—the Paste command won't be available if you have).
- Click Paste.
- Your file appears in the list.

To move more than one folder at once, hold down either the Ctrl key or the Shift key as you click. (Holding down the Ctrl key lets you select files one at a time in any order; holding down the Shift key selects every file between the first one you clicked and the second.)

To create a copy of a file in another folder, follow the same procedure, selecting Copy in the shortcut menu instead of Cut. The file keeps the same name. (Word won't let you put files with the same name in the same directory.)

You can use this procedure to move or copy files onto floppy and Zip disks. After you cut or copy the file, just click to your desktop, MyComputer, and click on the drive icon. When the drive is open, right-click inside the display window and click Paste.

You'd think Word would let you click-and-drag; maybe in the next version.

Working with More than One File at a Time

If you were working strictly with paper documents, I'm pretty sure you wouldn't take out one document at a time and then put each one away in your filing cabinet before you took out another one. That would be crazy.

Well, back in the dinosaur days, that's how word processors worked. Fortunately, those days are as dead as the dinos. Modern word processors let you open bunches of documents at once, and Word is no exception. Just open them at will. The last file you opened will fill your Document Window; the other files will be represented by buttons along the Task Bar.

To switch between open files: just click on the Task Bar buttons, or use the Menu Bar:

- **Click on the Task Bar buttons.**

Or . . .

- **Go to the Menu Bar.**
- **Open the Window menu.**
- **You'll see a list of open files.**
- **Select the file you want to open.**
- **The file fills your screen.**

Word also lets you work with more than one file displayed in your Document Window, complete with toolbars, in a split screen. This is an extremely useful feature, especially if you're moving or comparing text between documents. You can actually drag and drop hunks of text between the open windows. (See Figure 6-6.)

To open more than one document in the Document Window at once:

- **Open two or more files. (Unless you're plugged into a big screen TV, you probably want to keep it down to no more than three.)**
- **Go to the Menu Bar.**
- **Open Window.**
- **Select Arrange All.**
- **The open files are displayed on your screen at the same time. The active document's Title Bar is highlighted.**

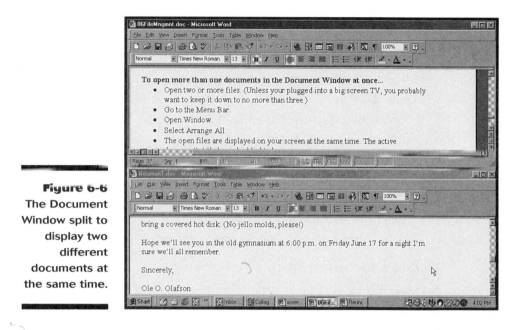

Figure 6-6
The Document Window split to display two different documents at the same time.

> To copy text between multiple documents open in a split screen, hold down the Shift key while you drag and drop.

TIP

- **To return a document window to its full size, click the Maximize button on one of the documents' Title Bar.**

Word lets you do a lot of dragging and dropping, which is very useful for the mouse-dependent among us. You can, for example, drag selected text from an open document into another open document, even if it's not open in the Document Window. Here's how:

- **Select the text you want to move to the other document.**
- **Click on it.**
- **Drag your mouse pointer to the Task Bar button of the target document.**
- **Hover over the document button without releasing the mouse button until the document opens (a couple of seconds).**
- **Position the mouse pointer where you want the text and drop it in place.**

Finding Files

Okay, you've got your files saved, disbursed among several usefully named subfolders. You know how to move them around, rename them, and copy them at will. Now all you have to do is *find* them. (See Figure 6-7.)

If you're just starting out in word processing, this may seem kind of silly. After all, you just open up My Documents, open up the condo newsletter subfolder, and there your documents are. I mean, how long could it take to riffle through a few files? But believe me, when you've been at it for a few years and built up some hefty file lists, you won't be laughing. Right now, I have hundreds of them, and I expect eventually to have thousands.

Luckily, Word has provided some very useful "find" tools.

To find a file using Word's Find feature:

- **Open the Open Dialog Box.**
- **Click on the Tools drop-down arrow on the Open dialog box toolbar.**
- **Select Find.**
- **Click on the drop-down list to select a drive or folder to search.**
- **To include subfolders in your search, click in the Search subfolders check box.**

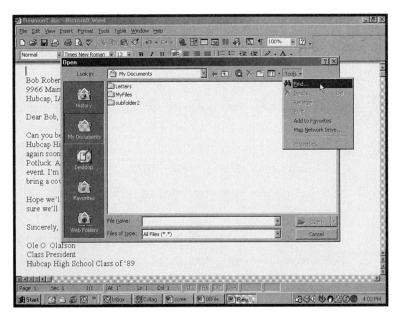

Figure 6-7
The Open dialog box with the Tools drop-down menu open and Find selected.

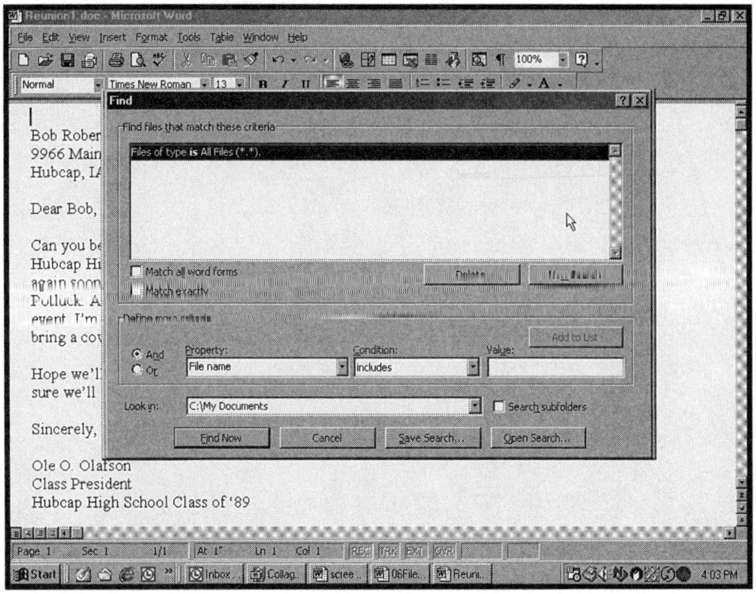

Figure 6-8
The Find dialog
box.

- In the "Define more criteria" area, use the Property, Condition, and Value drop-down lists to define your search criteria.
- Click Add to List to add the criteria to the search list.
- Click the Find Now button to start the search and return to the Open dialog box.
- Presently, the results of your search appear in the Open dialog box.
- Double-click on the filename to open the file.

7

More than Just the World's Greatest Typewriter

Writing and Editing in Word

Microsoft's Word has been accumulating bells and whistles for years, but behind all that noise, the fundamental purpose of this program is *word processing*. Without a doubt, Word 2000 has taken that function to a new level, but in the end, it all boils down to entering and editing text.

Entering Text

Your primary means of entering text in Word 2000 documents is, not surprisingly, your keyboard. The Document Window is analogous to a piece of paper in a typewriter (with some critical improvements). When you open a new Word document, the blinking insertion-point indicator appears automatically in the upper-left-hand corner of your Document Window, ready for you to begin typing.

In Word, you never have to hit the "return" key (Enter) at the end of a line; Word *wraps* the text, which means it automatically moves you to the next line when you reach the right-hand margin. You hit the Enter key when you want to break for a new paragraph or insert a blank line.

And you never have to stop to insert page 2 or do anything at all to continue from one page to the next. Word takes you from the last line of page 1 to the first line of page 2 and so on, automatically.

Click and Type

If you happen to be in Print Layout or Web Layout view, you can utilize Word 2000's brand new Click-and-Type feature and literally begin typing anywhere on the page. Just position your mouse pointer anywhere in the Document Window, double-click, and start typing.

> Let's say you reach the end of the text you want to put on, say, page 5, but you're in the middle of the page. Instead of hammering the Enter key until you get to the top of page 6, insert a manual page break right where you are by hitting Ctrl + Enter. When you print the document or look at it in Print Layout view, the proper number of blank lines will be there.
>
> **TIP**

You'll notice that the I-beam mouse pointer is different when you're using Click and Type. It has about four little lines next to it. These little lines indicate how the text you type will be aligned, that is, how it will line up between the margins. If you move the mouse pointer to the left, the lines align left; move it to the right, they align right; in the middle, you get a center-page alignment.

If you don't like the Click and Type feature, you can turn it off.

To turn off the Click and Type feature:

* Click on the Tools heading in the Menu Bar.
* Highlight and select Options.
* In the Options dialog box, click the Edit tab.
* Uncheck the Enable Click and Type check box.
* Click OK.

Typing Tricks

Most of the keyboard keys still serve their traditional functions. The Tab key, the space bar, and the Shift keys all do pretty much what they've always done. But some things are different. For example:

* The Cap Lock key allows you to type in all caps, but you have to hold down the Shift key to type the top characters on the numbers and punctuation keys.
* You can type the same character repeatedly by holding a key down. This trick works with any of the traditional "typing" keys, including numbers, punctuation marks, and the space bar.
* The Backspace key deletes characters to the immediate left of the cursor, or any amount of selected text.
* The Delete key deletes characters to the immediate right of the cursor or any amount of selected text.

Typing Modes

Insert Mode is Word 2000's default text-entry setting. In this mode, if you start typing in the middle of a sentence, the text to the right moves forward ahead of the new text and remains intact. In Overtype Mode, the text to the right in this example would have been typed over.

There are two ways to toggle back and forth between typing modes:

1. **Hit the Insert key.**

2. **Double-click on the OVR box in the Status Bar. The letters are black when this feature is turned on, gray when this feature is turned off. Technically, because Insert is the default mode, you're turning the Overtype Mode on and off.**

Selecting Text

Once you've entered some text into a Word document, Word lets you manipulate it in a number of different ways. You can change the font, apply different formatting, delete it, copy it, or pick it up and move it somewhere else. But before you can do any of these things, you have to "select" the text you want to manipulate. In other words, you have to tell Word exactly which text you want to move. (See Figure 7-1.)

To select text in Word, you simply highlight the letters, words, or sentences you want to change, move, or copy. Selected text appears on your screen in a black bar. You can select text using your mouse or your keyboard. Here's how to do it:

To select text using the mouse:

- **Position your I-beam mouse pointer at the beginning of the character, word, or group of words you want to select.**

- **Click and drag the pointer over the text.**

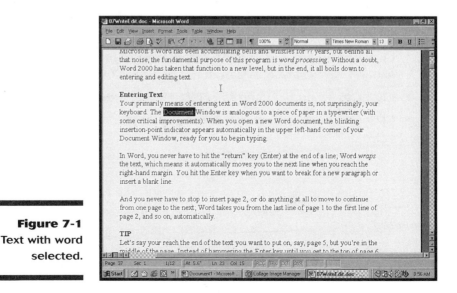

Figure 7-1
Text with word
selected.

- When the text you want to select is completely highlighted, release the mouse button.
- The highlighted text has been selected.

Or . . .

- Position your mouse pointer in the left margin of your document next to a line of text you want to select.
- Click to select that line.
- Double-click to select the entire paragraph.
- Triple-click to select the entire document.
- Clicking a fourth time re-selects the line only.

Or . . .

- Position your I-beam mouse pointer inside a word.
- Double-click to select that word.
- For single-letter words, such as "a" and "I," double-clicking on either side selects it.
- Triple-click to select the entire paragraph.
- Clicking a fourth time re-selects the word only.

To select text using the keyboard:

- Position your cursor next to the character, word, line, or group of words you want to select.
- Click Shift and use the Arrow key to highlight your selection one space at a time or one line at a time in any direction.
- Click Ctrl + Shift and use the Arrow keys to highlight one word at a time (right and left Arrows) or one paragraph at a time (up and down Arrows).
- Click Ctrl + End or Home to select all the text above or below your cursor.
- Click Ctrl + A to select the entire document.

To unselect text, click anywhere outside the highlighted text. You can also delete selected text either by hitting the Delete key, or by simply starting to type something new.

TIP

Rearranging Text

Whether your documents are large or small, sooner or later you're going to want to rearrange text. The ability to do this—to pick up a word, a sentence, a paragraph, or whole pages from one part of a document and then inset them intact into another part of that document, into a different document, or even into a different file—is the glory of word processors! This is definitely a procedure you are going to want to master. Luckily, it's easy.

Word 2000 offers you four techniques for rearranging existing text in a document:

1. **Cut or Copy, then Paste**
2. **Collect and Paste**
3. **Find and Replace**
4. **The Spike (covered in Chapter 16)**

Cut, Copy, and Paste

Can you believe that there was a time not that long ago when people literally *cut* sections of their paper documents apart, pasted them together with glue or cellophane tape, and then copied the cut-up sheet to create a newly organized page? Newspapers did it. Magazines did it. My mom did it with the family Christmas letter. Sheesh!

Rearranging text in Word 2000 is *muuuuuch* simpler. But though the process has changed, the language remains the same:

To cut text:

- **Select the text you want to cut.**
- **Click on the Cut button in the Standard Toolbar. Or . . .**
- **Hit Ctrl + X.**

"Cut" and "delete" are **not** synonymous terms, at least as far as Word is concerned. When you **cut** something, it still lives on the Clipboard, from which it can be retrieved; when you **delete** it, it's dead and can only be revived with the Undo feature.

TIP

To copy text:

- Select the text you want to copy.
- Click on the Copy button in the Standard Toolbar. Or . . .
- Hit Ctrl + C.
- The text you selected remains unaffected, but a copy of it is now available to you on the Clipboard.

To paste text:

- Position your cursor at the point in your document where you want to paste the text you've cut or copied using either your mouse or keyboard.

When you accumulate items on the Clipboard, **they stay on the Clipboard after you paste them into a document**. Even hitting "Paste All" won't scrape them off. You can paste the same items repeatedly throughout a document, or in several documents, as many times as you like, until you hit the "Clear Clipboard" button—the Xed-out clipboard icon—on the Clipboard itself.

TIP

- If you want to paste the text into a new document, you'll have to open it and position the cursor. (You probably ought to have the document open and available so you just have to switch to it.)
- Click the Paste button in the Standard Toolbar. Or . . .
- Hit Ctrl + V.
- Your copied or cut text inserts itself into your document, pushing text to the right of the insertion point forward.

Right-clicking over selected text invokes a shortcut menu of typical editorial tasks, including cut, paste, and copy.

TIP

Drag-and-Drop Copying

Word also lets you use your mouse to copy and reposition selected text.

To reposition selected text using your mouse:

- Click inside the selected text.
- Hold down the mouse button.
- Drag your mouse pointer to the insertion point.
- Notice that your pointer now has a ghostly box attached to it.
- Notice also, that a ghost cursor appears in the text near your mouse pointer to identify the insertion point.
- Release the mouse button.
- The selected text has disappeared from its old location and appeared at the insertion point.

To copy and insert text using your mouse:

- Click inside the selected text.
- Hold down the mouse button.
- Hold down the Ctrl key.
- Notice that your pointer now has a box with a plus sign in it next to the ghostly box.
- Drag your mouse pointer to position the ghost cursor at the insertion point.
- Release the mouse button.
- The selected text has disappeared from its old location and appeared at the insertion point.

When you're using your mouse pointer to copy and insert text, the order in which you click or hold down the Ctrl key matters. But if you release the Ctrl key before you release the mouse button, the operation becomes a cut-and-copy action.

Collect and Paste

The Clipboard has long been a part of Word's tool set, but in Word 2000 this feature has been improved considerably to allow a process called "collect and paste."

Collect and paste refers to the ability of the Word 2000 Clipboard to hold several copied items of various sizes and types and to then let you paste them into your document one at a time or as a group. This feature utilizes the Clipboard Toolbar

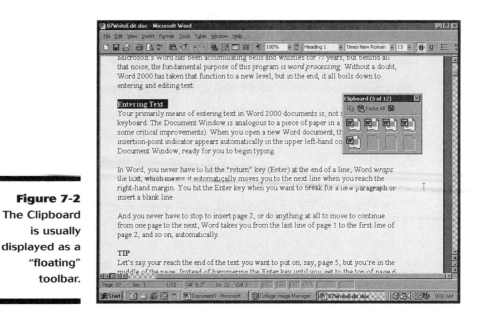

Figure 7-2
The Clipboard
is usually
displayed as a
"floating"
toolbar.

(it really looks more like a box), which displays the copied items and gives you access to this function. (See Figure 7-2.)

You can collect up to twelve copied items of virtually any size on the Clipboard toolbar. When you try to copy a thirteenth item, a warning window opens and let's you know that making another copy will bump the first item off the Clipboard to make room for the new item at the end.

Neither closing the Clipboard nor pasting items from the Clipboard, separately or as a group, clears collected items from the toolbar. To do this, you have to click on the Clear Clipboard key.

To use Word's Collect and Paste feature:

- **Begin cutting or copying text.**
- **When you cut or copy two items in a row, the Clipboard toolbar opens automatically in the Document Window.**
- **New icons appear in the Clipboard for each new item copied, up to twelve items total.**

When you hover your mouse pointer over a document icon in the Clipboard, a tip screen opens describing the item.

TIP

THE CLIPBOARD BUTTONS

CLEAR CLIPBOARD clears the Clipboard toolbar's contents.

PASTE ALL pastes every item in the Clipboard into the insertion point.

COPY lets you copy selected text in the document to the Clipboard.

CLOSE removes the Clipboard toolbar from the Document Window.

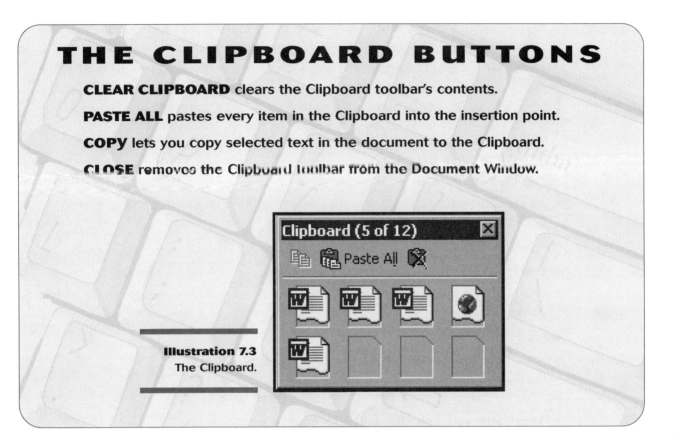

Illustration 7.3
The Clipboard.

- Position your curser at the insertion point.
- In the Clipboard, click on the icon for the text your want to paste.
- The text appears at the insertion point.
- Repeat to paste another item.
- Close the Clipboard by clicking the Close button.

Dragging the Clipboard toolbar over the toolbars at the top of your screen adds it on a separate line. To put it back in the Document Window, grab the Move Handle and drag it down.

You can move the Clipboard toolbar around the Program Window by clicking on the Clipboard Title Bar and dragging it with your mouse.

TIP

Is the Clipboard toolbar no longer appearing on your desk when you copy more than one item? The Clipboard is another of Word 2000's new "intuitive" toolbars. It automatically stops showing up in your Document Window if you fail to use it three times in a row to paste the items you cut and copy. To get it to start appearing again:

- **Go to the Menu Bar.**
- **Open View.**
- **Select Toolbars/Clipboard.**
- **The Clipboard will appear on your desk.**
- **As soon as you click Paste All or an individual item on the Clipboard, it'll go back to its old habits.**

Or . . .

- **Copy the same item two times consecutively.**
- **When you do this, the Clipboard appears and resumes appearing automatically.**

Or . . .

- **Reset the program tips.**

> Word lets you use the cut–and–copy operations to move or copy text to an entirely different program, such as Outlook. After the selected copy has been placed on the Clipboard through cutting or copying, switch to the other program and simply position your cursor and invoke the paste command as you would in Word. (This procedure works best with other Microsoft programs.)
>
> **TIP**

Undo and Redo

Two of Word's most useful editing commands are Undo and Redo. I can't tell you how many times I've thanked Heaven out loud when I realized I could get back that critical paragraph I just deleted, simply by invoking the Undo command. Or how often I've heaved a sigh of relief when I remembered that the thing I just undid I could redo with a couple of keystrokes.

The Undo command, not surprisingly, "undoes" your last typing action. If you invoke it again immediately, it undoes the action before that, and so on back to the first thing you typed after you opened the document. You can invoke this command three ways:

1. **Hit Ctrl + Z. (I know I've been hounding you to use the keyboard shortcuts, but you've got to admit, this is the simplest and most direct way to invoke this command.)**

2. **Click on the Edit heading in the Menu Bar and highlight and select Undo Typing.**

3. **Click on the Undo icon in the Standard Toolbar.**

The Redo command—guess what—"redoes" your last typing action. If the last thing you did was to type a group of words, Redo reproduces that group of words; if the last thing you did was to undo an action, Redo redoes it. This command, too, may be invoked in three ways:

1. **Hit Ctrl + Y. (Do I really need to say it?)**

2. **Click on the Edit heading in the Menu Bar and highlight and select Repeat Typing.**

3. **Click on the Redo Typing icon in the Standard Toolbar. (Notice that the Redo Typing icon is only accessible just after you've undone something.)**

One very cool thing about the Undo and Redo toolbar icons is they can display a complete record of your editorial actions, which then lets you undo or redo more than one action at a time. Click on the drop-down arrow next to the Undo icon, and you'll see a list of every typing action you've taken since you opened the document. You can't undo something you did earlier without undoing your more recent actions, but you can select a group of, say, your last five actions and undo them with a mouse click.

Notice that the Redo icon and drop-down arrow are only accessible after you've undone something. That list, of course, is much shorter.

TIP

8

Just in Case You Weren't Paying Attention in English Class Either

Checking for Errors in Word

Tools that help you check your documents for errors have been around almost since the first word processors began displaying those glowing amber letters on your black monitor screen. But, as it has done with many of its other features, Word 2000 takes these tools to a new level.

Word's Spelling and Grammar checkers work together to sift your text for errors—"proofing" in editor lingo.

Checking Your Spelling

Word's Spell Checker can monitor your spelling as you type, automatically pointing out errors as they occur. Whenever you misspell a word, the Spell Checker underscores it with a wavy red line. Word also notices if you repeat a word or capitalize it incorrectly and marks it with that wavy red line. (See Figures 8-1 and 8-2.)

To enable your Spell Checker to monitor your spelling as you type:

- **Go to the Menu Bar.**
- **Open Tools.**
- **Select Options to open the Options dialog box.**
- **Click on the Spelling and Grammar Tab.**

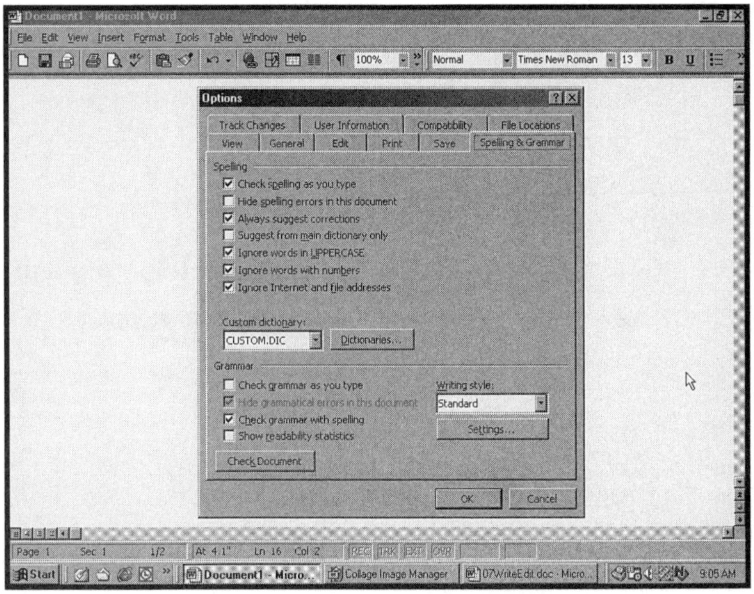

Figure 8-1
The Option dialog box with the Spelling tab selected.

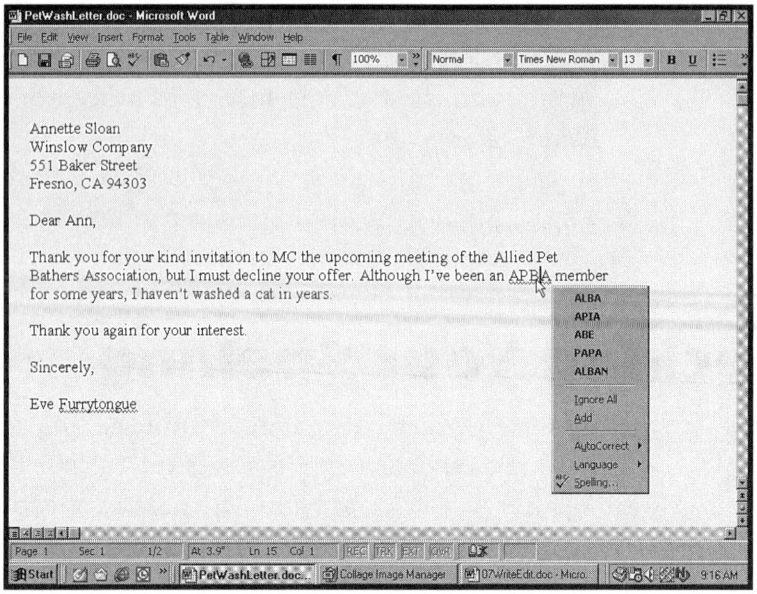

Figure 8-2
The Spelling
shortcut menu.

- **Click in the "Check spelling as you type" check box.**
- **Click OK.**

When Word marks something in your document with a wavy red line, it's pretty easy to get some alternative spelling suggestions. Just right-click the word to invoke a shortcut menu with a list of alternative spellings. To exchange the misspelled word for a word in the list, just click on the listed word. That menu also provides shortcuts to change the language you're using, proof your whole document, and add the misspelled word to your AutoCorrect file. (More on this shortly.)

You can run the Spell Checker for your entire document in three ways:

1. **Open the Tools menu and select Spelling and Grammar.**
2. **Click on the Spelling and Grammar button in the Standard toolbar.**
3. **Hit F7.**

As the Spell Checker "reads" your document, checking every word against its dictionary, it will stop whenever it finds something out of whack and present you with a dialog box. The dialog box displays the area of your document where the word was found, with the word in red. You then have the option of clicking on one of several buttons:

- **Ignore** skips that word and continues proofing.

- **Ignore Rule** stops worrying about the spelling rule the word broke—say, "it's" versus "its"—here and through the rest of the document.

- **Next Sentence** skips the current sentence without making any changes.

- **Change** substitutes the word you selected from the list in the "Suggestions" window.

- **Undo** takes you back to the last edit.

- **Options** opens the Spelling and Grammar options dialog box.

- **Cancel** stops this spell checking session.

Sometimes Word tells you something is misspelled when you know it's not. That is because computers are stupid. I know . . . I know . . . But it's true; computers only know what you tell them, and you haven't told yours that Mohan is your partner from India's name or that FLOGG is the acronym for your trade association. Uncommon names, abbreviations, acronyms, language specific to industries such as high tech or medicine—all can cause Word to wave it's wavy red flags. If you often use words that Word doesn't recognize, the Spell Checker can drive you nuts.

You can ignore those wavy red lines, or you can smarten up Word by adding special or oddly spelled words to its dictionary.

To add a word to the Word dictionary:

- Right-click the word underlined in wavy red to invoke the shortcut menu.

- Select Add.

- Word will now recognize that word as spelled correctly.

Spellcheckers are great, but they don't always catch misplaced homophones. **Homophones** are words that sound the same, but have different meanings and spellings, such as right and write, bare and bear, waste and waist, peak and peek (or pique), and so on. To be absolutely sure your catching this kind of error, you'll have to proof your documents the old fashioned way.

TIP

Checking Your Grammar

You might have noticed that nearly all of the command buttons and menu choices associated with the Spell Checker are labeled "Spelling and Grammar." That's because the Spell Checker and the Grammar Checker are designed to work together to find errors in your document.

Just like Word's Spell Checker, the Grammar Checker can monitor your work as you type. Whenever you make a grammatical error, the Grammar Checker underscores it with a wavy *green* line.

To enable your Grammar Checker to monitor your work as you type:

- Go to the Menu Bar.
- Open Tools.
- Select Options to open the Options dialog box.
- Click on the Spelling and Grammar Tab.
- Go to the Grammar area at the bottom of the box.
- Click in the "Check grammar as you type" check box.
- Click OK.

You can find grammatical alternatives the same way you found alternate spellings: just right-click the underlined text to invoke the shortcut menu. You'll find alternative wordings from which you may select a replacement or an explanation of what you did wrong highlighted in yellow. You'll also find a shortcut to start proofing the whole document and an Ignore button that removes the wavy green line.

Some of us find the wavy red and green lines distracting and prefer to spell- and grammar-check our documents after we've finished typing.

To turn the Spelling and Grammar Checkers off until your ready for them:

- Go to the Menu Bar.
- Open Tools.
- Select Options to open the Options dialog box.
- Click on the Spelling and Grammar Tab.
- Click in the "Check spelling as you type" check box to remove the checkmark.
- Click in the "Check grammar as you type" check box to remove the checkmark.
- Click OK.
- No more wavy lines!

You can also check the spelling and grammar of specified sections of your document. Here's how:

- **Select the section of text you want to proof.**
- **Invoke the Spelling and Grammar checker.**
- **Word proofs the text.**
- **When it's finished proofing the selected section, Word will ask whether you want to continue proofing the rest of the document.**
- **Click No.**

You can invoke the Spell Checker to proof your document without the Grammar Checker (although you can't do it the other way around). Here's how:

- **Go to the Menu Bar.**
- **Open Tools.**
- **Select Options to open the Options dialog box.**
- **Click on the Spelling and Grammar Tab.**
- **Click in the "Check grammar with spelling" check box to remove the check mark.**
- **Click OK.**

Or . . .

- **Start up the Spell Checker.**
- **When the Spelling and Grammar dialog box appears, uncheck the "Check grammar" check box.**

Making the Rules

Word allows you to select the grammatical rules and writing style parameters you want the Grammar checker to enforce when it checks your document. You can choose from preselected groups of options, or customize a list of your own unique preferences. (See Figure 8-3.)

By default, Word checks your document's grammar and writing style using the Standard group of options. (See Figure 8-4.)

To select another group:

- **Go to the Menu Bar.**
- **Open Tools.**
- **Select Options to open the Options dialog box.**

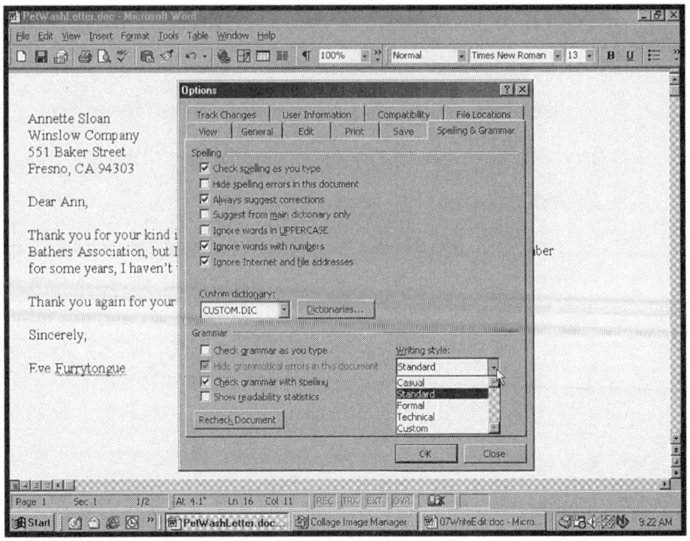

Figure 8-3
The Options dialog box with the Spelling and Grammar tab open and the Writing style drop-down menu open.

- Click on the Spelling and Grammar tab.
- Select a style from the "Writing Style" drop-down list.
- Select a style group.
- Click OK.
- The next time you invoke the Grammar checker, it will apply the options in the new group.

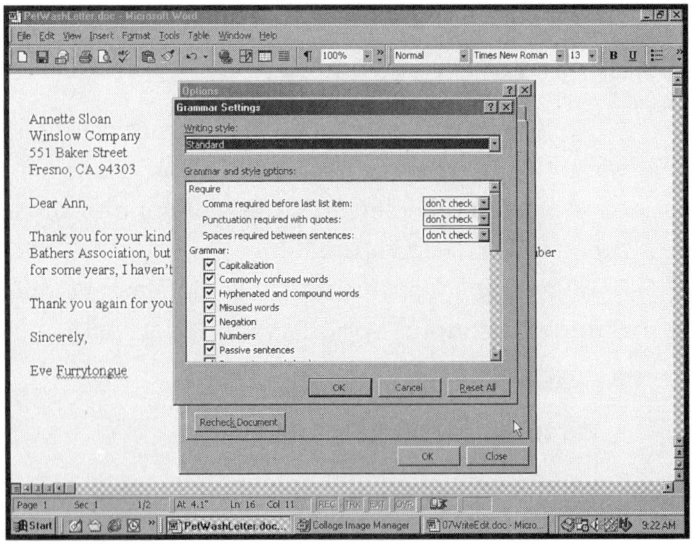

Figure 8-4
The Grammar Settings dialog box

To create a customized set of grammar and style parameters:

- Go to the Menu Bar.
- Open Tools.
- Select Options to open the Options dialog box.
- Click on the Spelling and Grammar tab.
- Select a style from the "Writing Style" drop-down list
- Click on the "Settings" button,
- Select Custom from the "Writing Style" drop-down list.
- Click in the check boxes next to the options you want Word's Grammar checker to use.

Word 2000's Writing Styles

STANDARD Checks all the Grammar options except Numbers and Sentence Structure. Checks none of the Style options.

CASUAL Checks for proper Capitalization, Verb-Subject Agreement, Commonly Confused and Misused Words, and Verb-Noun Phrases. Checks none of the Style options.

FORMAL Checks every Grammar option. Checks every Style option except Gender-Specific Words and use of First Person.

TECHNICAL Checks all the Grammar options except Passive Sentences, Possessives, and Plurals. Checks all the Style options except Contractions, Gender-specific Words, Jargon, Split Infinitives, Successive Nouns, and Prepositions.

CUSTOM Checks the grammar and writing style rules you set.

You can modify Word's grammatical style categories by checking and unchecking the boxes shown in the "Grammar and style options" window of the Grammar Settings dialog box. To reset the modified categories to their default settings, click the Reset All button.

TIP

Word's Grammar Checker Options

Word 2000 provides a number of Grammar Checker options, which you can tell Word to use or not when it proofreads your documents. They include:

CAPITALIZATION Makes sure that names and titles are capitalized. Also looks for overuse of capitalization.

COMMONLY CONFUSED WORDS Uses sentence context to ferret out misplaced homophones and other commonly misused words, such as "it's" (for "its"), "there" (for "their" or "they're"), and so one.

HYPHENATED AND COMPOUND WORDS Looks for improperly hyphenated words, words that should be hyphenated, improperly closed compounds (high school), and open compounds that should be closed (set up).

MISUSED WORDS Incorrect usage of adjectives and adverbs, comparatives and superlatives, such as "like" as a conjunction, "nor" versus "or," "what" versus "which," "who" versus "whom," units of measure, conjunctions, prepositions, and pronouns.

NEGATION The double negative killer. (Don't nobody care.)

NUMBERS Looks for numerals that should be spelled out ("nine" not "9"), and vice versa ("12" not "twelve"). Also detects incorrect usage of "%" in place of "percentage."

PASSIVE SENTENCES Highlights sentences written in the passive voice (The broom is used by janitors) and sometimes suggests alternative sentences in the active voice.

POSSESSIVES AND PLURALS Finds incorrectly written possessives and plurals.

PUNCTUATION Looks for proper use of commas, colons, periods, question marks, quotation marks, colons, semicolons, and spaces between words.

RELATIVE CLAUSES Watches for incorrect use of relative pronouns and punctuation (who, which, that, whatever, whichever, that's, whose).

SENTENCE STRUCTURE Shows sentence fragments, run-on sentences, overuse of conjunctions, shifts between the active and the passive voice within a sentence, incorrect sentence structure of questions, and misplaced modifiers.

SUBJECT-VERB AGREEMENT Monitors for disagreement between subject and verbs, subject-complement agreement, and subject–verb agreement with pronouns and quantifiers. (The players has won the game/Elvis have left the building.)

VERB AND NOUN PHRASES Finds incorrect noun and verb phrases; a/an misuse; incorrect verb tenses; transitive verbs used as intransitive verbs; number agreement errors in noun phrases ("five machine" instead of "five machines").

Word's Writing Style Options

Word also provides a number of Writing Style options, which you can tell Word to use when you invoke the Grammar Checker. They include:

CLICHÉS Finds words or phrases identified as clichés in the dictionary.

COLLOQUIALISMS Looks for colloquial words and phrases, including "real," "awfully," and "plenty" used as adverbs; two consecutive possessives; "get" used as a passive verb; "kind of" used in place of "somewhat"; "scared of" used in place of "afraid of"; and "how come" used in place of "why."

CONTRACTIONS Notices contractions that you might want to spell out or that are considered too informal for a formal writing style. For example (from Word Help): "We won't leave 'til tomorrow" instead of "We will not leave until tomorrow."

GENDER–SPECIFIC WORDS Tracks down words with "man" or "woman" in them and offers a non-gender-specific alternative. For example: "worker" instead of "workman," "mail carrier" instead of "mailman," but also, words such as "stewardess" for which it offers to substitute "flight attendant."

JARGON Ferrets out technical, business, or industry lingo.

SENTENCE LENGTH Highlights sentences more than sixty words long.

SENTENCES BEGINNING WITH "AND," "BUT," AND "HOPEFULLY"
Use of conjunctions at the beginning of sentences has become fairly widely accepted practice, but stands out like a sore thumb in formal writing. Also nixes the use of "plus" as a conjunction between two independent clauses.

SUCCESSIVE NOUNS (MORE THAN THREE) Watches out for strings of nouns that may leave the reader scratching his/her head. For example (from Word Help): "The income tax office business practices remained the same."

SUCCESSIVE PREPOSITIONAL PHRASES (MORE THAN THREE) The book on the shelf in the corner at the library on the edge of town was checked out."

UNCLEAR PHRASING Notes ambiguous phrasing, such as "more" followed by an adjective and a plural or mass noun ("We need more thorough employees," instead of "We need more employees who are thorough"), or sentences in which there is more than one possible referent for a pronoun ("All of the departments did not file a report" instead of "Not all of the departments filed a report").

USE OF FIRST PERSON Makes sure that you've used the pronouns "I" and "me" properly. If you're using Technical style, it prompts you to recast your sentence without them.

WORDINESS Reacts to wordy relative clauses or vague modifiers (such as "fairly" or "pretty"), redundant adverbs, too many negatives, the unnecessary use of "or not" in the phrase "whether or not," or the use of "possible . . . may" in place of "possible . . . will."

SPLIT INFINITIVES Although Word allows a split infinitive, which is so commonly used nowadays it's almost accepted, it won't let you squeeze in more than one between the "to" and the infinitive form of the verb. Captain Picard can admonish the crew of the Enterprise "to boldly go where no one has gone before," but in Word at least, he can't tell them "to very boldly go" anywhere.

9

Minding Your Ps and Qs . . . And Your Xs, Ys, and Zs

Formatting Text in Word

Formatting, in the word–processing world, refers to a host of features and functions that affect the way your documents look—from the size of your fonts to the width of your margins, from the line spacing to the text alignment, from columns to bulleted lists. Word 2000 is loaded with tools for formatting individual characters, blocks of text, and entire pages.

The ability to apply formatting to the documents it creates is what transformed computer word processing from glorified typing to desktop publishing. We've come to take these changes for granted, but think about it! Until just a few years ago, the only way you could do any of the things described in the next three chapters— things you can do just sitting at your desk—was with a printing press!

The next three chapters explain all but a few of the formatting techniques available to you in Word 2000. (You'll find a handful of advanced techniques in Chapter 16, on working with Word's advanced features. Master these tools and you'll be able to create truly sophisticated documents.

Chapters 10 and 11 look at Word's paragraph and page formatting options. But let's start with what you might think of as the smallest formatting unit: the font.

What Are Fonts?

A *font* is a type style that is applied to words, numbers, and punctuation; it refers to the design of the typeface. The characteristics of a font—serifed or non-serifed, monospaced or proportionally spaced, etc.—remain consistent for all the letters of the alphabet, numbers, punctuation marks, and many special characters, such as asterisks. Some of the better-known fonts are Helvetica, Courier, and Arial. When I talk about "character formatting," I'm talking about changing the kind, size, and look of fonts.

> **Word's fonts are TrueType fonts, which means the way they look on your monitor screen is the way they're going to look on the page coming out of your printer. You can recognize TrueType fonts by the logo that precedes them in the font menu. You can use other font types in Word, but they won't necessarily look the same on the printed page.**
>
> **TIP**

Word 2000 comes with 44 different fonts that you can apply to the text of any document you create. The program's default font is Times New Roman, which happens to be my personal favorite for most of the work I do in Word. It's a proportionally spaced, serifed font that I find very easy to read. Unless you change it (and you can), the text in every Word document would be Times New Roman.

> Some of Word's 44 TrueTypo fonts aren't letters or numbers, but, rather, are symbols that correspond to keyboard keys. The phrase **"Now I lay me down to sleep,"** looks like this in Marlett:
>
> ⬚⬚ ╱╱ ‹ ⬚⬚⬚ ⌐ ✔ ◥ ⬚ ⌐⌐ ⌐⌐ ╱╱ ‹ ●⬚▲ ╱╱⬚ ? ⌐⌐⌐ ╱╱⬚⬚
>
> **TIP**

Changing Fonts

You can change fonts any time. You can start a new document with a new font, or you can change fonts when you're halfway finished. You can use a dozen different fonts in a single document (but you've got to be careful not to go crazy), or you can apply a different font to each letter of a word (I recently did this on a birthday card for my one of my nieces). (See Figure 9-1.)

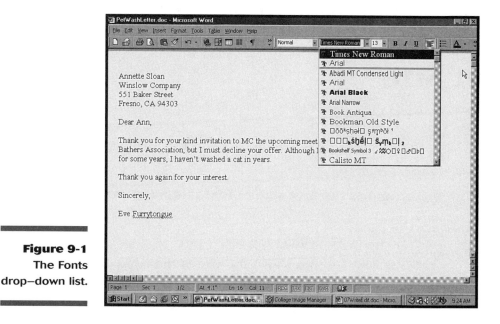

Figure 9-1
The Fonts drop–down list.

To change the font of text and numbers:

- Select the text in your document that you want to display in a different font. Or . . .

- Hit Ctrl + A if you want to change the font for the entire document.

- Go to the Formatting toolbar.

- The Font box shows the type of font currently applied to the text where your cursor is located—in this example, it's the default font, Times New Roman.

- Click on the down arrow next to the Font box to display the Font List.

- The Font List displays the last five fonts you selected in the upper portion, and the complete font selection in alphabetical order below that.

- Scroll down the list until you find the font you want to apply to the selected text.

- Click on the font.

- The selected text in your document is now displayed in your chosen font.

If you want to change the font in a new document, just select the new font as explained here before you start typing.

Word 2000 is the first version of this program to display its selection of fonts in the fonts listed. Arial Black looks like **Arial Black**, Hattenschweiller looks like Hattenschweiller, and Lucinda Console looks like—you guessed it— Lucinda Console.

TIP

Font Size

By default, Word's gives you a 12-point font. (Fonts are measured in "points," on a 72-points-per-inch scale. Because 12 points is the default font size, whichever fonts you assign to the text in your documents will all be in 12-point type—until you change it. (See Figure 9-2.)

To change the font size of text and numbers:

- Select the text you want to resize.

- Go to the Formatting toolbar.

- The Font Size box shows the size of the font currently applied to the text where your cursor is located—in this example, 12 points.

- Click the down arrow next to the Font Size box to display a list of font sizes.

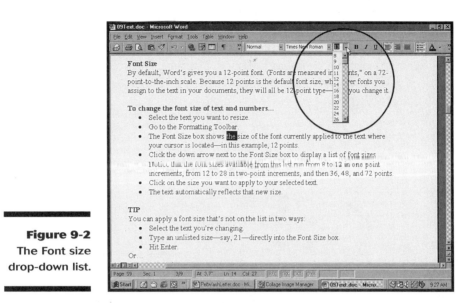

Figure 9-2
The Font size
drop-down list.

- Notice that the font sizes available from this list run from 8 to 12 in one-point increments, from 12 to 28 in two-point increments, and then 36, 48, and 72 points.
- Click on the size you want to apply to your selected text.
- The text automatically reflects that new size.

You can apply a font size that's not on the list in one of two ways:

- Select the text you're changing.
- Type an unlisted size—say, 21—directly into the Font Size box.
- Hit Enter.

Or . . .

- Select the text.
- Hit Ctrl +] (the right bracket key) to increase the text size by one point, or Ctrl + [(the left bracket key) to reduce the text size by one point. You can hold down the Ctrl key and continue hitting the bracket keys until the text is the size you want. You'll see the sizes change in the Font Size box on the Formatting toolbar.

Font Styles and Effects

Just as fonts can be resized, so can different "styles" be applied to almost any font. A font *style*, in the context of this chapter, simply means that the selected text is bold, *italicized*, *underlined*, or not (in Word lingo, "regular.") (Word's Styles, which apply to document formats, are completely different animals, as we'll see in Chapter 15, Word Magic: Working with Styles, Themes, Templates, and Wizards).

Font *effects* are special characteristics that may be applied to your text in Word 2000. These include:

- Superscript
- Subscript
- Strikethrough
- Double Strikethrough
- Shadow

- Outline
- Emboss
- Engrave
- Small Caps
- All Caps

Bold, Italics, and Underline

These three are the simplest styles to apply to the text in your document. Here's how you do it:

- Select the text you want to modify.
- Go to the Formatting toolbar, and click on the Bold, Italics, or Underline button. Or . . .
- Hit Ctrl + B for bold, Ctrl + I for italics, or Ctrl + U for underline.
- Your text changes instantly.
- Hitting the toolbar button or key combinations again when the modified text is selected toggles the style off.

Most fonts in Word 2000 will accept all three style modifications at the same time. In other words, your text can be **bold,** *italicized bold,* and **underlined *italicized bold***. Some of the special effects can be piled on, too, for example: **underlined italicized bold superscript**. But some fonts balk at too many styles and effects, which makes sense: Why would you want **Arial Black bold**.

TIP

Font Colors

And the Lords of Technology said, "Let there be color!" Okay . . . probably not . . . but with advances in color printing technology and the advent of inexpensive color printers, color was bound to find it's way into the tool set of word processors.

The capabilities of your printer notwithstanding, text displayed in the Word 2000 Document Window can take on a variety of hues. (See Figure 9-3.)

To change the color of text and numbers:

* Select the text you want to modify.
* Go to the Formatting toolbar.
* By default, the Font Color button displays the automatic setting for black text.
* Click on the down arrow next to the Font Color button.
* Click on the color you want.
* The selected text changes color.

Notice that this action changes the color of the little bar on the Font Color button. Now, to change selected text to that color, all you have to do is click the button.

To apply a different color to selected text:

* Click the down arrow next to the Font Color button.
* Click on a different color.

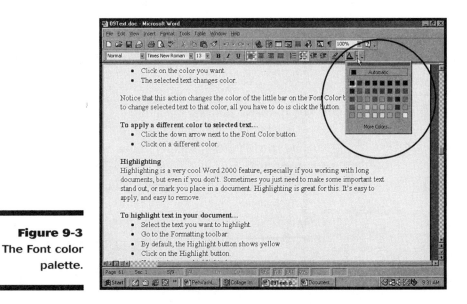

Figure 9-3
The Font color palette.

92 *Everything Microsoft® Word 2000*

Highlighting

Highlighting is a very cool Word 2000 feature, especially if you work with long documents, but even if you don't. Sometimes you just need to make some important text stand out or mark your place in a document. Highlighting is great for this. It's easy to apply and easy to remove. (See Figure 9-4.)

To highlight text in your document:

* Select the text you want to highlight.
* Go to the Formatting toolbar.
* Click on the Highlight button. (By default, the Highlight button shows yellow.)

Or, if you want a different color of highlighting . . .

* Click on the down arrow next to the Highlight button.
* Click on a highlight color. Notice that the color on the Highlight button changes.
* Your selected text is now highlighted.

Or . . .

* Click on the Highlight button.

Or, if you want a different color of highlighting . . .

* Click on the down arrow next to the Highlight button.
* Click on a highlight color.

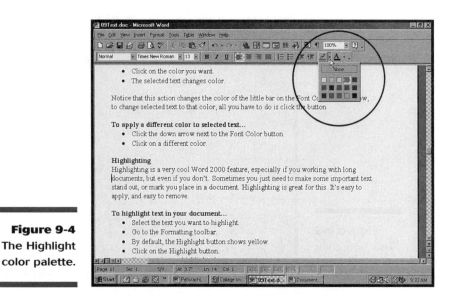

Figure 9-4
The Highlight color palette.

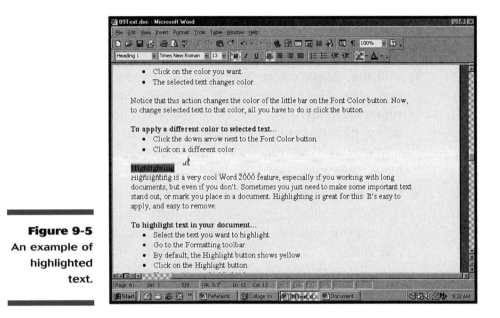

Figure 9-5
An example of
highlighted
text.

- Now your mouse pointer looks like a highlighter.
- Select the text you want to highlight by dragging the mouse pointer over it or by clicking on it as described in Chapter 4 (Word basics).
- Your text is now highlighted. (See Figure 9-5.)

To remove highlighting from text and numbers:

- Select the text.
- Go to the Formatting toolbar.
- Click on the down arrow next to the Highlight button.
- Click on the "None" box.
- Your selected text is now free of highlighting.

Or . . .

- Before selecting any text, click on the Highlight button to toggle on the highlighter pointer.
- Select the highlighted text using the mouse pointer.
- Your text is now highlightless.

To get rid of the highlighter mouse pointer, click on the Highlight button again or hit Esc. You can also highlight graphics using any of the text-highlighting techniques.

Word 2000's highlighting feature really works best onscreen. When you need to print highlighted text, stick with the lighter colors: yellow, bright green, turquoise, and pink. This suggestion is especially important to remember when using a black-and-white printer. The lighter highlight colors will print as pale gray screens on noncolor printers; the darker ones will print as bars of black, obscuring the highlighted sections.

TIP

You can display or hide the highlighting effect, both on your monitor screen and in your printed documents, without changing the text itself. Here's how:

- **Go to the Menu Bar.**
- **Open Tools.**
- **Select Options.**
- **Click on the View tab.**
- **In the "Show" area, click in the "Highlights" check box to remove the checkmark.**
- **No highlights will appear in your documents.**

The Font Dialog Box

To get to the special effects, you have to open the Font dialog box, which is also another way to apply the other character formatting options. In fact, everything you can do to fonts in Word 2000, you can do from the Font dialog box. (See Figure 9-6.)

You can change the color of all the highlighting in your document or remove it entirely. Here's how you do it:

- 📁 Hit Ctrl + A to select the whole document.
- 📁 Go to the Formatting toolbar.
- 📁 Click on the down arrow next to the Highlight button.
- 📁 Click on a different color. Or . . .
- 📁 Click the "None" box to remove all highlighting.

TIP

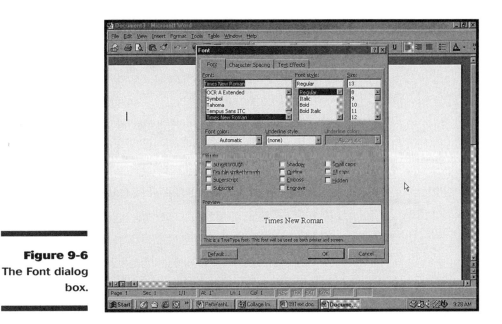

Figure 9-6
The Font dialog
box.

To open the Font Dialog Box:

- Go the Menu Bar.
- Open Format.
- Select Font to open the Font dialog box.
- Click on the Font tab.

Now you have access not only to the special text effects but also to every font option in Word: font types, sizes, styles, color, and some effects you haven't seen yet.

To apply any of the effects shown:

- Select the text you want to modify.
- Click on the check box next to the effect you want to apply.
- A preview of the modified text appears in the Preview box.
- Click OK.

The Font Dialog box gives you access to some very cool effects. (See Figure 9-7.)

To change the style of an underline:

- Select the underlined text you want to modify.
- Click the down arrow next to the "Underline style" list box.

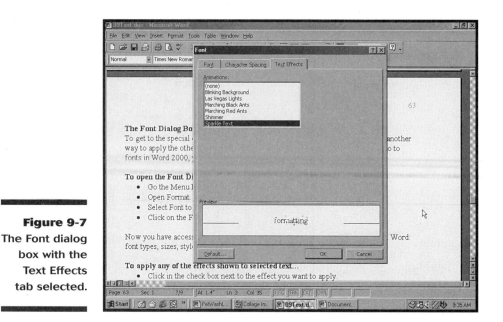

Figure 9-7
The Font dialog
box with the
Text Effects
tab selected.

- Click on an underline style.
- Click OK.
- The new underline is applied to the selected text.

To change the color of an underline in selected text:

- Click the down arrow next to the "Underline color" list box (not available unless you've selected some underlined text).
- Click on a color.
- Click OK.
- The new color is applied to the underline in the selected text.

The Font dialog box also gives you access to some interesting *animated* text effects. Click on the Text Effects tab to get a list of these, which includes:

- **Blinking Background**
- **Las Vegas Lights**
- **Marching Black Ants**
- **Marching Red Ants**
- **Shimmer**
- **Sparkle Text (my fave)**

To apply these effects to selected text:

- Click in the check box next to the effect you want.
- A preview of the modified text appears in the Preview box.
- Click OK.

Obviously, these effects won't be showing up in the printed document . . . yet.

Font Spacing

There are only a few other things you can do to the text in your Word 2000 documents: You can expand or condense it, expand or condense the spaces between characters, and shift it up and down a bit.

The Character Spacing Tab

To get to these options, click on the Character Spacing tab in the Formatting dialog box. The Scale list box gives you percentage options that let you stretch and squeeze your text like an accordion. Select one, and you'll see the effect in the Preview window. To apply this option to selected text, just click on a percentage and click OK.

The Spacing list box gives you three character-spacing options: Normal, Expanded, and Condensed. You have to select some text to see the effect of these options in the Preview box. The Expanded option pulls the letters apart evenly; the Condensed option pushes them together evenly. Click on the up and down arrows next to the "By" list box to specify by how much space you want the characters expanded or condensed. Click OK to implement the changes.

The Position list box also gives you three options: Normal, Raised, and Lowered. You don't need to have selected some text to see the affect of these options in the Preview box. The Raised option bumps the selected text up above the line by the number of points you specify in the "By" list box; the Lowered option drops it down. Click OK to implement the changes.

Kerning

Here's Word's definition of "kerning": *The adjustment of text that involves slightly decreasing or increasing the amount of space between any two adjacent letters to improve the overall appearance of text. The amount of kerning depends on the font design and the specific pair of letters. You can use automatic kerning only with proportionally spaced TrueType fonts or similar scalable fonts that are larger than a certain minimum size. The minimum size varies from font to font.*

In other words, while the Scale feature alters the spacing between all selected letters by the same amount, the kerning feature alters the spacing between particular *pairs* of letters. To kern characters that are above a particular point size, select the "Kerning for fonts" check box, and then enter the point size in the "Points and above" box.

> **You can change the case of selected text from all caps to all lower case or to title (each word capitalized) simply and quickly by hitting Shift + F3. If you hold down the Shift key, you can toggle through the different text cases by repeatedly hitting F3.**
>
> **TIP**

You can remove any of these character-formatting changes in selected text by returning to the Formatting dialog box, unselecting the various check boxes, and clicking OK.

The font used in the Word 2000 dialog boxes and other interface components is known as the Office Interface Font. This is the font used in all the program's dialog boxes, toolbars, rulers, buttons, messages, and menus.

If you don't like it, you can change it. Here's how:

- **Go to the Menu Bar.**
- **Open Help.**
- **Select Microsoft® Word Help to open the Help dialog box.**
- **Click on the Index tab.**
- **Type "font" in the "Type keywords" window.**
- **Click on the Search button.**
- **In the "Choose a topic" window, click on "About the Office interface font."**
- **In the display window, click on the "Change the Office interface font" hyperlink.**
- **Follow the steps described.**

Keep in mind that the dialog boxes in Word 2000 are designed for the Office Interface Font; Impact Bold might not fit, and Calisto might not have the necessary characters. Also, some of the Office interface items might continue to be displayed in the default font. What's more, Microsoft advises against doing this, because it changes some things in the Windows registry. As Microsoft puts it, "Unexpected results might occur."

10

A Plethora of Pretty Paragraphs
Formatting Paragraphs in Word

Word 2000 gives you several formatting tools that allow you to change the alignment, positioning, and spacing of individual lines of text and whole paragraphs in your documents. You can change the way you work with tabs and indents, expand or contract the line spacing, modify the text alignment, use bulleted lists, and separate sections of text with borders, boxes and shading.

What's a Paragraph?

Beyond the font, there's the paragraph. This might be overkill, but let's take just a few moments to define exactly what Word means by "paragraph." Word 2000 recognizes a *paragraph* as a distinct unit of information with its own formatting characteristics (alignment, spacing, etc.). A Word paragraph is always followed by a paragraph mark—sometimes they're hidden, but they're there. A paragraph in Word can be a single line of text—the title of your term paper, for example—or 50 lines, if you're William Faulkner.

Word 2000 lets you apply different formatting to different paragraphs within the same document, which comes in very handy when you're centering titles, citing long passages that require single spacing, or using footnotes.

Under the heading of "More Information Than I Really Needed," add this: Paragraph marks in Word actually contain all of the formatting information for that paragraph. You usually change a paragraph's formatting by selecting the entire paragraph, which, whether you realize it or not, includes the paragraph mark. But you can also change a paragraph's formatting by selecting its paragraph mark and setting its formatting attributes before you start typing. Hitting the Enter key marks the paragraph and pulls the formatting into the next paragraph you type.

TIP

Line Spacing

By default, Word documents are single spaced, but it's easy to change that. You can change the line spacing of a few lines, a paragraph, several paragraphs, or your whole document. (See Figure 10-1.)

To change line spacing in your documents using the Keyboard:

- Select the text you want to change.
- Click on Ctrl + 1 for single-line spacing, Ctrl + 2 for double-line spacing, or Ctrl + 5 for one-and-a-half-line spacing.
- Your new line spacing is reflected in your document.

To change line spacing in your documents using the Menu Bar:

- Select the text you want to change.
- Go to the Menu Bar.
- Open Format.
- Select Paragraph to open the Paragraph dialog box.
- Click on the Indents and Spacing tab.
- Click on the down arrow next to the "Line spacing" list box.
- The box displays a list of line-spacing options.

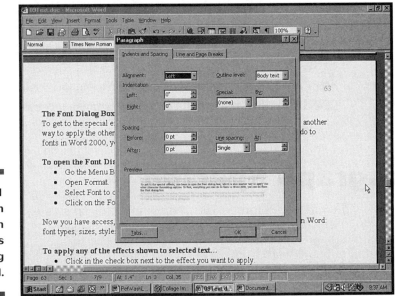

Figure 10-1
The Paragraph dialog box with the Indents and Spacing tab selected.

- **Select Single, 1.5 lines, or Double to apply standard options.**
- **Click OK**
- **You new spacing is applied.**

You might have noticed that, just as the Font dialog box gave you access to every Word text-formatting option, the Paragraph dialog box gives you access to all the paragraph formatting options.

The "At least," "Exactly," and "Multiple" Line Spacing Options

The roles of the "Single," "Double," and "1.5" line-spacing options are pretty obvious, but the other three take some explaining.

- **"At least" refers to the minimum line spacing Word can handle, given the font sizes and graphics of your document.**
- **The "Exactly" option creates fixed line spacing that you specify. Characters and graphics larger than this fixed space get cut off.**
- **"Multiple" refers to line spacing based on a mathematical formula, the multiple for which you designate. For example, if you select Multiple and set your line spacing at 1.2, the line spacing in your document will increase by a factor of 1.2, or 20 percent; if you set your line spacing at .08, the line spacing in your document will decrease by 20 percent. You set these factors in the "At" box.**

If a line in your document contains a large text character or graphic, Word automatically accommodates the character by increasing the spacing for that entire line—unless you've imposed fixed line spacing with the Exactly option. To keep the larger characters from being cut off while keeping the line spacing even, select the line spacing in the At box that is large enough to fit the largest character or graphic in the line.

Paragraph Spacing

Word, by default, also places no extra spaces (or lines) between paragraphs in a document. But many people like to stick a half-space or even a whole space between their paragraphs to make their documents easier to read. Word lets you change the spacing between individual (selected) paragraphs or between all

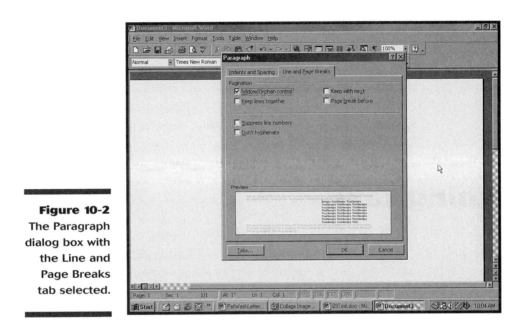

Figure 10-2
The Paragraph
dialog box with
the Line and
Page Breaks
tab selected.

paragraphs in your document; it lets you change the spacing before and after a paragraph. (See Figure 10-2.)

To change the spacing between paragraphs:

- Select the paragraph you want to modify. (Or you can select multiple consecutive paragraphs or the whole document.)
- Go to the Menu Bar.
- Open Format.
- Select Paragraph to open the Paragraph dialog box.
- Click on the "Indents and spacing" tab.
- Click on the up and down arrows next to the "Before" list box to set the spacing above a paragraph.
- Click on up and down arrows next to the "After" list box to set the spacing below a paragraph.
- Click OK.
- The selected paragraphs reflect the spacing changes.

Once you have set spacing options for all lines and paragraphs in your Word document, those settings travel with you to the next paragraph inside the paragraph mark. All you have to do is hit Enter at the end of one paragraph to carry the

> **Click Ctrl + 0 (zero) to remove one line space preceding a paragraph.**
>
> **TIP**

settings down into the next one. (This does not apply to paragraph spacing that you set for selected text only.)

Aligning Text

By default, Word aligns your text automatically with the left margin, which is where you'll want it for standard letters, memos, and other such documents you create with this program. But sometimes you need to line up text differently. Fortunately, Word lets you position the text in your document anywhere you want it.

When we talk about Word's *alignment* commands, we're talking about tools that deal with how your text is positioned on the page. *Horizontal* alignment refers to the position of the text between the right and left margins. *Margins*, of course, determine the overall width of the main text area. Word lets you center your text between the margins, align it with the right margin, or "justify" it so that it lines up equidistant from both margins. And you can mix and match these positions throughout your document (though not within a paragraph).

Word also lets you change the vertical alignment. *Vertical alignment* refers to a paragraph's position relative to the top and bottom page margins. For example, you might want to adjust the vertical alignment of text on the title page of a report or term paper so the title sits dead center. Or you might want to position paragraphs in a newsletter so they are vertically justified and spaced evenly down the page.

To change the horizontal text alignment of a Word document:

- Select the paragraph or paragraphs you want to modify.
- Go to the Menu Bar.
- Open Format.
- Select Paragraph to open the Paragraph Dialog Box.
- Click on the "Indents and Spacing" tab.
- Click on the Alignment drop–down arrow to display a list of alignment options.
- Select Left, Centered, Right, or Justified.
- Check the effect of the change in the Preview window.

- Click OK.
- Your paragraph is realigned.

To change the vertical text alignment of a Word document:

- Go to the Menu Bar.
- Open File.
- Select Page Setup to open the Page Setup dialog box.
- Click the Layout tab to display the layout options
- Click the Vertical Alignment drop-down list.
- Select a new alignment: Top (default), Center, Justified, or Bottom.
- Click OK to exit and apply the new alignment to your document.

To change the vertical text alignment of a Word document back to what it was before, use the Undo command.

Indenting

When you indent a paragraph or a group of paragraphs in Word, what you're really doing is setting up different margins for that block of text. Thoughtfully used indents can make a document easier to read and better organized. Indents are used to set off quotes or special text in reports and term papers.

Word allows you to set the exact length of left and right indents; you can indent the first line *only*, or every line *except* the first one (called a hanging indent), or the entire paragraph as a unified chunk.

If you want to modify only one paragraph, you can "select" it by simply positioning your cursor at the front of the first line. If you want to affect more than one paragraph, you must highlight the entire block of text.

The standard Word Tab-key indent is one-half (0.5) inch.

To indent a single line at the beginning of a paragraph using the Menu Bar:

- Place your cursor at the beginning of the first line.
- Go to the Menu Bar.
- Open Format.
- Select Paragraph to open the Paragraph Dialog Box
- Click on the "Indents and Spacing" tab.

> Whatever indents you impose on one paragraph will show up in a new paragraph created "inside" the paragraph marker. In other words, if you indent the first line of a paragraph, and then move your cursor to the last character of that paragraph and hit the Enter key, you'll find that your cursor automatically indents the first line of the next paragraph.
>
> **TIP**

- Click on the down arrow next to the "Special" list box.
- Select "First line."
- By default the By box reads "0.5," but you can click on the up and down arrows to change that number.
- Check the effect of your indent in the Preview window.
- Click OK.
- Your indent takes effect.

To create a hanging indent:

- Place your cursor at the beginning of the first line.
- Go to the Menu Bar.
- Open Format.
- Select Paragraph to open the Paragraph Dialog Box.
- Click on the "Indents and Spacing" tab.
- Click on the down arrow next to the "Special" list box.
- Select "Hanging."
- By default the By box reads "0.5," but you can click on the up and down arrows to change that number.
- Check the effect of your indent in the Preview window.
- Click OK.
- Your indent takes effect.

You can set both single-line and hanging indents using the Word's horizontal Ruler. Here's how:

📁 Enable the Ruler (see Chapter 4).

📁 Notice the three triangular drag buttons. These buttons are the **indent markers**. The bottom one on the right is for a right indent; the bottom one on the left is for a left indent, the top one is for a hanging indent.

📁 Use you mouse pointer to drag an indent marker to your desired indent.

📁 Viola! Indent applied!

TIP

To change tabs using the Ruler:

* Set your cursor at the beginning of the line you want to tab. The line can be blank or it can be a line of text.

* Find the tab drag box at the far left end of the Ruler.

* By default, the Left Tab alignment is selected (looks like a letter L.).

* To select another, click the button and cycle through the selections. (To select the Left Tab options, you'll have to click all the way through to the beginning.)

* Hover your mouse pointer over the button to display the name of each tab alignment.

* On the Ruler, click where you want the selected tab type inserted.

* The same tab symbol appears on the Ruler at that spot. (With your mouse pointer, you can slide that tab stop back and forth along the Ruler.)

* When you hit the Tab button, the cursor moves to the new tab stop.

* Now, when you tab from the beginning of a line, your new tab applies.

To remove your custom tabs, just drag them off the Ruler with your mouse pointer. (See Figure 10-3.)

To change tabs using the Tabs dialog box:

* Position your cursor where you want to insert a tab in your document.

* Go to the Menu Bar.

* Open Format.

* Select Tabs to open the Tabs dialog box.

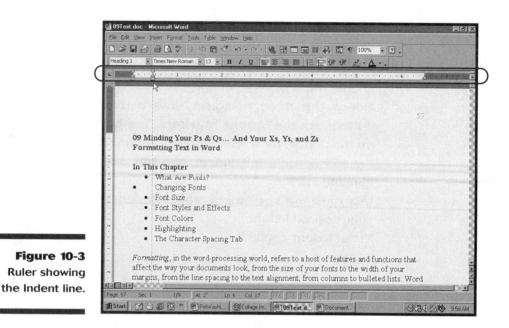

Figure 10-3
Ruler showing
the Indent line.

- Enter a new tab stop measurement in the "Tab stop position" text box. (Think inches.)

- The default alignment setting is left, but you can click on a radio button in the "Alignment" option to change it.

- After setting a tab stop, you can add it to Word's list box by clicking the Set button. Word keeps track of the tabs you set in this dialog box. When you set tabs in the Tabs dialog box, you can always reapply the setting to a new document or to another area in your existing document.

- Click OK.

- The new tab stop is ready to go. (See Figure 10-4.)

TABS

Word uses tabs to indent and to create vertically aligned columns of text. By default, Word's tab stops are set at half-inch intervals along each line in your document. Hitting the Tab key moves the cursor to the next tab column. The tabbed text is always aligned left.

Fortunately, we don't have to use the default tab stop. Word lets you create custom tab stops and change how the tabbed text is aligned at a tab stop in two ways: using the Ruler and using the Format Tabs dialog box.

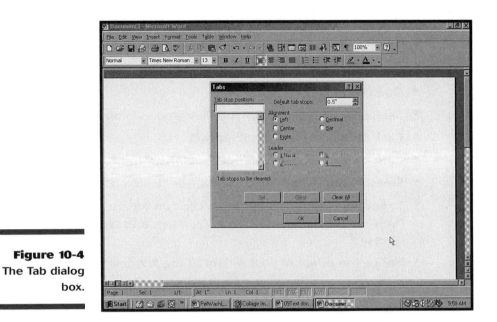

Figure 10-4
The Tab dialog
box.

To remove the tab setting you've added to the list box:

- Go back to the Tabs dialog box.
- Select the tab from the list box.
- Click the Clear button.

Or . . .

- Remove all the tab stops you've set by clicking the Clear All button.
- Word lets you set as many custom tabs per line as your Ruler will hold.

To indent blocks (paragraphs or groups of paragraphs) of text using the Keyboard:

- Select the paragraph or paragraphs you want to modify.
- Hit the Tab key or Ctrl + M. (+ Shift to move back.)
- Your paragraph jumps to the right by a tab length each time you hit these keys.

To indent blocks of text using the Toolbars:

- Select the paragraph or paragraphs you want to modify.
- Go to the Formatting toolbar.
- Click on one of the two Indent buttons to increase or decrease the indent.
- Your paragraph moves a tab length each time you click on a button.

To indent blocks of text using the Menu bar:

- Select the paragraph or paragraphs you want to modify.
- Go to the Menu Bar.
- Open Format.
- Select Paragraph to open the Paragraph dialog box.
- Click on the "Indents and Spacing" tab.
- Click on the Alignment drop-down arrow to display a list of alignment options.
- Select "Left," "Centered," "Right," or "Justified."
- To set the length of the indent, click on the up and down arrows next to the "Left" or "Right" indent boxes. (You can also type a number directly into the boxes.)
- Notice the effect of your indent in the Preview window.
- Click OK.
- Your paragraph is realigned.

Bulleted and Numbered Lists

Word lets you set off lists of information in your documents with numerals, letters, and "bullets." *Bullets* are line markers for lists in your documents; Word gives you several to choose from, including dots, arrows, checkmarks, boxes, and a whole catalog of "picture" bullets. You can use Word's Bullets and Numbering commands before or after you type a list. (See Figure 10-5.)

To apply bullets or numbering to existing text using the using the Toolbars:

- Select the text you want to number or bullet.
- Go to the Formatting toolbar.
- Click the Numbering button to turn the selected text into a numbered list, or click on the Bullets button to create a bulleted list.
- Your text is now indented and in numbered or bulleted list form.

To apply bullets or numbering to existing text using the Menu Bar:

- Select the text you want to number or bullet.
- Go to the Menu Bar.
- Open Format.

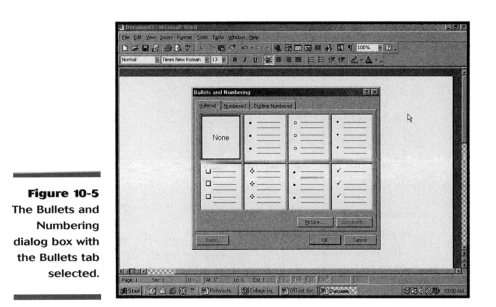

Figure 10-5
The Bullets and Numbering dialog box with the Bullets tab selected.

- **Select Bullets and Numbering to open the Bullets and Numbering dialog box.**
- **Click the "Bulleted" or "Numbered" tab.**
- **Click on the bullet or numbering style you want.**
- **Click OK.**
- **Your text is now indented and in numbered or bulleted list form.**

You can add to the list by positioning your cursor at the end of the last item on the list and hitting Enter to begin a new item, or by clicking at the end of an item inside the list. Word will automatically attach the right bullet in a bulleted list, and it will adjust the number sequence in a numbered list.

To turn off the list and to continue typing normally, hit Enter twice or click the Numbering or Bullets button on the toolbar.

Customized Bullet Options

Word provides you with an additional selection of exotic bullets (all of which look great in a Web page). In the Bullets and Numbering dialog box, click on the "Picture" button to access the Picture Bullet window and a large database of colored, artsy, and animated bullets. Just scroll through the selection and click on the one you want to apply to your list. (See Figure 10-6.)

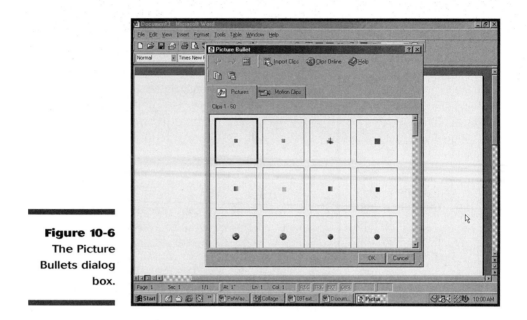

Figure 10-6
The Picture
Bullets dialog
box.

Word also lets you designate another font for the bullets and numbers you use, and to customize the way in which they are positioned in your document.

To customize the placement of the bullets or numbers in your list:

- Select some text and open the Bullets and Numbering dialog box using your keyboard or mouse.
- Select a bullet style.
- Use the Customize button to open the Customize Bulleted List dialog box.
- Enter a new measurement in the Indent At text box.

By default, Word creates numbered lists automatically if you type a certain combination of keys that suggests to the computer you are making a list. If you type the numeral 1 followed by a period, a space, and some text, and then hit Enter, Word shifts into numbered list mode.

If you type an asterisk (*) followed by a space and some type, and then hit Enter, Word shifts into bullet mode.

TIP

WIDOWS AND ORPHANS

In Word, a **widow** is the last line of a paragraph printed by itself at the top of a page; an **orphan** is the first line of a paragraph printed by itself at the bottom of a page. By default, Word saves widows and orphans from their lonely fate. But your heart is so cold you just don't care about widows and orphans. Well, Snidely Whiplash, you can leave them out in the cold by changing the default setting. To turn off the widows and orphans control:

- Go to the Menu Bar.
- Open Format.
- Select Paragraph.
- Click on the Line and Page Breaks tab.

- Uncheck the box next to Widow/Orphan Control.

If you have a change of heart, just recheck the box.

- Check the Preview window.
- Exit to apply the new indents.

To assign a Picture Bullet to your list:

- Select some text—either bulleted or not—and open the Bullets and Numbering dialog box using your keyboard or mouse.
- Select a bullet style.
- Use the Picture button to open the Picture Bullet dialog box.
- Scroll through the list of picture bullets in the Pictures tab and select one.
- A balloon list pops up.
- Select the Insert Clip icon to apply the new bullets to your list.

11

Just so We're on the Same Page
Formatting Pages in Word

The concept of a "page" seems almost anachronistic in a book about computer software, but it's still the standard for digital wordsmiths everywhere, even in a world of virtual documents like the ones created with Word 2000. Besides, eventually most of this stuff is probably going to be running through someone's printer. (More on that subject later.)

Now for a little jargon hair splitting: A "page" and a "document" aren't the same thing. I know . . . I know . . . I promised no jargon, but just so we're on the same . . . um . . . page, let me explain the difference: *Document* refers to the entire file—the chapter of your book, the section of your report, that letter to your Uncle Juanito—whatever its length; a *page* is a unit of that document defined by "margins."

That said, for the sake of simplicity and (I hope) clarity, this chapter is about a group of Word 2000 formatting tools that allow you to modify what you might call "whole-document" characteristics, including commands that affect the parts and the whole—page breaks, margins, headers and footers, page numbers, and columns.

That said, let's start with the page.

Margins

Pages in Word are defined by margins. *Margins* are the boundaries marking the edges of your document's typing area. Because most printing takes place on standard 8½ by 11-inch sheets of paper, that's pretty much how Word defines a page too. Within those confines, Word's default margin settings are 1 inch across the top and bottom, and 1.25 inches on the sides. (See Figure 11-1.)

That page setup is fine for most situations, but once in a while you need a little more wagon room; other times you need to tighten up things—and sometimes you need both in the same document. Fortunately, Word lets you change margins as often as you change your socks.

To change your page margins:

- **Go to the Menu Bar.**
- **Open File.**
- **Select Page Setup to open the Page Setup dialog box.**
- **Click on the Margins tab.**
- **Click on the up and down arrows next to the "Top," "Bottom," "Left," and "Right" boxes to choose margin settings incrementally. Or . . .**

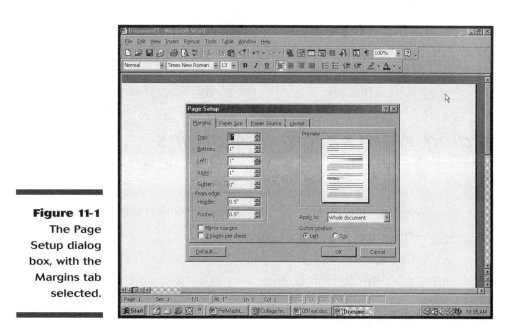

Figure 11-1
The Page
Setup dialog
box, with the
Margins tab
selected.

- Type new margin settings directly into the boxes.
- Check the Preview window to see the effect your new settings will have on your document.
- Click OK to exit the dialog box and to apply the new margins to your document.

If the Preview window in the Page Setup dialog box didn't give you an adequate look at how the new margins are going to affect the pages in your final document, click the Print Preview button in the Standard toolbar to pull back and look at a whole page. This view allows you to scroll through your whole document to see how the new margins look and it's a great way to visually check your margin settings. Click the Close button in the toolbar to return to Normal view. (You can also get to Print Preview through the Menu Bar: File/Print Preview.)

Changing Your Margins with the Ruler

While you were in Print Preview, you might have noticed the Rulers. If you don't like your margins, you can use the Rulers to adjust them. It's one of the easiest ways to do it (there's no trying to visualize how a 1.21-inch right margin is going to look).

The margins are displayed as gray bars at each end of the horizontal and vertical Rulers. Just reach up with your mouse pointer and click and drag a margin marker to reset the margin.

Assuming your Ruler is visible, this approach works in every view but Outline.

Changing Word's Default Margins

Have you found margin settings you really like and use repeatedly? Tired of having to reset them every time you fire up a new document? Well, you're in luck: Word is *sooooo* flexible, it lets you change the default margin settings. Here's how you do it:

- **Open the Page Setup dialog box.**
- **Change the Margin settings.**
- **Click the Default button.**
- **When Word asks whether you want to change the default settings for page setup, answer "Yes."**
- **Click OK.**

Word lets you change the default margins as often as you like. But keep in mind that they are there for a reason: to accommodate the limitations of desktop printers. Although most printers will allow you to juggle your margins a bit, they're just not as flexible as Word, and you might end up with text in an unprintable area.

Page Breaks

Probably the greatest single feature of word processors like Word is their ability to wrap text so you never have to hit a Return key; a close second is their ability to make automatic page breaks. If you're working in Normal view, it feels like you're typing on one continuous role of paper. (Makes me feel a little like Jack Keroac.) (See Figure 11-2.)

But sometimes you want to skip to the top of the next page, before you've reached the end of the page you've just finished working on—maybe you finished a chapter or a section, or maybe you're creating a title page with lots of white space—and you don't feel like pounding the Enter key to get there.

As it happens, inserting page breaks manually is extremely easy in Word.

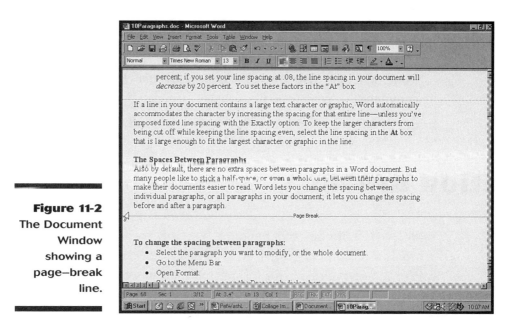

Figure 11-2
The Document
Window
showing a
page—break
line.

To insert a manual page break using the Keyboard:

- Position your cursor where you want the break.

- Hit Ctrl + Enter.

- In Normal view, a dotted line labeled "Page Break" appears, and your cursor is positioned in the first space of the first line of the second page. (In Print Layout view, you skip to the top of the next page.)

- You can skip forward as many pages as you like this way.

To insert a manual page break using the Menu Bar:

- Position your cursor where you want the break.

- Go to the Menu Bar.

- Open Insert.

- Select Break to open the Break dialog box.

- You'll see a list of page break types.

- Click on the "Page break" radio button.

- Click OK.

- The page-break line appears in your document.

Section Breaks

While you were working in the Break dialog box, you probably noticed a column of radio buttons under the heading "Section break types." A *section*, as defined in Word, is a separately formatted area of your document, for which the formatting is totally independent of the formatting parameters of the rest of the document. A *section break* is a mark you insert to show the end of a section.

According to Word Help: A section break stores the section formatting elements, such as the margins, page orientation, headers and footers, and sequence of page numbers. A section break appears as a double dotted line that contains the words "Section Break."

You can insert section breaks in your document to vary the layout. You can create double columns in one section, triple columns in another, and surround them with normally formatted text.

Word lets you insert four different types of section breaks in your documents:

- **Next page**, which inserts a section break and starts the new section on the next page.

- **Continuous**, which inserts a section break and starts the new section on the same page.

- **Odd page**, which inserts a section break and starts the new section on the next odd-numbered page.

- **Even page**, which inserts a section break and starts the new section on the next even-numbered page.

You can use section breaks to organize your newsletters, brochures, and any document that must contain more than one formatting scheme.

You can remove section breaks in the same way you remove page breaks, with the Backspace and Delete keys.

Page Numbers

I never thought I'd have occasion to use this phrase, but while we're inserting things, let's talk about page numbers. It's easy to forget about numbering your pages in a program that lets you know, second by second, exactly which column of which line of which page of how many pages that blinking little cursor is on. But if you were whipping up a long document, you would be well advised to number your pages before sending it to the printer. (See Figure 11-3.)

Inserting page numbers is a fairly straightforward process in Word. You only have to do it once, and your whole document is automatically numbered. As you work, making the document longer or shorter, cutting or adding paragraphs or pages, Word makes all the adjustments.

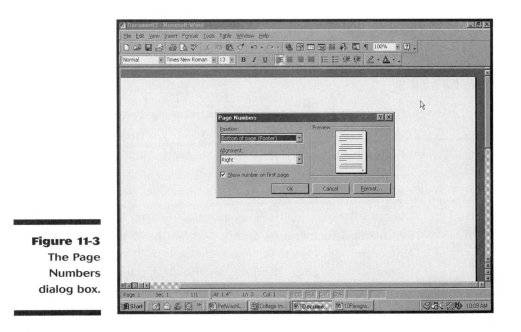

Figure 11-3
The Page
Numbers
dialog box.

To insert page numbers in your Word documents:

- Go to the Menu Bar.
- Open Insert.
- Select Page Numbers to open the Page Numbers dialog box.
- Click on the up and down arrows next to the "Position" and "Alignment" drop-down lists to place the numbers at the top or bottom of the page and to align them. (The Preview window shows you where you're putting them.)
- Check or uncheck the "Show numbers on first page" box.
- Click OK.
- Your pages are now numbered, though you won't be able to see them in Normal view.

Formatting Page Numbers

While you were working in the Page Numbers dialog box, you might have noticed a Format button. This button accesses the Page Number Format dialog box, where you can specify a number style and control the page and chapter numbering schemes. For example, you might want to use Roman numerals for chapters and Arabic page numbers for sections. If you're going to print a large document that spans several files, you can specify exactly which pages start with which numbers, so that the whole thing will come out numbered correctly.

Columns

Whether you're using this program to write letters home, to construct business reports, to build brochures, or to organize your monthly alien-abduction newsletter, I think you'll find Word's Column feature surprisingly handy.

I know I listed it in the walk-through instructions, but I just wanted to throw in another reminder to notice the "Show numbers on first page" check box. If you prefer to not print a page number on the first page of your document, make sure to deselect the "Show number on first page" check box in the Page Numbers dialog box.

TIP

Word lets you create double and triple columns that allow the text to flow from column to column, just like a newspaper. You can add breaks to control how your columns look on the page. You also can insert them virtually anywhere in a document and with different formatting. (See Figure 11-4.)

To create columns in your Word document using the toolbars:

- Select the text you want to reformat
- Click on the Columns button on the Standard toolbar. A tiny toolbar featuring four document icons drops down.
- With the button still depressed, drag your mouse pointer across the document icons to select the number of columns you want to use.
- Release the mouse button and the format is applied.

To create columns in your Word document using the Menu Bar:

- Select the text you want to reformat.
- Go to the Menu Bar.
- Open Format.
- Select Columns to open the Columns dialog box.
- Under the "Presets" area, click on the column type you want to use. Or . . .

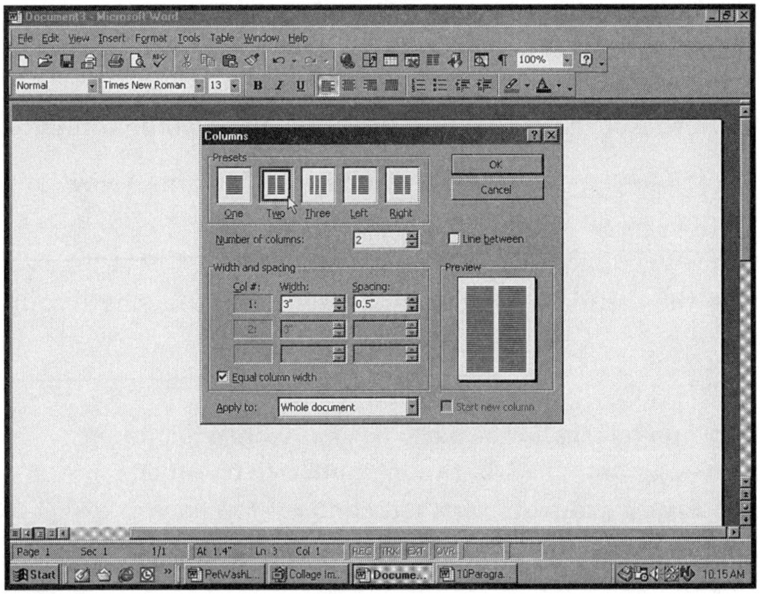

Figure 11-4
The Columns dialog box with the two—column format selected.

A QUICK PERSONAL NOTE TO MICROSOFT ABOUT WORD'S DEFAULT PAGE NUMBER SETTING:

Dear Big Bill and Company,

For some reason, the default setting for page–number placement in Word is the lower right corner. Yet, virtually every editor and publisher I've ever worked with in nearly two decades has asked to receive manuscripts with the pages numbered in the upper left corner.

Just thought you ought to know.

—JKW

- Click on the up and down arrows next to the "Number of columns" drop-down list to select a column type.
- Under "Width" and "Spacing" click the up and down arrows to set an exact measurement for the columns and the space between them (or go with the default settings).
- The Preview window displays what the columns will look like.
- The "Apply to" drop-down list lets you apply the columns to either the entire document or from "This point forward" (if you haven't already selected text you want to convert to columns).
- Click OK to exit the dialog box and apply the column format to your text.

You can't see your new column formatting in Normal view. You can see columns only in Print Layout view.

To turn your column text back into normal text, select the text, click the Columns button on the Standard toolbar, and drag to select a single column.

The Columns dialog box includes two more options: "Equal column width" and "Line between," both with on-off check boxes. **Equal column width** essentially forces you to choose one of the first three column types. **Line between** adds a divider line between the columns.

TIP

Headers and Footers

I took a header off my parents' front porch when I was about ten years old and nearly broke my neck. As I remember, it was a lot more painful than inserting headers and footers into a Word document. (I've never taken a footer, but it sounds almost as painful.) (See Figure 11-5.)

A *header* in a Word document is text you see at the very top of every page, just above the margin, a *footer* appears—you guessed it—at the bottom of every page, just below the margin. Headers and footers are used to display things like the document title, date, author's name, the company name . . . and, of course, *page numbers*. Footers, which are not the same as *footnotes*, can contain virtually the same stuff. You insert headers and footers into your document almost the same way.

To insert headers and footers into your Word document using the Menu Bar:

- **Go to the Menu Bar.**
- **Open View.**
- **Select Header and Footer. (In this case, I've selected Header.)**

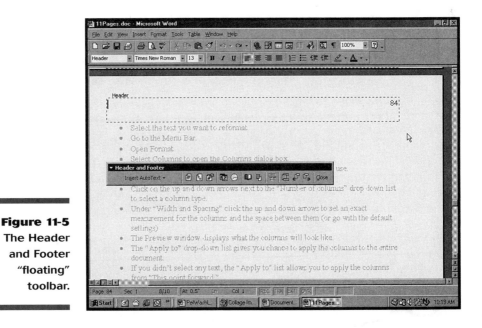

Figure 11-5
The Header and Footer "floating" toolbar.

- Word automatically switches to Print Layout View and displays the Header and Footer toolbar, with the insertion point at the beginning of the header or footer.

- Enter text into the header.

- Click the Close button in the Header and Footer toolbar to return to the body of the document.

> You can insert fields in headers and footers. **Fields** are holding places for information that Word updates automatically, such as the current date or time. (More on fields in Chapter 19, where we look at Word's Mail Merge features.)
>
> **TIP**

Headers and footers are yet another thing you can't see in the Normal view. You've got to be in Print Layout or Print preview to see them.

The Header and Footer Toolbar has a few features worth underscoring.

- To move back and forth between a footer and a header, click the Switch Between Header and Footer button on the Header and Footer toolbar.

- To insert fields—such as the current date—or to select built-in Header and Footer entries, use the AutoText button.

- To insert the current page number from the Header and Footer toolbar, click the Page Number button.

- To space out several fields on a single line, click the Tab key between entries, as shown in this figure.

Bound documents sometimes need different headers placed on the odd and even pages. You can set this up in Word by opening File/Page Setup/Layout. Under "Headers and Footers," click the "Different Odd and Even" check box, and then click OK. Use the "Show Next" and "Show Previous" buttons in the Header and Footer toolbar to switch between the headers and footers for odd and even pages.

Double-click the pale-gray header or footer text at the upper and lower ends of your page to switch back and forth between Header and Footer. (You've got to be in Print Layout view. Switch back to the body text by double-clicking the pale-gray body text.

TIP

12

Through a Glass Brightly
Working with Word's Document Views

Word 2000 provides you with four "views" or display modes that affect the way your document looks on your computer screen. These views—Normal, Print Layout, Web Layout, and Outline—affect only what happened in the Document Window.

All four views may be activated by clicking on the View heading of the Menu Bar, and then highlighting and selecting the view you want in the pull-down menu. Now, let's look at how they look and how they work.

Normal View

Normal is the Word 2000 default view. In this view, the Document Window displays only text, with no document edges visible. Your graphics and special objects aren't visible in this view, either, though they often take up space anyway. (See Figure 12-1.)

Print Layout

This view shows you exactly what you're going to see on the printed page. It displays text, clip art, page margins, headers, footers—everything you stuffed into

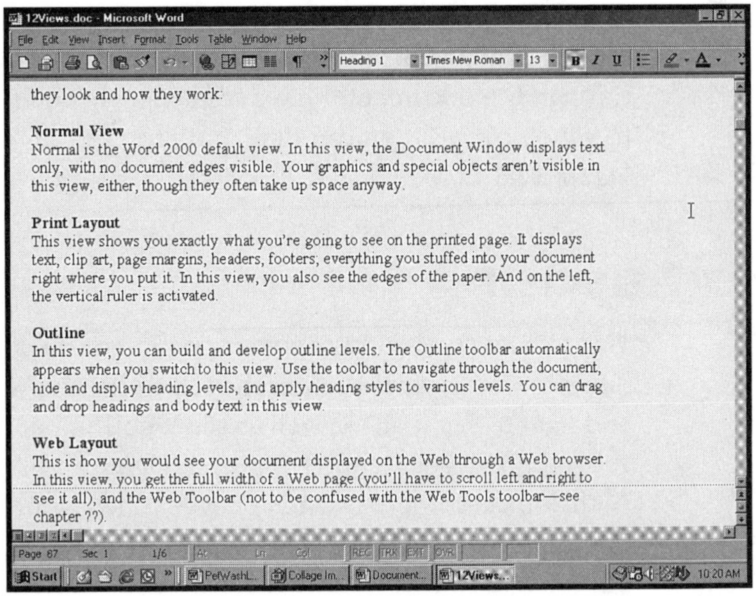

Figure 12-1
The Normal document view.

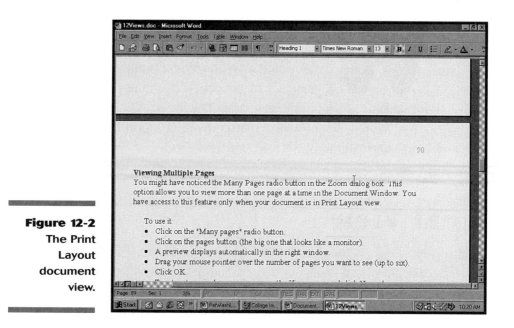

Figure 12-2
The Print
Layout
document
view.

your document, right where you put it. In this view, you also see the edges of the paper. And on the left, the vertical Ruler is activated. (See Figure 12-2.)

Outline

In this view, you can build and develop outline levels. The Outline toolbar automatically appears when you switch to this view. Use the toolbar to navigate through the document, hide and display heading levels, and apply heading styles to various levels. You can drag and drop headings and body text in this view. (See Figure 12-3.)

Web Layout

This is how you would see your document displayed on the Web through a Web browser. In this view, you get the full width of a Web page (you'll have to scroll left and right to see it all) as well as the Web Toolbar (not to be confused with the Web Tools toolbar; see Chapter 21). (See Figure 12-4.)

The quickest way to switch between these four views is by clicking on the teeny-tiny buttons located at the left end of the horizontal scroll bar. Just click on a button, and your view changes instantly.

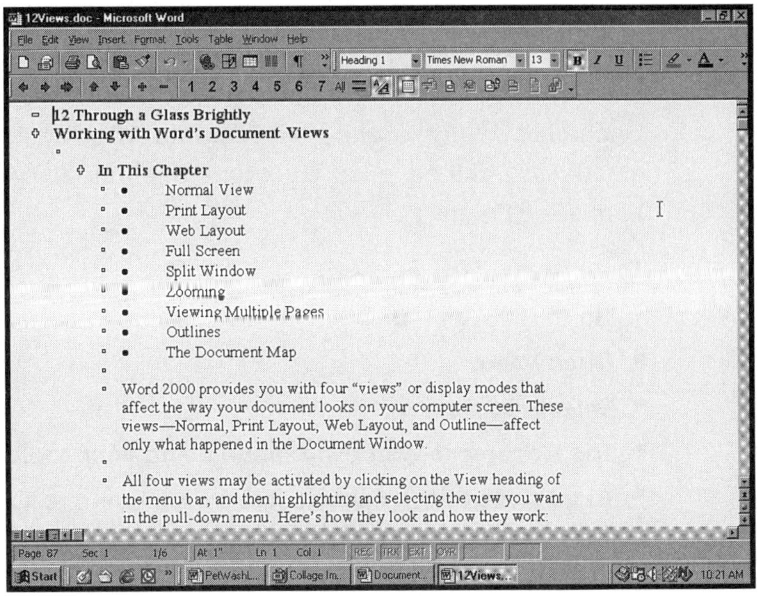

Figure 12-3
The Outline
document
view.

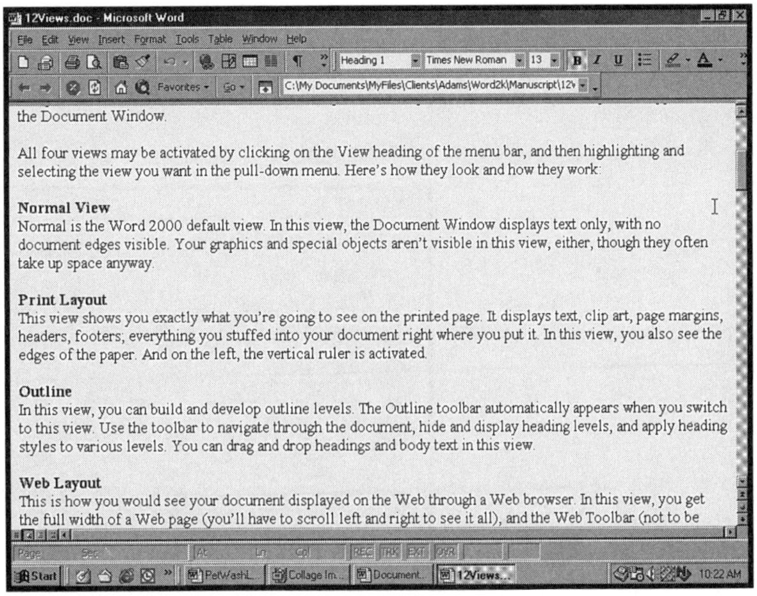

Figure 12-4
The Web
Layout
document
view.

Full Screen

There's really a fifth view: Full Screen. This view affects the appearance of both the Document Window and the Program Window. In Full Screen, your document explodes to the edges of your screen, eliminating menu bars, toolbars, and scroll bars. (See Figure 12-5.)

To activate Full Screen:

- Go to the Menu Bar.
- Open View.
- Select Full Screen.
- The Document Window expands, and your toolbars disappear.
- To go back to the normal screen, click on the Close Full Screen button in the little floating menu.

Split Window

Yet another Word 2000 view option allows you to cut your Document Window in half horizontally to display different portions of the same document at the same time. (See Figure 12-6.)

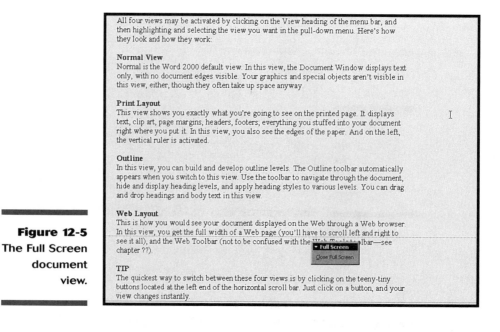

Figure 12-5
The Full Screen document view.

All four views may be activated by clicking on the View heading of the menu bar, and then highlighting and selecting the view you want in the pull-down menu. Here's how they look and how they work:

Normal View
Normal is the Word 2000 default view. In this view, the Document Window displays text only, with no document edges visible. Your graphics and special objects aren't visible in this view, either, though they often take up space anyway.

Print Layout
This view shows you exactly what you're going to see on the printed page. It displays text, clip art, page margins, headers, footers; everything you stuffed into your document right where you put it. In this view, you also see the edges of the paper. And on the left, the vertical ruler is activated.

Outline
In this view, you can build and develop outline levels. The Outline toolbar automatically appears when you switch to this view. Use the toolbar to navigate through the document, hide and display heading levels, and apply heading styles to various levels. You can drag and drop headings and body text in this view.

Web Layout
This is how you would see your document displayed on the Web through a Web browser. In this view, you get the full width of a Web page (you'll have to scroll left and right to see it all), and the Web Toolbar (not to be confused with the Web Tools toolbar—see chapter ??).

▾ Full Screen
Close Full Screen

TIP
The quickest way to switch between these four views is by clicking on the teeny-tiny buttons located at the left end of the horizontal scroll bar. Just click on a button, and your view changes instantly.

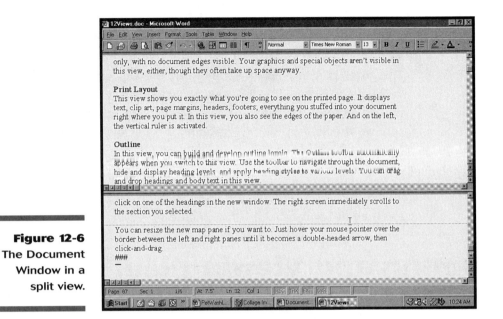

Figure 12-6
The Document
Window in a
split view.

To split your Document window to display two docs at the same time:

- Go to the Menu Bar.
- Open Window.
- Select Split.
- Your mouse pointer now controls a horizontal bar.
- Drag this bar to the place in the window where you want the split. (Where you put the bar is strictly a matter of preference.)
- Click the bar in place.
- You now have a split screen displaying your document.
- You move back and forth between screens by clicking inside them.

One of the coolest things about this view is how easy it makes copying and pasting text from different pages in a long document. You can cut and copy or drag and drop between screens.

To get back your old (whole) screen:

- Go to the Menu Bar.
- Open Window.
- Select Remove Split.
- The split screen disappears.

Another way to split your screen is to grab the splitter bar with your mouse and drag it onto your Document Window. The "bar" is a tiny little rectangle at the top end of the vertical scroll bar. You'll know you've got it when your mouse pointer changes to the double-arrow. You can remove the split by simply dragging the bar off screen.

TIP

Remember: two screens; *one* document. Whatever you do to your document in one screen happens in the other, including saves.

Zooming and Viewing Multiple Pages

The Zoom feature allows you to magnify or reduce your document. You're not actually making anything larger or smaller with this feature (as you would with the font size controls). All you're changing is the way the document looks on your screen. Zooming does not affect the way your document prints.

Word lets you select from a list of zoom percentages listed in the Zoom dialog box: 200% (which makes your text look huge), 100% (the normal view of your document), and 75% (which makes your document look smaller). The "Page Width" setting zooms back a little (90%) to show your document from left to right margins. The "Text Width" setting (116%) zooms in a little to show your document with the margins at the edges of the Document Window. The "Whole Page" setting (39%) pulls way back to display an entire document page. The "Two Page" setting backs out to squeeze two whole pages onto your screen. The "Many Pages" setting (10%) gives you nearly four eight–page rows.

Word allows you to set virtually any zoom percentage (say, 101%) by clicking on the up-down arrows next to the "Percent" text box in Zoom dialog box. (See Figure 12-7.)

To use the Zoom feature:

- Go to the Menu Bar.
- Open View.
- Select Zoom to open the Zoom dialog box.
- Select a percentage by clicking on one of the radio buttons beside the percentage list.

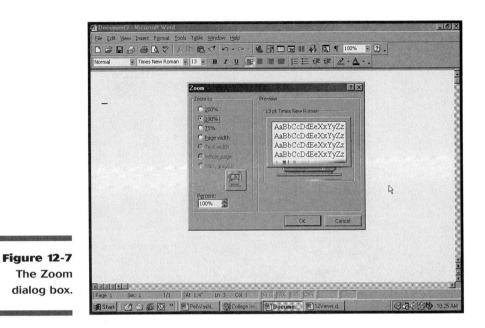

Figure 12-7
The Zoom
dialog box.

- Or use the up-down arrows next to the "Percentage" text box to set a zoom percentage of your own.
- You'll see your zoomed page previewed in the monitor-shaped window on the right.
- Click OK.
- Your document appears in the Document Window at your chosen percentage.

You can also use the toolbar icon to change the Zoom:

- Click on the down arrow next to the Zoom drop-down list on the Standard toolbar.
- You'll see a list of zoom percentages and settings.
- Click on a zoom percentage or setting.
- Your document view changes immediately to reflect your selection.

The Zoom controls work in any of the four View modes, as well as Print Preview. But the multiple-pages features work only when your document is in Print Layout view. (See Figure 12-8.)

In the Zoom dialog box, you might have noticed a large button illustrated with a monitor showing several document pages. (It's just beneath the "Many Pages" radio button.) Clicking on this button opens a pallet of multiple page views. You can drag

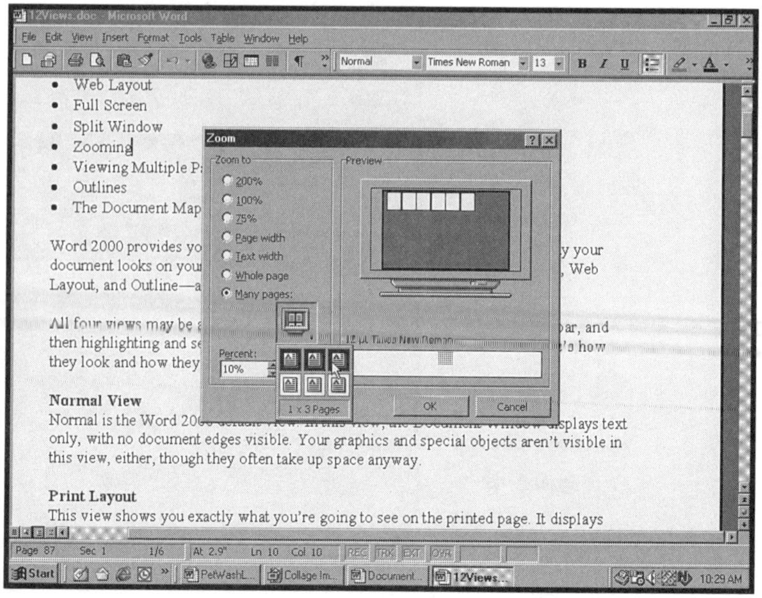

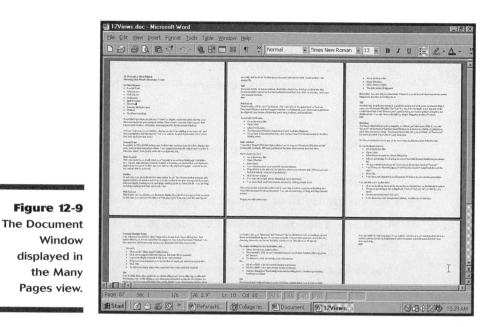

Figure 12-8
The Zoom dialog box with the multiple page drop-down menu open.

Figure 12-9
The Document Window displayed in the Many Pages view.

your mouse pointer over the number of pages you want to see (up to six), click inside the pallet, and then click on the OK button to change to this view. To return to a single page view, open the View menu and click Normal. (See Figure 12-9.)

Outlines

When you're working on a long, complicated document, Word's Outline view can be a godsend. This view takes large amounts of material and organizes it into a manageable hierarchy of subheadings and "body text" (everything that's not a heading). It's just easier to organize information with an outline. There's even an Outlining toolbar that lets you click a button to assign heading levels and to zip to sections of your document.

To switch to Outline view:

• Click the Outline View button in the bottom–left corner of the Document Window (it's on the same line as the horizontal scroll bar).

Or . . .

• Go to the Menu Bar.
• Open View.
• Select Outline.

When you make this switch, the Outline toolbar appears, docked at the top of your Document Window. You can switch to Outline view anytime to impose an outline page format on an existing document.

In Outline view, you "promote" and "demote" text to different levels of headings up and down the hierarchical layout. *Promoting* text pulls it up the hierarchal structure and moves it to the left; *demoting* it moves your text to the right, one level at a time (about a tab space).

To assign headings to text in Outline view:

• Select the text you want to effect.
• To promote it, click on the Promote button in the Outline toolbar (the big, green left arrow).
• To demote it, click on the big green right arrow. Or . . .
• Hit Alt + Shift + the Left Arrow key to promote.
• Hit Alt + Shift + the Right Arrow key to demote.
• The text changes as Word assigns the new heading level.
• Continue promoting headings as needed.

> The Expand and Collapse buttons on the Outline toolbar allow you to view or hide subheadings and body text. The toolbar also lets you display only certain heading levels (the big number buttons). When you move collapsed headings in a document in Outline view, you take all of its subheading with it.
>
> **TIP**

The Document Map

While we're looking at document views, lets talk about the Document Map, also known as the Map view. This is a great feature for navigating large documents with lots of headings. When you switch to the Document Map, Word inserts a new frame (see Chapter 21 on Web features) called the "map pane" into your Document Window. The second frame is sort of like a table of contents filled with document headings and subheadings. (See Figure 12-10.)

To switch to the Document Map view:

* **Go to the Menu Bar.**
* **Open View.**

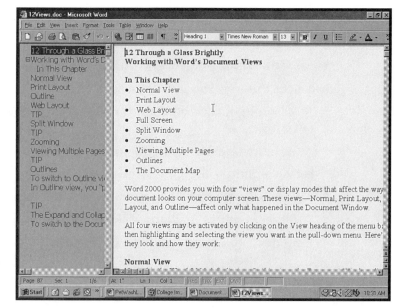

Figure 12-10
The Document
Map view.

- **Select Document Map.**
- **You are now looking at two panes in one window.**
- **To get rid of this view, go back to the View menu and reselect Document Map.**

Once you have the Map on, it's easy to navigate to various parts of your document: Just click on one of the headings in the new window. The right screen immediately scrolls to the section you selected.

If you'd like, you can resize the new map pane. Just hover your mouse pointer over the border between the left and right panes until it becomes a double-headed arrow, then click and drag.

13

Start the Presses!
Printing Documents Created in Word

By now you've created at least a few documents in Word 2000. You've named them and saved them in file folders. You've resized and restyled the fonts, adjusted the paragraph alignments, and tweaked the page layouts. Now, let's get these bad boys out in the real world and see how they perform!

I don't know whatever became of the "paperless office" we were promised about ten years ago. I have *three* computers in my office, and I'm buried in paper about half the time. The fact is, for the foreseeable future printed documents are the end to which most of your Word work is heading.

When it comes to printing options, Word has a full inkwell. The program let's you change the paper size you want your document printed on—including envelopes and labels—and specify which pages to print and the number of copies printed. It even lets you print more than one Word document to a page.

Previewing Your Files

Before you send that first stream of electrons off to your printer, you should probably stop to preview how it's all going to look when the toner has cooled. Word's Print Preview mode shows you just what you can expect and gives you a chance to make last-minute tweaks. You'll want to check things like page numbers, paragraph alignment and spacing, and graphics placement. (See Figure 13-1.)

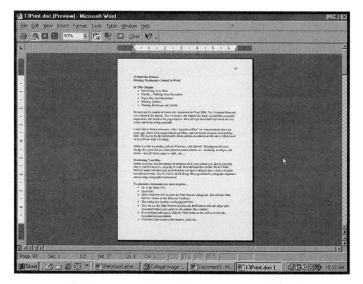

Figure 13-1
Print Preview
document
view.

To preview a document you want to print:

- Go to the Menu Bar.
- Open File.
- Select Print Preview to open the Print Preview dialog box. (Or click the Print Preview button on the Standard toolbar.)
- The dialog box displays a full-page preview.
- You can use the Print Preview toolbar and the Rulers to edit and adjust your document before your send it to the printer. (See sidebar.)
- If everything looks good, click the Print button on the toolbar to send the document to your printer.
- Click the Close button in the toolbar, or hit Esc.

Printing Options

You're not always going to want to print out an entire document. Sometimes you just want to grab a couple of pages from the middle of a much longer doc. Sometimes you need to print a few lines of text or specific pages scattered throughout your document. Word provides you with a number of ways to print your documents. You can print a single page, selected text, groups of pages, only odd or only even pages, specified elements of the document (such as Comments), or the whole document. You can print multiple copies of everything. You can also direct the document to print on a machine other than the default printer.

All printing option changes must be made *before* you click OK or hit Enter—otherwise, the document will print only with whatever change you made before you sent the thing to the printer.

You can open the Print dialog box to change printing options in one of two ways:

- Go to the Menu Bar.
- Open File and select Print

Or...

- Hit the Ctrl + P keys.

To change the printer:

- Open the Print dialog box.
- Click on the arrow next to the "Name" to open the drop-down menu.
- Select the printer or multifunction printer/fax machine you wish to print on.

THE PRINT PREVIEW TOOLBAR

The Print Preview toolbar helps you make last-minute adjustments to your documents on their way to the printer.

🗁 The Many Pages button lets your see more than one page at once (up to four at a time).

🗁 The Shrink to Fit button tries to get your whole document onto one page for printing.

🗁 The Full Screen button jumps you into Full Screen view for editing.

🗁 The Magnify button lets you zoom in on sections of your document, which you can then edit.

🗁 And the Ruler lets your readjust your paragraph alignments.

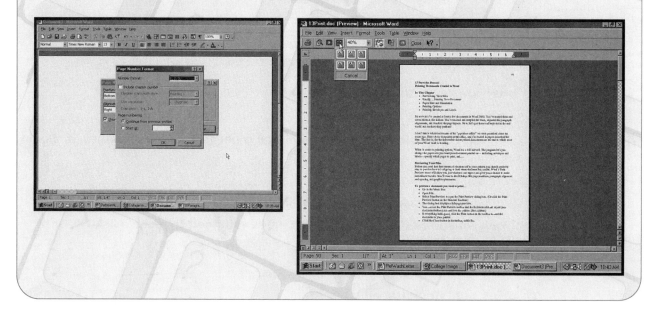

- If you've made all the Print option changes you need to make, hit OK or Enter to print the document.

To print specific elements of the document:

- Open the Print dialog box. (If you've made other Print option changes, it should already be open.)

- Click on the down arrow next to the "Print what" drop-down list (bottom-left of dialog box) and select the document or document feature (e.g., Comment) you want to print.

- If you've made all the Print option changes you need to make, click **OK** or hit **Enter** to print the document.

To print only the current page:

- Make sure the cursor is positioned in the page you want to print.

- Open the Print dialog box. (If you've made other Print option changes, it should already be open.)

- Make sure the "Print what" and "Print" fields in the bottom-left of the dialog box are set to "Document" and "All pages in range" (the defaults).

- Go to the Page Range section.

- Click the "Current" page radio button.

- If you've made all the Print option changes you need to make, click **OK** or hit **Enter** to print the document.

- The page where your cursor is will print.

To print selected text only:

- Select the text you want to print.

- Open the Print dialog box. (If you've made other Print option changes, it should already be open.)

- Go to the Page Range section.

- The "Selection" radio button is available. Click it.

- If you've made all the Print option changes you need to make, click **OK** or hit **Enter** to print the document.

- Your selected text will print.

To print only designated pages:

- Open the Print dialog box. (If you've made other Print option changes, it should already be open.)

- Make sure the "Print" field in the bottom-left dialog box is set to "All pages in range." Use the arrow to the right of the box to change the setting, if needed.

- Go to the Page Range section.

- Click the "Pages" radio button, and a cursor appears in the text box.

- Type in the number of a single page, or the number ranges of the groups of pages you want to print, or scattered single pages. For example, typing in a number "6" prints the sixth page of your document; typing in "6–10" prints pages six through ten of your doc; typing in "6–10, 15, 42–45" prints pages 6 through 10, page 15, and pages 42 through 45. (The comma works as a separator.)

Note: *You don't have to insert page numbers for this to work.*

- If you've made all the Print option changes you need to make, click OK or hit Enter to print the document.
- Your designated pages will print.

To print more than one copy:

- Open the Print dialog box. (If you've made other Print option changes, it should already be open.)
- Select the part or parts of the document you want to print. (See instructions, above.)
- In the Copies area, click on the up/down arrow next to the text box to set the number of copies you want printed.
- If you want your printed copies collated, click on the "Collate" check box.
- If you've made all the Print option changes you need to make, click OK or hit Enter to print the document.
- The specified number of copies will print.

Finally . . . Printing Your Document

I'm assuming you have a printer connected to your computer, it is turned on, and it is working properly. I realize this last assumption is not always a fair one, but it would be silly to try to dispense nuggets of printer tech wisdom in these pages. If you do everything explained in this chapter and your printer doesn't cough up Rembrandt-like documents, your only option is to call (misery-laden groan) tech support. (See Figure 13-2.)

If you've previewed your document, and you're satisfied that it's ready to go, and you don't need to change any of the Print options—you can send your document to your printer with no further ado, using the default printer settings, in one of two ways:

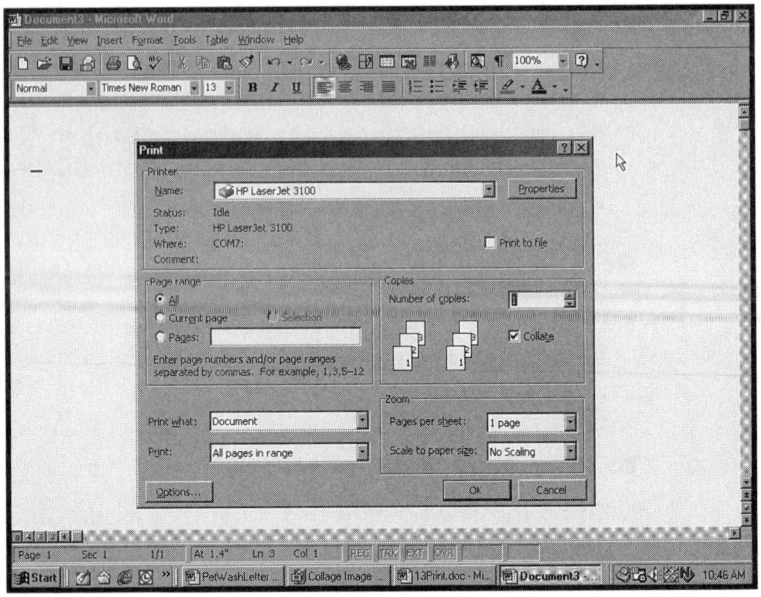

Figure 13-2
The Print
dialog box.

- Click on the Print button (the printer icon) in the Standard toolbar.

Or . . .

- Hit Ctrl + P keys or select File and then Print from the Menu Bar to open the Print dialog box.

- Hit Enter or click OK.

  If you need to specify certain print options before printing your document:

- Open the Print dialog box (with either the Menu Bar or the keyboard shortcut).

- Make whatever Print option changes you need to make, using the instructions given earlier.

- Click OK on the printer dialog box or hit the Enter key.

Printing Envelopes and Labels

Word also lets you apply your formidable formatting expertise to the task of addressing envelopes and creating labels. This is actually a much cooler set of tools than you might at first think. Word not only lets you perfectly center a mailing address and a return address on about two dozen different sizes of envelopes for a very professional look; it not only lets your create more than sixty different types and sizes of labels, including business cards, rolodex cards, and standard Avery labels; it also—get this—lets you include the postal delivery point *bar code*. Very cool.

Paper Size and Orientation

As I mentioned before, Word automatically assumes that your document is a standard 8 ½" by 11" page. If you need to create a document that uses a different paper size, you can change your margins in the Page Setup dialog box and change the settings. From the Paper Size tab, you can change the paper size or page orientation or enter the measurements for a custom paper size. It's best to select a paper size and orientation before building your document. If you change the settings after your document is created, you may have to adjust the text to fit the new size or orientation. (See Figure 13-3.)

To adjust the text to fit the new size or orientation of your document:

- **Go to the Menu Bar.**
- **Open File.**
- **Select Page Setup to open the Page Setup dialog box.**
- **Click the Paper Size tab to view the paper sizes and orientation options.**
- **Click on the down arrow to open the "Use the Paper Size" drop-down list.**
- **Select a paper size.**
- **The Preview pane displays your selection.**

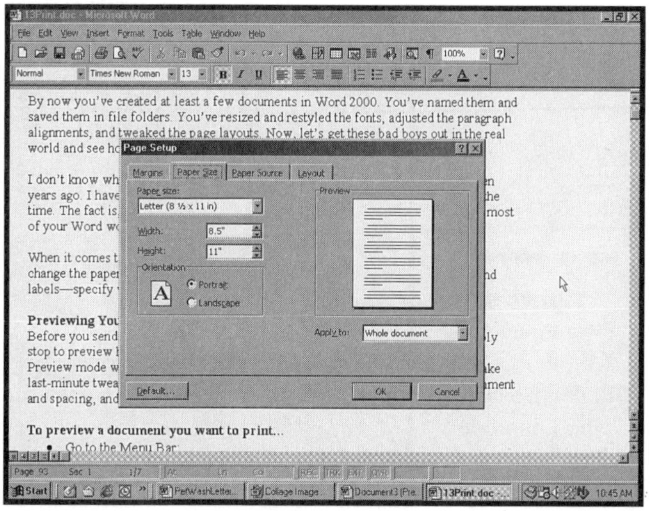

Figure 13-3
The Page Setup dialog box with the Page Size tab selected.

If it looks like you're going to be using your new Page Setup settings a lot, you can make them your default printer settings. Just click on the default key and answer Yes.

TIP

Or . . .

- Create a custom size by selecting Custom from the list.
- Enter your custom measurements in the Width and Height text boxes.
- In the Orientation area, click on a radio button to choose how you want your print to appear on the page. ("Portrait," the default setting, is the normal upright orientation; "Landscape" prints things sideways.)
- Your choice is reflected both in the icon on the left and the Preview pane.
- If you need to designate a paper source—say, your printer has multiple paper trays with letter- and legal-sized paper or different colored sheets—click on the Paper Source tab.
- Select the appropriate tray.
- Click OK to exit the Page Setup dialog box.
- The changes will be reflected when you print your document.

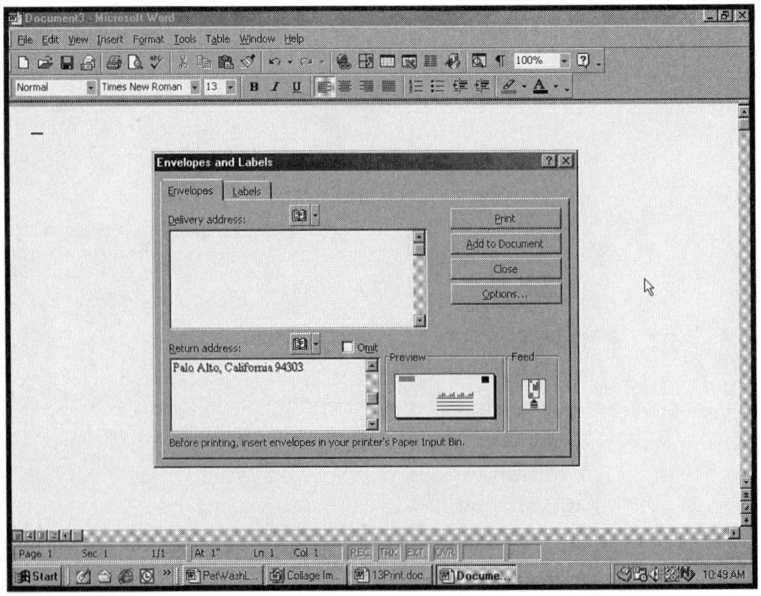

Figure 13-4
The Envelopes and Labels dialog box with the Envelopes tab selected.

Make sure to check how the changes you made have affected your document in Print Preview. A new paper size, for example, could make a huge difference that you just have to see to understand. Print Preview lets you make additional tweaks before you sent the document to the printer. (See Figure 13-4.)

Word also takes the addresses you type into your letter document and transfers them to the envelope without you having to retype them. Also very cool.

Most of the action here takes place in the Envelopes and Labels dialog box so. . . . (See Figure 13-5.)

To Open the Envelopes and Labels dialog box:

- Hit Alt + T + E

Or . . .

- Go to the Menu Bar.
- Open Tools.
- Select Envelopes and Labels.

Printing Envelopes

Make sure you have an envelope in your printer, ready to go. Word automatically copies the delivery and return addresses from an open letter document to the

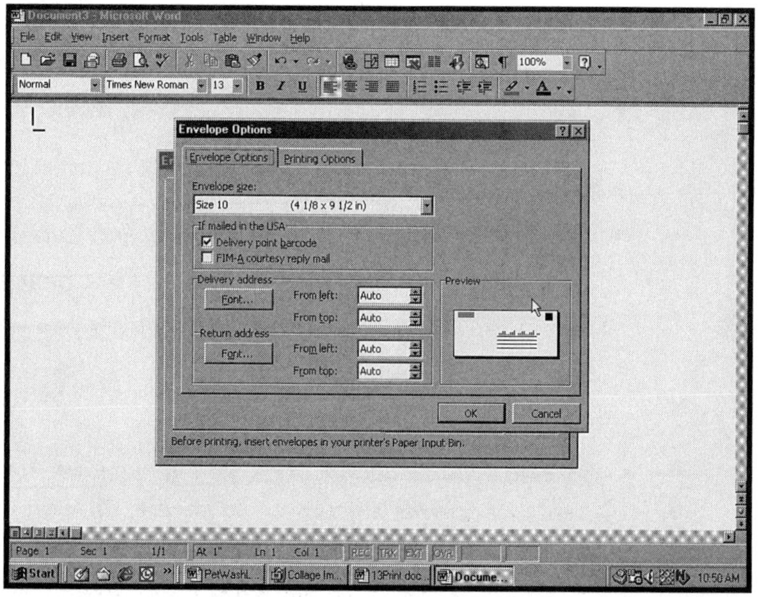

Figure 13-5
The Envelopes and Labels dialog box with the Envelope Options tab selected.

Envelope dialog box for printing. But if you don't have a letter open in your Document Window, you can type the addresses you want printed on an envelope at the top of a new (otherwise blank) document, or you can just type the addresses into the text boxes in the Envelopes and Labels dialog box.

Word also has an advanced feature that stores the return address you normally use and then automatically retrieves it whenever you create and print an envelope (or label). Of course, you can always change the saved (default) return address, as needed. See Chapter 19 on Word's Mail features.

To print an address on an envelope:

- Make sure you have an envelope in your printer, ready to go.
- Word automatically uses the delivery and return addresses from an open letter document. But if you don't have a letter open in your Document Window, you can type the addresses you want printed on an envelope at the top of a document, or you can just type them into the text boxes in the Envelopes and Labels dialog box.
- Open the Envelopes and Labels dialog box.
- Click on the Envelopes tab.
- If needed, type in the delivery address and the return address in the appropriate text boxes.
- If you want to print the return address, make sure the little "Omit" text box is unchecked.
- Click the Options button to open the Envelopes Options dialog box.
- Notice that the default envelope size is a standard number 10.
- To change the envelope size, click on the arrow button next to the "Envelope size" drop-down list.
- Select an envelope size.
- Click OK to return to the Envelopes and Labels dialog box.
- Click on the Font buttons to open a Font dialog box for each of the addresses.
- Select the fonts, font styles, and effects you want.
- Click OK.

To add the envelope style you've just created and its contents to your document to save it click on the Add to Document button in the Envelopes and Labels dialog box.

Printing envelopes can be a tricky business. Basically, they're folded up pieces of paper in very odd sizes. If anything could go wrong with your printing, here's where it might happen. Make sure you've read the documentation that came with your printer and you understand how to feed envelopes into your machine.

TIP

- Click on the up and down arrows next to the spacing text boxes to adjust the spacing between the addresses and the edges of the envelope.
- The Preview Window displays the effect of your actions.
- Definitely click on the bar code check box.
- The FIM—A courtesy reply mail is definitely optional.
- Click OK to return to the Envelopes and Labels dialog box.
- Click the Print button.

Printing Labels

Printing labels in Word is a little trickier than printing envelopes, but just as straightforward. The problems usually lie with the printers and their ability to

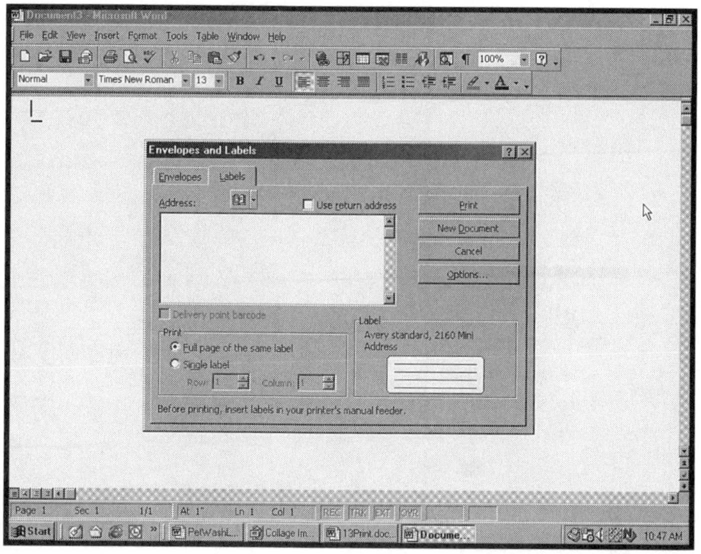

Figure 13-6
The Envelopes and Labels dialog box with the Labels tab selected

handle the label sheets. Setting things up carefully at the printer and then in the Envelopes and Labels dialog box before you hit the print button will help to smooth out the experience. (See Figure 13-6.)

Word lets you print a single label or a full page of labels, and it supports a variety of standard Avery Label sizes. If you're using Outlook, Word will let you import addresses to use as labels. (This feature works with other address databases, as well.) (See Figure 13-7.)

To print a label:

- Open the Envelopes and Labels dialog box.
- Click on the Labels tab.
- If needed, type in the address in the Address text box.
- To import an address, click the Address Book icon and open the address database you want to use. (Outlook's Personal Address Book works very well.)
- Select the address you want to use as label.
- In the "Print" area, click on either the "Full page of the same label" or the "Single label" radio buttons to select your printing option. (If you selected the "Single label" option to print a specific label on your label sheet, use the Row and Column settings to specify the label's location on the sheet.)
- To print a return address label, click in the "Use return address" check box.

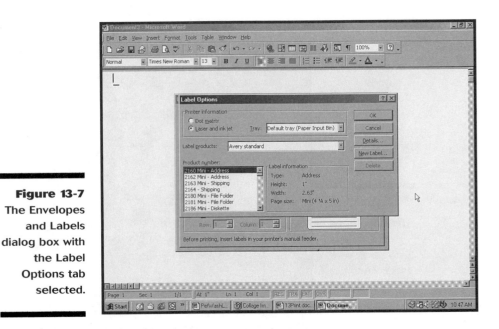

Figure 13-7
The Envelopes and Labels dialog box with the Label Options tab selected.

- Click the Options button to open the Label Options dialog box.
- Click on the arrow button next to the "Label products" drop-down list.
- Select a product.
- Click on the arrow button next to the "Product number" list box.
- Select the product number. The label information area displays the dimensions of the label and label page.
- Click OK to return to the Envelopes and Labels dialog box.
- To print the label, click the Print button.

14

Having it Your Way
Customizing Word's Menus and Toolbars

Just about everything in Word 2000 is customizable: the templates, the document views, the things you see on the screen as you type, and nearly every default setting. But Word's menus and toolbars offer particularly juicy opportunities to tweak this thing so it's even more responsive to your needs and the way you like to work.

Word lets you customize your menus quit a bit, and your toolbars a lot—you can change and rearrange them virtually any way you want. You can add or remove buttons, move Standard buttons to the Formatting toolbar (and vice versa), drag whole toolbars to different parts of the Program window, even create a brand spanking new toolbar of your own unique design.

Customizing Your Toolbars

Word 2000 includes 16 different "built-in" toolbars—that is, toolbars that came with the program and that you can't delete. Each built-in toolbar contains shortcut buttons to a set of related tools and commands. For example, there's a Drawing toolbar, a Web toolbar, and a Reviewing toolbar. (See Figure 14-1.)

WHERE THE ACTION IS

Most of the action in this chapter takes place in the Toolbars submenu and the Customize dialog box. Here's how to open them:

Using the keyboard:

- Hit Alt + V.
- Use the Up-Down Arrow keys to select Tools.
- Use the Right-Left Arrow keys to open the Tools submenu.
- Use the Up-Down Arrow keys to select Customize.
- Hit Enter.

Using the Toolbars:

- Right-click on any toolbar to open the Toolbars submenu.
- Click Customize to open the Customize dialog box.

Using the Menu Bar:

- Open View.

Select Toolbars to open the Toolbars submenu. Click Customize to open the Customize dialog box.

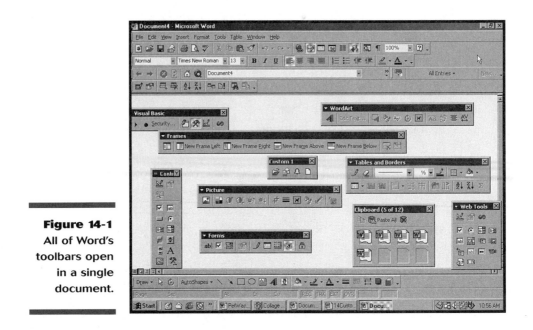

Figure 14-1
All of Word's toolbars open in a single document.

Word's built-in toolbars can be expanded, reshaped, filled with additional buttons and drop-down menus, and moved just about anywhere in the Program Window. (See Figure 14-2.)

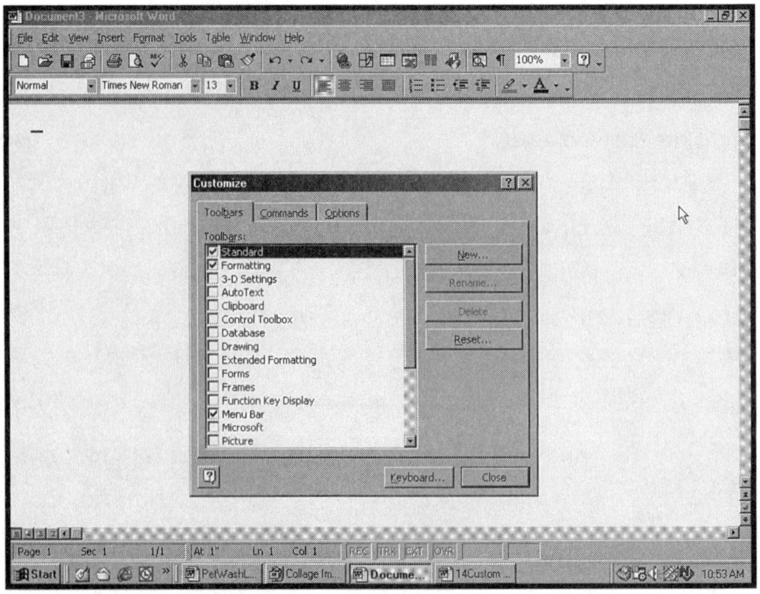

Figure 14-2
Customized toolbars dialog box.

Showing and Hiding Toolbars

You've got at least 16 tool bars in this program, but Word knows that you're not going to want to leave them all on the screen at once. Word makes it easy to show and hide its toolbars, as you need them.

To hide or show a toolbar:

- Open the Toolbars submenu

- Click in the check box next to the toolbar you want to hide to remove the check.

Or . . .

- Click in the check box next to the toolbar you want to show to inset a check.

- If you don't see the toolbar you want, click open the Customize dialog box.

- Click on the Toolbars tab.

- Click in the check box next to the toolbars you want to show or hide.

Note: *To hide a floating toolbar without going through all this, just click on the Close button on that toolbar's Title Bar.*

Repositioning Your Toolbars

By default the Standard and Formatting toolbars share a row at the top of your Program Window. Microsoft describes this arrangement as "side by side," but really one toolbar sits "on top" of the other. This arrangement hides some of the buttons of each toolbar. To get to the hidden buttons, you have to click on the More Buttons button at the right-most visible end of the toolbar or grab the nubs at the left-most end of the "front" toolbar and slide it out of the way. Even though the responsive nature of Word 2000 toolbars puts the buttons you use most frequently where you can see them, this arrangement can be a real pain. (See Figure 14-3.)

And there's no rule that says your toolbars have to be docked at the top of your Program window. Word lets you put them anywhere. I know Word users who put their toolbars and Menu Bar at the bottom of their screens; I know at least one Word user who prefers having his toolbars on the *sides* of the Document Window.

To move the Standard and Formatting toolbars to different rows:

- Open the Customize dialog box.

- Click on the Options tab.

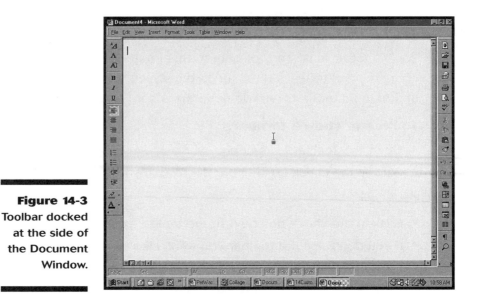

Figure 14-3
Toolbar docked
at the side of
the Document
Window.

- Click in "Standard and Formatting toolbars share one row" to clear the check box.
- Click OK.

Or . . .

- Use your mouse pointer to grab the nub of one of the toolbars.
- Pull the toolbar downward to position it beneath the other toolbar or upward to position it above.

Note: _You can even position a toolbar above the Menu Bar by moving either the toolbar or the Menu Bar until it unfolds in its new location._

Note: _The one thing you can't do is put a toolbar on the same row as the Menu Bar._

To move your toolbars to the sides or bottom of your Program Window:

- Use your mouse pointer to grab the nub of the toolbar you want to move.
- Pull it downward to the bottom or over to side of your Document Window until it unfolds and snaps into its new position.

Note: _Most monitors are wider than they are tall, so your Standard and Formatting toolbars will be truncated if you dock them on the side of the Program Window; you can still get to all of the buttons on the Standard toolbar, but the drop-down text formatting lists of the Formatting toolbar disappear._

You don't have to anchor your toolbars at the edges of your Document Window. You can "float" them inside the window, like the Clipboard.

To let your toolbars "float" in the Document Window:

- **Use your mouse pointer to grab the nub of the bar you want to move.**
- **Pull the toolbar into the Document Window.**
- **Release the button and the bar unfolds.**
- **To move the floating toolbars around your Document Window, click on the Title Bars and drag.**

Floating toolbars unfold by default into boxy, two–row configurations. But you can resize them easily.

To resize a floating toolbar:

- **Move your pointer to any edge of the floating toolbar until it changes to a double-headed arrow.**
- **Click and drag the edge of the toolbar to resize it.**
- **Release the button to set the new size.**

Note: *You can make the toolbar wider or taller.*

Creating, Adding, and Removing Buttons

Word won't let you make completely new toolbar buttons, but it will let you add virtually any of its built-in buttons to different toolbars, change their size, change their appearance, and change their names. (See Figure 14-4.)

To add a button to a toolbar:

- **Make sure the toolbar you want to add a button to is showing.**
- **Open the Customize dialog box.**
- **Click the Commands tab.**
- **Select a category in the Categories list box on the left.**
- **A list of commands and button icons for that category is shown in the Commands list box on the right.**
- **Click on a command.**
- **Drag and drop it to your toolbar.**

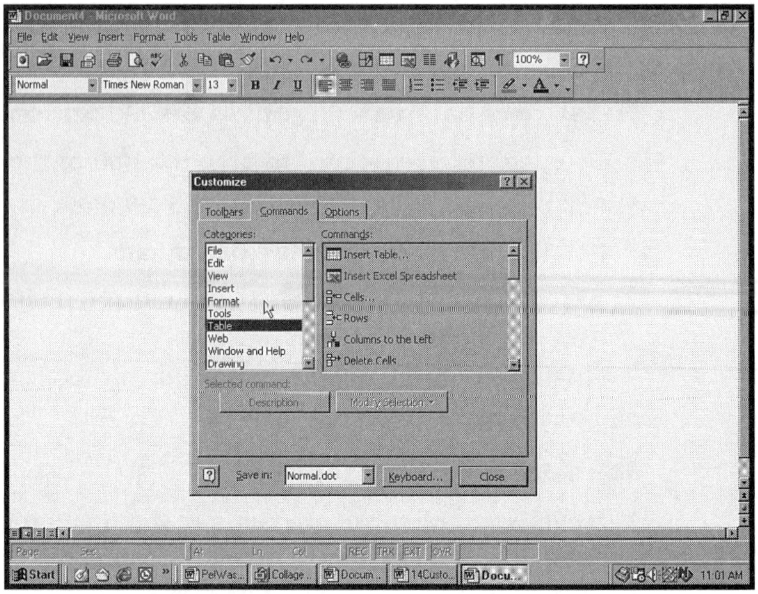

Figure 14-4
The Customize
dialog box with
the Commands
tab selected.

To remove a button from a toolbar:

- Click on the button you want to remove.
- Hold down the Alt key.
- Drag the button off the toolbar.

Or . . .

- Click on the More Buttons down arrow.
- Click on Add or Remove Buttons.

Note: *In floating toolbars, click the arrow in the upper-left corner of its Title Bar.*

- Click in the check box in to uncheck the button you want to remove.
- The button vanishes from your toolbar.

Built-in buttons deleted from built-in toolbars never really go away. They're always available in the Customize dialog box. Delete a custom button, and it goes to Toolbar Button Heaven—unless you create a storage toolbar for custom buttons. Here's how you do it:

- Make sure the toolbar containing your custom button is showing on your screen.
- Create a new toolbar as described in this chapter; call it something like "Buttons" or "Storage."

- Your new storage toolbar remains showing on the screen.
- Drag and drop the buttons you want to save into it.
- To hide the storage toolbar, right-click on it to open the Toolbars submenu and then click to remove the checkmark.

You can create a storage toolbar for customer menus too or just drag them into the one you just created.

Word also lets you rename your toolbar buttons.

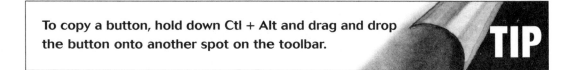

To copy a button, hold down Ctl + Alt and drag and drop the button onto another spot on the toolbar. **TIP**

To rename a toolbar button:

- Make sure that the menu or toolbar you want to change is showing on your screen.
- Open the Customize dialog box.
- Leave the Customize dialog box open.
- Right-click the button on the toolbar to open a shortcut menu.
- Type the name in the "Name" text box.
- Hit Enter.

Note: *If your toolbar button isn't displaying a label, you'll have to activate a ScreenTip to see the new name. (Just hover your mouse pointer over the button, and the ScreenTip pops up.)*

Word lets you change the button graphics and provides you with a list of alternatives. (See Figure 14-5.)

To change a button graphic:

- Make sure the toolbar you want to add a button to is showing.
- Open the Customize dialog box.
- Right-click on the button you want (on the toolbar) to open a shortcut menu.
- Select the Change Button Image to display a palette of button graphics. (It won't be available on buttons you can't change.)
- Click on the graphic you want.
- The button changes, and the palette and shortcut menus close.
- Close the Customize dialog box.

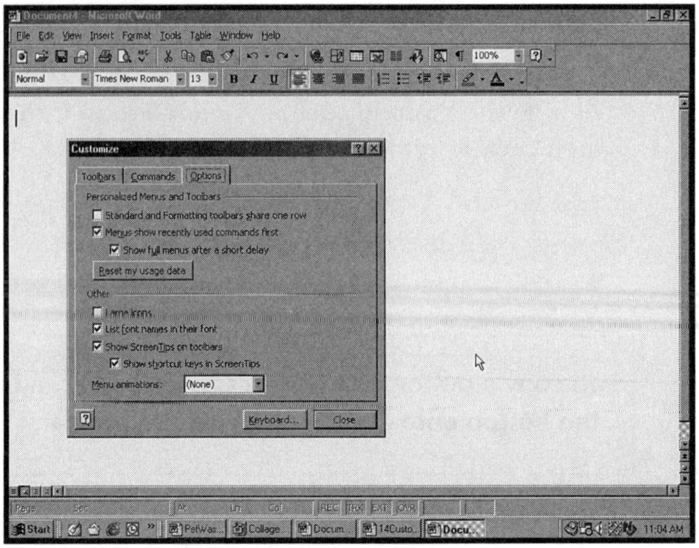

Figure 14-5
The Customize
dialog box with
the Options
tab selected.

And, although I'm not sure why you would want to do it, Word also lets you use large toolbar buttons that fill half the screen.

To change the size of toolbar buttons:

- Open the Customize dialog box.
- Click the Options tab.
- Click in the "Large icons" check box.
- Your toolbar buttons instantly reflect the change to large icons.

To give your toolbars a more organized look, you might want to add a separator bar between groups of similar buttons.

To add a separator between buttons on a toolbar:

- Make sure the toolbar you want to modify is showing.
- Open the Customize dialog box.
- Right-click on a button (on the toolbar) to open a floating menu.

Note: *Usually, right-clicking on a toolbar button opens the Toolbars submenu. When the Customize dialog box is open, a different menu materializes.*

- Click in "Begin a Group."
- A separator bar appears to the left of the button on a horizontal toolbar and above it on a vertical toolbar.

Or . . .

* Hold down the Alt key and click and drag the toolbar button slightly away from the one next to it.
* A separator bar will appear between the buttons.

Note: *To remove the separator bar, hold down the Alt key and drag one of the buttons next to it closer to the one of the other side.*

> To rearrange buttons on a toolbar, hold down the Alt key and click and drag them. A bold I-beam cursor marks the insertion spot.
>
> **TIP**

Let's say you've tweaked Word's built-in toolbars until you don't know what's what anymore, and now you just want things back the way they were when you first installed the program. No problem.

To restore a built-in toolbar to its default buttons, menus, and submenus:

* Open the Toolbars submenu.
* Select Customize.
* Click on the Toolbars tab.
* Find the toolbar in the Toolbars display window.
* Select it.
* Click the Reset button.
* Word's original settings are restored.

Creating New Toolbars

All this pushing and yanking and rearranging and button adding to Word's built-in toolbars can get confusing and messy. Why not start with a clean, fresh toolbar of your own? You can leave the built-ins intact, while customizing and recustomizing to your heart's content. (See Figure 14-6.)

To create a new toolbar:

* Open the Customize dialog box.
* Click on the Toolbars tab.

- Click on the New button to open the New Toolbar dialog box.
- Type a name for your new toolbar in the "Toolbar name" textbox. (Click inside the box if it's not already selected.)
- Click the document template in which you want to save the toolbar in the "Make toolbar available to" list box.
- Click OK to return to the Customize dialog box.
- A new, empty toolbar bearing the name you typed appears in your Document Window.

Note: *Your new toolbar is just a baby box, because there are no buttons in it.*

- Click the Commands tab.
- Select a Category from the list on the left to display a group of commands in the Command window on the right.
- Click on a command and drag and drop it into your baby toolbar.
- The command appears as a button on your new toolbar.

Note: *You can continue dragging and dropping to add as many commands to your new toolbar as you like.*

You can show or hide your custom toolbar, just as you can show and hide the built-ins. But if you're sick of your toolbar and just want it to go away forever, you can give it the ax.

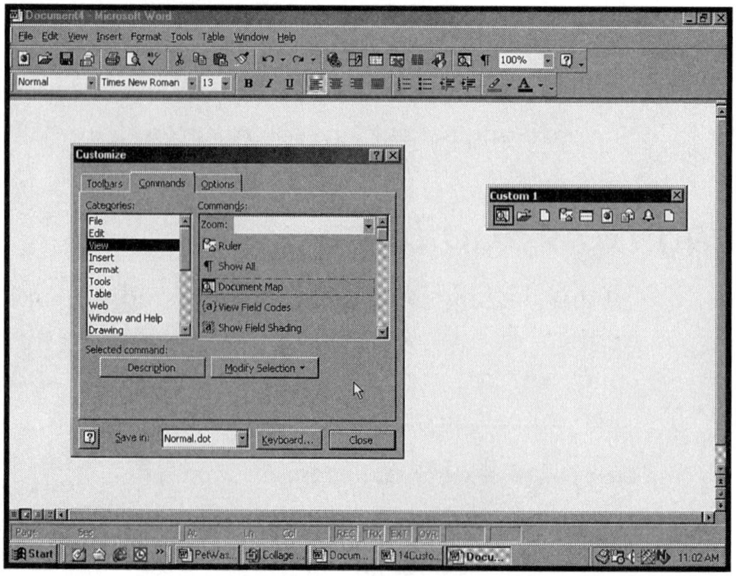

Figure 14-6
The Customize dialog box with the custom toolbar

To delete a custom toolbar:

- Open the Toolbars submenu.

- Select Customize.

- Click on the Toolbars tab.

- Find the toolbar in the Toolbars display window.

- Select it.

- Click the Delete button.

- The toolbar disappears from the list.

Note: *The Delete button is not available if you select a built-in Word toolbar.*

The Options tab of the Customize dialog box lets you further customize Word with some additional feature selections:

- **Large icons**—Checking this box gives you huge toolbar icons. Go ahead and check it to see an immediate effect. If you don't like it, just clear the check box.

- **List font names in their font**—With this box checked, the fonts list presents the font names in the actual font. I like this feature, but if you don't, just clear the check box to turn it off.

- **Show ScreenTips on toolbars**—With this box checked, you can hover your mouse pointer over a toolbar button and cause a little box with that button's name to pop up. Clear the box if you want this feature turned off.

- **Show shortcut keys on ScreenTips**—If you like the ScreenTips feature, you might as well check this box; it doesn't cost you anything, and it's a great way to learn some keyboard shortcuts.

Customizing Your Menus Bar

Word's Menu Bar is almost as customizable as its built-in toolbars; you can move it around the Document Window, resize it, and add buttons to it. You can't hide it the way you hide toolbars (though it does disappear in Full Screen view), and you can't delete the default menu headings, but you can rename them.

Turning Off the Intuitive Menus

Some people like Word's intuitive menus; some people don't. I'm neutral on the subject, but I have a friend who hates them. She finds Word's shuffling of the menu choices quite annoying—she wants her menus to look the same every time she opens them—and she doesn't like the way they open up fully after a couple of seconds.

Fortunately for my friend—and maybe for you—it's simple to turn off this feature.

To turn off Word's customized menu features:

- **Open the Customize dialog box.**
- **Click on the Options tab.**
- **Click in the "Menus show recently used commands first" check box to remove the check mark and to turn off the intuitive menus completely.**

Note: *If you like the shorter menus but you hate the way they open up suddenly after a couple of seconds, click the "Show full menus after a short delay" check box to remove the check mark. You can still see the full menus, but now you have to click on the arrow buttons to open them up.*

Moving the Menu Bar

The Menu Bar doesn't have to be docked at the top of your Program window any more than do your toolbars. You can grab the nub with your mouse pointer and move the Menu Bar around your screen, dock it at different edges, or leave it floating in the middle, just as you moved your toolbars.

The Customize Shortcut Menu

The Customize dialog box must be open whenever you are editing menu commands and toolbar buttons. When the dialog box is open, right-clicking on a menu command, a menu heading, or a toolbar button summons a shortcut menu loaded with editing options, including:

- **Reset**—Reinstates the default settings.
- **Delete**—Removes a toolbar button or menu command.
- **Copy Button Image**—Copies the look of a selected button to a clipboard.
- **Paste Button Image**—Replaces one button's image with the one you copied.
- **Reset Button Image**—Changes back a button to its default image.
- **Change Button Image**—Opens a palette of icons you can apply to a button.
- **Default Style**—Applies Word's default style to the button or command.

- **Text Only (Always)**—Replaces the default icon with text.
- **Text Only (in Menus)**—Replaces the default menu icons.
- **Image and Text**—Puts both text and icons on buttons and menus.
- **Begin a Group**—Sets a divider to the left of the selected button.
- **Assign a Hyperlink**—Assigns a hyperlink to that button.

To apply any of these options, click on the command button, and then click on the option.

Adding and Removing Menu Bar Buttons and Commands

You also can add buttons to the Menu Bar. If Document Window space is a consideration, putting your most used toolbar buttons up on your Menu Bar could allow you to hide your toolbar and increase your typing real estate.

To add a button to the Menu Bar:

- Open the Customize dialog box.
- Click the Commands tab.
- Select a category in the Categories list box on the left.
- A list of commands and button icons for that category is shown in the Commands list box on the right.
- Click on a command.
- Drag and drop it to your Menu Bar.

To remove a button from your Menu Bar:

- Click on the button you want to remove.
- Hold down the Alt key.
- Drag the button off the toolbar.
- Word lets you add commands to your Menu Bar menus.

To add a menu command:

- Open the Customize dialog box.
- Click on the Command tab.
- Select a category to display a list in the Command window.
- Click and drag a command to the Menu Bar over a heading (View, Format, etc.) to open the menu.

- Drag the command into the menu and release the mouse button.
- That command now appears in the list.

And it lets you rename the command.

To rename a menu command:

- Open the Customize dialog box.
- Open the menu that contains the command you want to change.
- Right-click the command to open the shortcut menu.
- Type the new name in the "Name" text box.
- Hit Enter.

You rename Menu Bar headings in Word the same way you rename commands.

TIP

Creating New Menus

Finally, Word lets you create entirely new menus that you can place in custom or built-in toolbars or in the Menu Bar. Placed in toolbars, they look like standard drop-down menus, complete with down arrow; in the Menu Bar, they look like your old faves, sans underlined letter.

To create a new drop-down menu:

- Open the Customize dialog box.
- Click on the Commands tab.
- Select New Menu in the Categories window. (Keep clicking that down arrow; it's the last item on the list.)
- In the Commands window, click New Menu.
- Drag New Menu from the Commands window to the toolbar or the Menu Bar.
- Release the mouse button, and a new menu button called "New Menu" appears. (It's a regular heading in the Menu Bar.)
- With the Customize dialog box still open, right-click the New Menu button to open the shortcut menu.

- Type a new name in the "Name" text box.
- Hit Enter.

To add command buttons to your custom menu:

- Open the Customize dialog box.
- Click on the Commands tab.
- Right-click on your new menu icon (on the toolbar) to open a blank drop-down menu.
- Select a category to display a list of commands.
- Click-and-drag the command you want from the Commands box into your empty drop-down menu.
- Release the button, and the command appears.
- Repeat to add more commands.

15

Word Magic
Working with Styles, Themes, Templates, and Wizards

n earlier chapters, we looked at Word's extensive formatting options. Word lets you select and apply different fonts and typeface styles, expand or contract the spaces between lines, adjust the alignment of paragraphs and page margins—just about anything you can think of to tweak and tug your documents into shape.

You can apply these formatting characteristics manually, either as you type or after you've finished, by selecting text and invoking commands. Or, you can automatically apply collections of formatting specifications using Word's styles, themes, and templates tools. And you can get Word to walk you through the process with a wizard.

Styles

A *style* is a cluster of text and paragraph formatting choices that you can apply to any section or sections of your document. Each Word template comprises several styles. If you open a new document without choosing a template, Word actually chooses a template for you: the Normal template. Click on the down arrow next to the Style drop-down list in the Format toolbar, and you'll see a list of styles that are part of the Normal template. For example, the "Heading 1" Style in the Normal template is 16-point, double-spaced Arial font, aligned flush left. If you select some text and then click on "heading 1" from the Style drop–down list, that text will change to 16-point, double-spaced Arial, and it will be aligned flush left. To add a bit of confusion, Word also includes a "Normal" style within its "Normal" template. Sheesh! (See Figure 15-1.).

Here's a real example: applying the predefined Word style named *Heading* 1 converts the selected text into a 16-point, bold Arial font, aligned flush-left, with some extra spacing before and after it. Here's another one: the pre-defined Word style named *Title* converts the selected text into 16-point bold Arial, centered on the page, 12 spaces from the top margin.

Once you figure out how to use them, styles can considerably cut down on your typing and clicking, and really streamline your common formatting tasks.

Most of the style action takes place in the Styles dialog box. To open it, click on Format, then Style in the Menu Bar, or hit Alt + O + S and use the up-down Arrow keys to select Style.

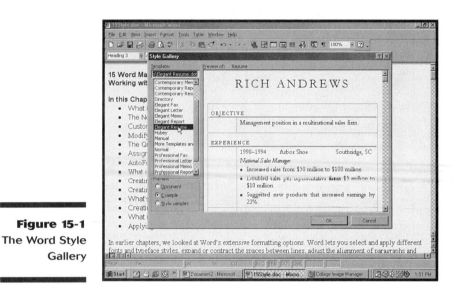

Figure 15-1
The Word Style
Gallery

The Normal Style

When you open up a new blank document in Word, the program automatically assigns the so-called N*ormal* style to that document. By default, the Normal style sets the font as 12-point Times New Roman and imposes single-line spacing and flush-left paragraph alignment. It also turns on the widows-orphans control and lets your Word Grammar and Spelling checker know you're using English. Unless you change it, all the text you type into that document will conform to those formatting parameters. (See Figure 15-2.)

The Normal style is part of the Normal template (also known as NORMAL.DOT), which includes a number of other styles besides good old Normal. Heading 1, which I mentioned earlier, is one of the styles available in the Normal template. (More on templates shortly.)

Word comes with over a hundred existing predefined, or "built-in," styles that allow you to transform your text into section headings, title pages, footnotes, and much more. And Word lets you create custom styles tailored to your specific needs.

You can see a list of all styles currently available in your document by going to the Styles dialog box and selecting "Styles in use" from the drop-down list. Or you can open the Styles drop-down list on the Formatting toolbar. The style names in this list appear in their font types and styles; each style's font size and an illustration of its paragraph alignment appears in gray boxes on the right.

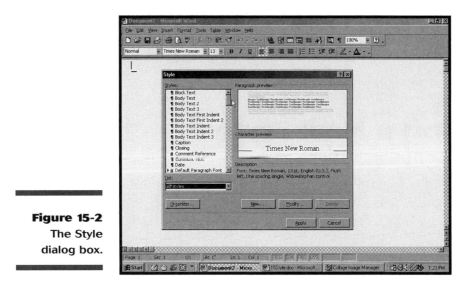

Figure 15-2
The Style
dialog box.

To apply a built-in style:

- Select the text you want to modify. (You can highlight the text or position your cursor at the beginning of a line to modify the whole paragraph.)
- In the Formatting toolbar, click on the down arrow next to the Style drop-down list.
- Select the style you want to apply.
- The new style is instantly applied to your text.

Or . . .

- Open the Style dialog box.
- The Styles list box shows a list of the Styles.
- Select a style from the list.

Note: *The "Paragraph" and "Character" preview windows show an example of the style.*

- Click on the Apply button.
- The style changes are implemented in the selected text.

Customizing Styles

Anyone who works with Word for very long eventually begins to tinker with the Normal style. The idea behind styles is to save you from unnecessary typing and clicking as you format your document. If you find that every time you start a new document you have to change the font or create an automatic indent, maybe you should create a style of your own. You can create a style by building one from scratch or by modifying an existing style.

Creating a New Style

Once you've got the basics of formatting down, you can custom-build a style that gives certain text whatever page style, paragraph style, and/or font style you want. You do this by creating a style that includes all the formatting specs you want for a specific hunk of text, which might be, say, a line of text you select or a special type of paragraph you use repeatedly in your document, such as a subject heading. You also name and save the style, so you can use it later in the document or even in other documents. (See Figure 15-3.)

To create a new style from scratch:

- **Open the Style dialog box.**
- **Click on the New button to open the New Style dialog box.**
- **Type a name for your new style in the "Name" list box.**

Note: *Try to make your names descriptive and take care not to use any of the existing style names.*

- **Make sure that Paragraph is showing in the "Style type" drop-down list.**

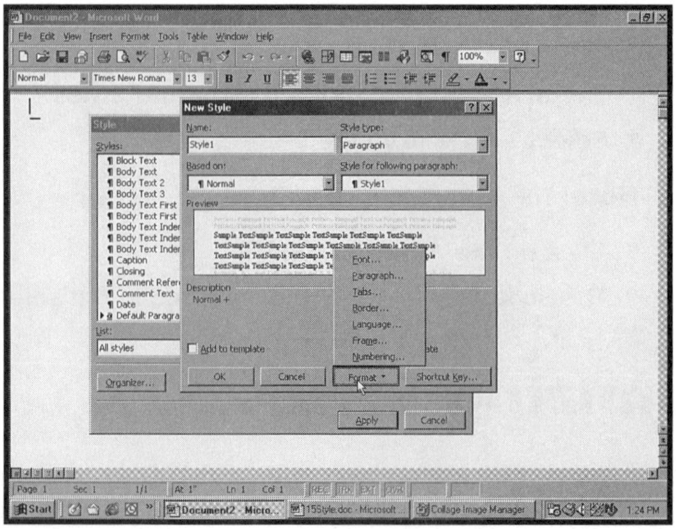

Figure 15-3
The New Style
dialog box.

> Basing your new style on an existing style is a real time-saver. **TIP**

Note: *You'll probably want to create most of your styles at the paragraph level, but you can create character-only styles too. (More on this shortly.)*

- Click on the Format button to display a list of formatting options.
- Select the type of formatting you want to modify to open the corresponding formatting dialog box (Font, Paragraph, Tabs, Borders, Language, Frame, Numbering).
- Make your changes by clicking on the options you want.
- Click OK to return to the New Style dialog box.
- Click OK to return to the Style dialog box.
- Click Apply to apply your changes to the style.
- Notice your changes are now reflected in all specified text of that style in your document.

Modifying an Existing Style

You can make changes both to Word's built-in styles and to styles you create. Any changes you make to a style are applied automatically wherever the style was used in the document.

> If your cursor is on any text or if any text is highlighted when you activate the Style dialog box, the formatting for that text carries over to your new style. After you click on "New," you'll see the formatting specs under "Description." So, if you want to create a brand-spanking new style without having to modify any existing formatting, make sure your cursor is on a blank space in your document. Or, create the style before you start typing. **TIP**

To create a new style by modifying an existing Style:

- Open the Style dialog box.
- From the Styles list box, select the style you want to change.
- Click on the Modify button to open the Modify Style dialog box.
- Click on the Format button to display a list of formatting options.
- Select the type of formatting you want to change to open a formatting dialog box (Font, Paragraph, Tabs, Borders, Language, Frame, Numbering).
- Make your changes by clicking on the options you want.
- Click OK to return to the Modify Style dialog box
- Click OK to return to the Style dialog box.
- Click Apply to apply your changes to the style.

By default, Word saves any new or modified styles to the Normal template. You can, however, select a different template or create a new one for your document. More on templates later in this chapter.

The Quickest Way to Custom-Build a Style

A quicker way to create a new style, either from scratch or by modifying an existing one, is to format a hunk of text the way you want it, select the text, and then base the new style on the formatting you just used. You can format the text with existing formatting and then add the modifications you want. And you don't even have to open up the Style dialog box to do it. Here's how: (See Figure 15-4.)

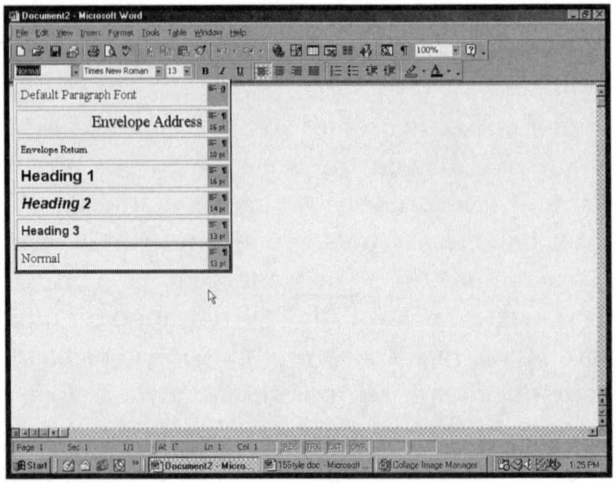

Figure 15-4
The Style toolbar drop-down list.

- Select the text that contains the formatting you want to use for your style.
- Click on the down arrow next to the Style box in the Formatting toolbar.
- Click inside the drop-down list and type over an existing style name.

Note: *Don't worry; that style just gets moved out.*

- Hit Enter.

You can create styles that modify only characters and leave the paragraph formatting intact. To do this, follow the steps under "To create a new style...," but you want "Character" showing in the "Style type" drop-down list.

For one reason or another, you might decide you want to get rid of a style for good. Here's how you do it:

- Open the Style dialog box.
- Select the style you want to remove in the Styles list box.
- Click the Delete button.
- Click on the Apply button to exit the dialog box.
- The style is history.

> To see a list of the formatting commands used by a particular style, open the Style dialog box and select the Style. Below the Character box is a Description that tells what formatting is assigned to the style.
>
> **TIP**

Assigning a Style Shortcut Key

As I've mentioned, probably *ad naseum* by now, using keyboard commands is much more efficient than using the mouse for most tasks. You can speed up the way you assign styles to your text by creating shortcut keys to the Styles you use most. (See Figure 15-5.)

To assign a shortcut key to a style:

- Open the Style dialog box.
- Click on the Modify button to open the Modify Style dialog box.
- Click on the Shortcut Key button to open the Customize Keyboard dialog box.

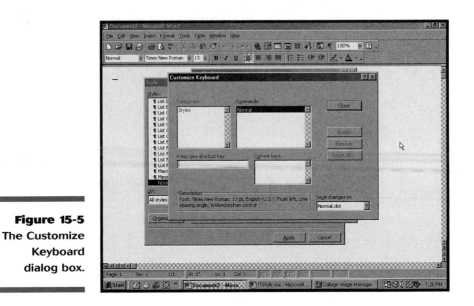

Figure 15-5
The Customize
Keyboard
dialog box.

- Click inside the "Press new shortcut key" text box.
- Type in a shortcut key combination.
- Word will let you know if the key combination is currently in use.
- When you find a key combo that's available, click the Assign button.
- Click Close to return to the Modify Style dialog box.
- Click OK to return to the Style dialog box.
- Click Apply to put your shortcut into effect.

AutoFormat

If you'd rather just leave all the formatting chores to Word, AutoFormat is for you. Word's AutoFormat feature applies formatting to your document . . . well . . . automatically. (See Figure 15-6.)

To enable AutoFormat:

- Make sure the document you want AutoFormat to modify is open.
- Open the Format menu.
- Select AutoFormat to open the AutoFormat dialog box.
- Notice that the dialog box lets you know which document the AutoFormatting will apply to.

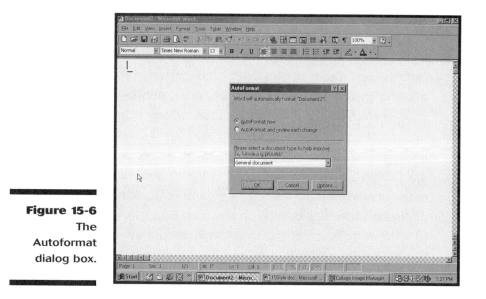

- If you want to review each formatting option AutoFormat wants to impose on your document, click on the "AutoFormat and review each change" radio button. (If you don't, click "AutoFormat now.")
- Click the drop-down arrow next to the list box.
- Select the type of document you're trying to create.
- Click OK.

Note: *If you selected "AutoFormat and review each change," a second AutoFormat dialog box appears. If you didn't, the new formatting is automatically applied to your document.*

- In the second AutoFormat dialog box, click on the Style Gallery button to open the Style Gallery dialog box.
- From the Template list box, select a document style.

Note: *The Preview area lets you see what the template style looks like.*

- Click OK to exit and to apply the formatting to your document.

Note: *If you selected "AutoFormat and review each change," AutoFormat lets you accept or reject each formatting change to your document, or you can click the Accept All button.*

Templates

Word 2000 makes the process of creating documents easier and more efficient with Templates. Word's predesigned and customizable templates let you do the formatting groundwork once for many documents—or skip it altogether.

A *template* is a collection of *styles* yoked together to create specific types of documents, such as memos, fax cover sheets, and resumes. Think of a template as a formatting pattern or page blueprint. Every document you create in Word 2000 uses some kind of a template. As I mentioned before, the NORMAL.DOT template is the one Word uses on all new documents created when you hit the Ctrl + N keys or click on the New button on the New Blank Document on your Standard toolbar. (It's the template behind the Blank Document icon in the New template dialog box.) (See Figure 15-7.)

Word 2000 comes with a substantial list of commonly used document templates, including:

- **Business and Personal Letters**
- **Fax Cover Sheets**
- **Mailing Labels**
- **Envelopes**
- **Memos**
- **Resumes**
- **Calendars**
- **Agendas**

- **Brochures**
- **Manuals**
- **Theses**
- **Legal Pleadings**
- **Reports**
- **E-mail Messages**
- **Web Pages**

Creating a Document from a Built-in Template

Word lets you chose from a list of predesigned templates or design your own. If you don't choose a template, Word chooses one for you: the default NORMAL.DOT, known as the Normal template. (See Figure 15-8.)

To create a document from an existing template:

- **Go to the Menu Bar.**
- **Open File.**
- **Select New to open the New dialog box.**

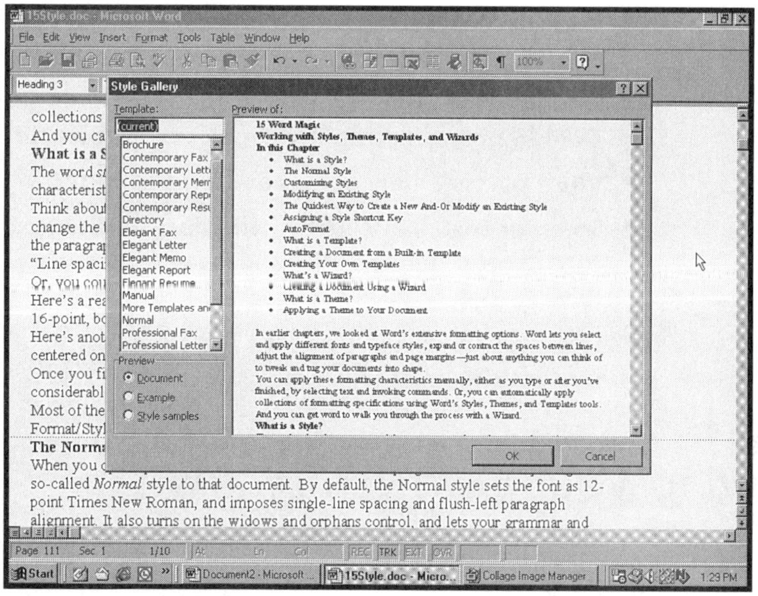

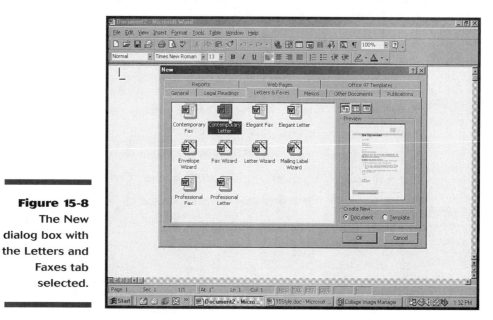

Figure 15-7
The Style
Gallery dialog
box.

Figure 15-8
The New
dialog box with
the Letters and
Faxes tab
selected.

- Click on a document category tab—in this example, Letters & Faxes—to display the template icons.

- Clicking on an icon once displays the template in the Preview window.

- Don't select an icon with "wizard" in its label; we'll get to those later in this chapter.

- Click on the Document radio button in the "Create New" area in the lower right corner.

- Double-click on a template icon in the main window—in this example, Contemporary Letter. (Or click once to select it and then click OK.)

- Word opens a new document, preformatted with "placeholder text" in brackets.

- To enter text, just click on the placeholder text and start typing. (In most cases, the placeholder text disappears when you begin typing, but once in awhile, you have to delete it.)

- Use your mouse to navigate from section to section, and you end up with a perfectly formatted letter. (See Figure 15-9.)

Creating Your Own Templates

You can also design a template from scratch or modify an existing template. You can create your document within the template structure from the start or impose a template on your document as you save it. (See Figure 15-10.)

To create a new template from scratch:

- Go to the Menu Bar.

- Open File.

- Select New to open the New dialog box.

- Click on the General tab.

- Find the Blank Document icon in the main window.

- Click on the Template radio button in the "Create New" area.

- Double-click the Blank Document icon (or click it once and click OK).

- Word opens what looks like a new document, but in the Title Bar it's identified as a template—in this example, Template 1.

> Depending on how Word was installed on your hard drive, some templates may be available only on the Office 2000 CD. You might click on, say, Legal Pleadings, and see this message in the Preview window: "Click Okay to install additional templates and create a new file." If you do, just pop the program CD into the drive and click "Next."

TIP

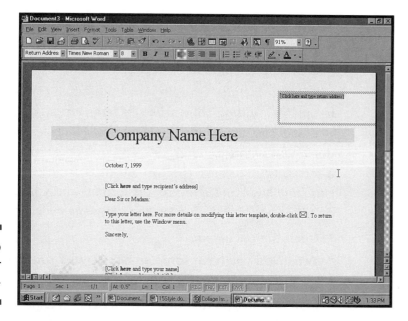

Figure 15-9
Letter
template.

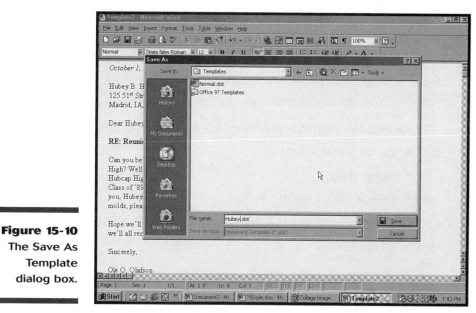

Figure 15-10
The Save As
Template
dialog box.

- Set up the formatting parameters—margins, font sizes and types, headings, tabs, etc.—and style you want.

- Hit F12 to open the Save As dialog box. Notice that you're in the Templates Folder.

- Type a name in the appropriate text box.

- Click OK.
- Your new template is now stored in the Templates folder.
- Close the document.

You can include virtually any amount of text and/or graphics in your custom templates. Adding things like letterheads, logos, departments, salutations, and closings can up your efficiency considerably. To do it, just add them to the document before you save it as a template. Probably the simplest way to "create" a template is to save the formatting settings in an existing document. Say your company has a preferred report format, and you have a properly formatted report on file in your computer. Do the following:

- Open the document.
- Tweak it if you have some small changes you want to make.
- Hit F12 to open the Save As dialog box.
- In the File Name text box, type a name for the new template (say, MyReports).
- In the Save As Type box, select Document Template.
- Click OK.
- Your new template is now stored in the Templates folder.

Another approach to templates is to create your document first (using the Normal template) and then impose a different template configuration.

To access additional Word templates on the Web:

- Go to the Menu Bar.
- Open Help.
- Select Office on the Web.
- You're computer will fire up your browser, dials up you ISP, and open the Office Update Web site.

Wizards

Templates are great, and every Word users should learn how to design and use them, but wizards make the process of creating commonly used document types even easier.

A *wizard*, as anyone who has worked very much with computer software will tell you, is a little program that guides you through some process, typically by asking you to answer questions and to make choices at key points along the way. Most programs nowadays include an install wizard, for example, that steers you along the often pothole-riddled set-up and installation process.

Word's template wizards are designed to guide you through the process of creating specific categories of documents, such as letters, fax cover sheets, memos, calendars, reports, and Web pages, among others. (See Figure 15-11.)

Creating a Document Using a Wizard

The process of engaging and using a Word template wizard is very straightforward. (See Figures 15-12 and 15-13.)

- **Go to the Menu Bar.**
- **Open File.**

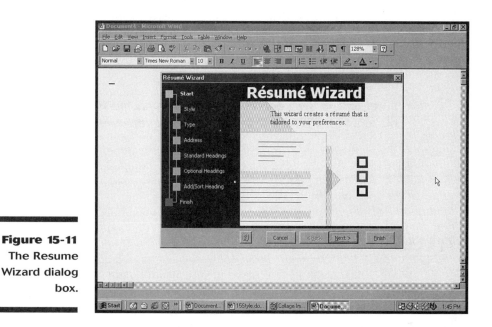

Figure 15-11
The Resume Wizard dialog box.

- Select New to open the New dialog box.
- Click on a tab to select a category of document you'd like to create—in this example, Other Documents.
- Find the icon with "Wizard" in its label.
- Click on the Document radio button in the "Create New" area.
- Double-click the Wizard icon—in this example, Resumes—to start the Wizard and open the Wizard dialog box. (Or click once to select it and then click OK.)
- Now you just click through the process, answering questions posed in each Wizard dialog box and typing in text along the way. The box displays a list of steps, from Start to Finish, along the left side. As you click through the process, each new step will be highlighted.
- In this example, the first dialog box asks which resume style you prefer. If "Professional" is okay with you, click the Next button at the bottom of the box to continue on to the next step.
- The next dialog box wants to know which type of resume you'd like to create. Click the option you prefer—in this example, "Professional."
- Click Next.
- The next box wants name and address information. Click on each text box and type in the appropriate information.
- Click "Next."
- The next three boxes ask which headings you prefer. Click on the ones you want—in the example, "Education," "Professional Experience," and "Objective."
- Click Finish to exit the wizard.
- Word opens a new customized document based on the selections you entered using the wizard.
- Enter text in the document by clicking on the placeholder text and typing. The placeholder text will disappear and be replaced by your new text entry.

If you change your mind about something you did in a previous step, just click the Back button to return to the previous dialog box and change your selections or the text you entered. You can also skip steps and go to the end by clicking Finish at any time.

Themes

Word 2000 takes all this style and template stuff to a spiffy new level with themes. *Themes*, like styles, are collections of formatting specifications. The difference is

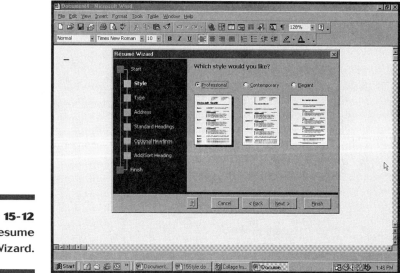

Figure 15-12
Resume
Wizard.

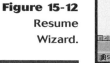

Figure 15-13
Resume
Template.

If you like using wizards, you'll want to check out the Microsoft Web site (**www.microsoft.com**). The company lists dozens of additional wizards, as well as other tips, tools, and info that Word 2000 users may download for fee.

TIP

themes include what Microsoft calls "unified design elements." They've got color! They've got backgrounds! They've got cool bullets, flashy fonts, and stylish partitioning lines!

Clearly, themes are meant to help you create a Web page (more on this in Chapter 21), but they also can help you fancy up other kinds of documents, from the family Christmas letter, to the condo association newsletter.

Themes differ from templates in that they don't provide AutoText entries, custom toolbars, macros, menu settings, or shortcut keys. A theme is all about providing a *look* for your document. Something bright! Something colorful, maybe with a blinking button! (See Figure 15-14.)

All the theme commands may be found in the Theme dialog box:

- **Go to the Menu Bar.**
- **Open Format.**
- **Select Theme.**

Applying a Theme to Your Document

Word comes with two dozen themes, all listed in the Theme dialog box. From there, you can apply a new theme, change themes, or remove a theme. The Preview

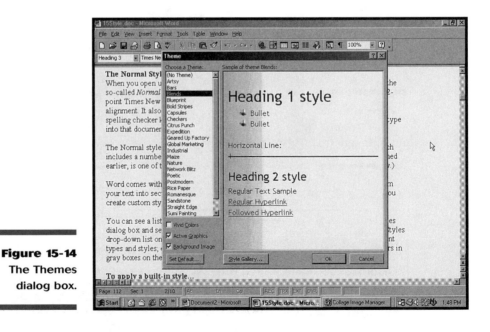

Figure 15-14
The Themes
dialog box.

window lets you see just what design elements you'll be getting with each theme. You can even enhance a theme elements by checking "Vivid colors," "Active graphics," or "Background Image." (See Figure 15-5.)

To apply a Theme to an existing document:

- Make sure the document you want to modify is open on your screen.
- Open the Theme dialog box.
- Select a Theme from the "Choose a theme" list box.
- Click inside the check boxes next to the options you want ("Vivid colors," "Active graphics," or "Background Image").

Note: *You can see the effects of each option in the Preview window.*

Bingo! Your document immediately sports a fresh, new look. (All are happy.)

Note: *You need a Web browser to see the graphic in action.*

If a particular theme turns out not to be your cup of tea, you can remove it easily.

To remove a Theme from a document:

- Open the Theme dialog box.
- Select "No theme" in the "Choose a theme list."
- Poof! Your theme is gone. (All are sad.)

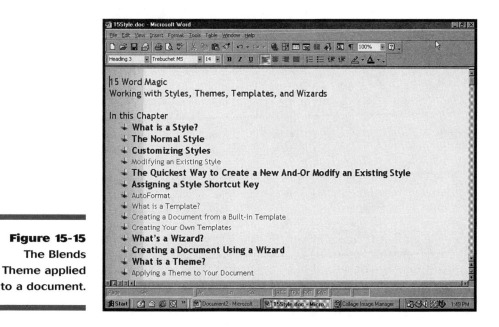

Figure 15-15
The Blends
Theme applied
to a document.

16

Now That You've Snatched the Pebble from My Hand, Grasshopper . . .

Working with Word's Advanced Features

The title of this chapter is a bit of a misnomer. "Advanced" implies that this is where I've stashed the really tough stuff, that you have to be a serious student of Word even to consider attempting these complicated tasks, that only experienced veterans need bother with these Byzantine procedures.

The truth is *nothing* in Word 2000 is *that* complicated. It's not the intuitive walk in the park that Microsoft would like you to believe it is, but for most of the things most of us want to do with it, it's pretty logical and straightforward.

The features explained in this chapter aren't so advanced that you have to be a slouching, deskbound, carpal-tunnel-syndromed Wordiac to use them, but you do need to have some experience with the program to put them in context. Some of them—like Tracking Document Changes Between Users or Inserting Footnotes—you might never use; others, like Find and Replace and creating simple Macros—you might use everyday.

The tools and features you'll learn about in this chapter could probably have fit into other chapters, but I thought they were important enough and *specialized* enough to pull out of the scramble to master the more basic functions of the program.

Find and Replace

Sometimes you need to search your document for bits of information, key references, or specific words. Sometimes you need to change a recurring word that the Spell checker wouldn't catch, like the day you discovered the annual report you just finished for Big Shirts R Us had some pretty important Rs left out of the company name. Sometimes you're looking for information, like when you were searching through your graduate thesis for that cool analogy about Zen and golf.

Whenever you need to search for something in your documents, long or short, there's just no need to reach for the scroll bar when you can invoke the Find and Replace feature. Find and Replace lets you search for and replace every occurrence of a word. You can replace it with another word or delete it by replacing it with nothing. It will replace characters, punctuation, spacing, and even entire phrases.

Or you can use it to search your document for data or just to move through it more efficiently than you can with a scrollbar.

Where the Action Is

All the action here takes place in the Find and Replace dialog box. (See Figure 16-1.) Here's how to open it to its three tab settings:

- **Go to the Menu Bar.**
- **Open Edit.**
- **Select Find, Replace, or Go To.**

Or . . .

- **Hit Ctrl + F (Find), H (Replace), or G (Go To).**

To use Find and Replace to find text:

- **Open the Find and Replace dialog box and select the Find tab. The Find tab will be in front.**
- **Type in the word or phrase you want to find in the "Find what" text box.**
- **Click on the "More" button for additional search parameter options.**

Note: *You can narrow your search considerably with these "More" options. For example, you can make your search case sensitive ("Match case"), so can search for the name "Will" and not have to see every occurrence of the word "will;" you can search only for whole words, so that a search for "nation" won't also seek out "condemnation" and "pagination."*

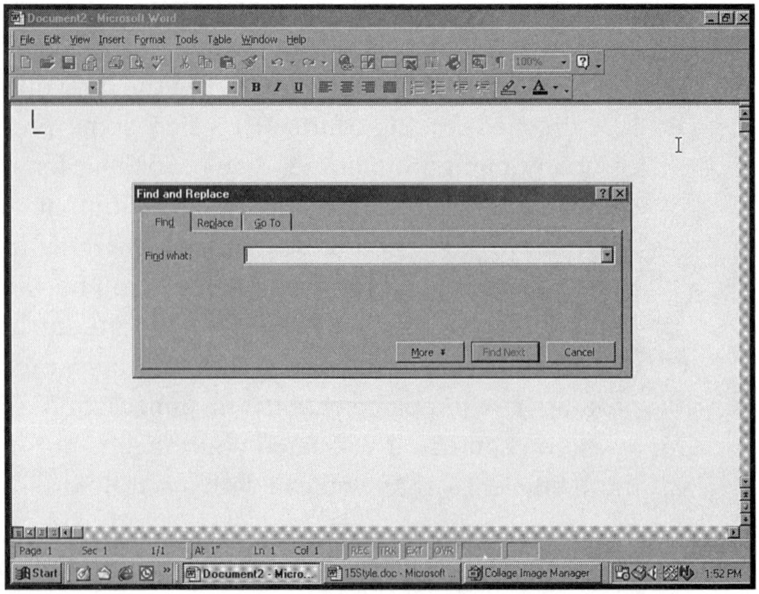

Figure 16-1
The Find and Replace dialog box with the Find tab selected.

- Click the Find Next button to locate the first occurrence of the word or phrase. To find the next one, click the button again, and so on.

Note: *Each time you click the Find Next button, Word jumps to the next occurrence of the word or phrase in your search and highlights it.*

Note: *The Find and Replace dialog box remains open on your screen throughout your search.*

- When you're finished searching, click the Cancel button to close the dialog box and stop the search. (See Figure 16-2.)

To use Find and Replace to find and replace text:

- Open the Find and Replace dialog box with the Replace tab in front.
- Type in the word or phrase you want to replace in the "Find what" text box.
- Type the word or phrase you want to replace it with in the "Replace with" text box.
- Click on the "More" button for access to the same additional search parameter options you had in the Find tab.
- To find the next occurrence in your document of the text in the "Find what" box, click the Replace button.
- Word finds and highlights the text in your document.

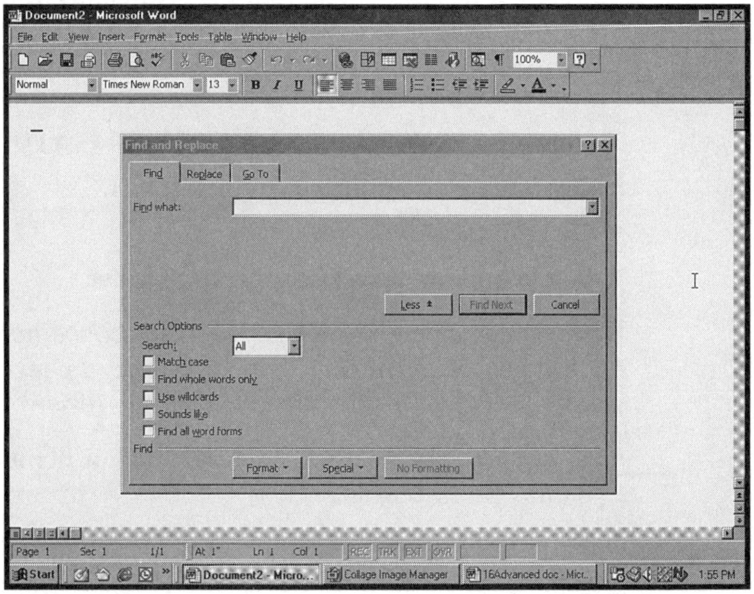

Figure 16-2
The Find and Replace dialog box with the Replace tab selected.

- To replace the highlighted text with the text in the "Replace with" box, click the Replace button again.
- Clicking this button also moves you on to the next occurrence of the word.

Note: *Whenever you want to skip an occurrence of the text without replacing it, click the Find Next button.*

- To find every occurrence of the text in the "Find what" box and replace it with the text in the "Replace with" box, click the Replace All button.
- When Word completes a search, it displays a prompt box telling you the search is complete. If the search didn't find any occurrences of the text, a prompt box alerts you to that too.

To remove repeated occurrences of text in your document, type a space and then the word you're looking for in the "Find what" text box, but leave the "Replace with" text box empty. Word will scrape the offending locutions from your document.

TIP

Go To

While we're talking about easier ways to search your documents, lets look at Word's Go To tool. If you're searching for things like a page, a bookmark, a comment, an endnote, an object, or other similar document elements, you can't beat Go To. (See Figure 16-3.)

To search for different types of items in your document:

- Open the Find and Replace dialog box.
- Click on the Go To tab.
- Select an item type from the display list.

Note: *Depending on which item you select, the name of the "Enter" text box changes. For example, if you're searching for a Page, the text box wants a page number; if you're looking for a Comment, it wants the reviewer's name, and so on.*

- To go to a specific item, type its name or number in the text box, and then click on the Go To button.
- To move from item to item in your document, leave the text box empty and click on the "Next" or "Previous" button. Keep clicking to move on to the next item.

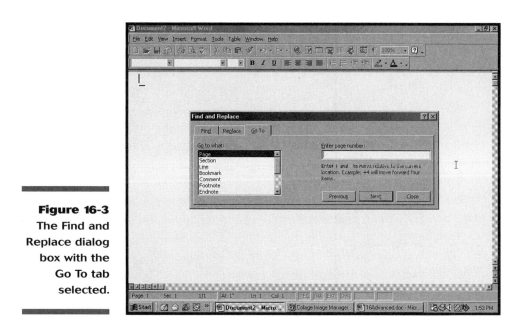

Figure 16-3
The Find and
Replace dialog
box with the
Go To tab
selected.

AutoCorrect

If you find you habitually misspell or mistype certain words—say, you can't seem to help hitting "a-d-n" instead of "a-n-d," or the whole "I before E except after C" thing causes your brain to seize every time you type "Einstein perceived" in your *Relativity Isn't Relative* monthly newsletter—no need to wait for the Spell checker to make things right. Word's AutoCorrect feature can automatically rewrite your common mistakes as you type.

But wait! There's more! AutoCorrect comes with a list of common misspellings, but you can tailor that list to reflect your habits. And, while you're doing that, you can throw in some shorthand keywords for words or short phrases you type a lot. (See Figure 16-4.)

Where the Action Is

All the action here takes place in the AutoCorrect dialog box. Here's how to open it with the AutoCorrect tab already selected:

- **Go to the Menu Bar.**
- **Open Tools.**

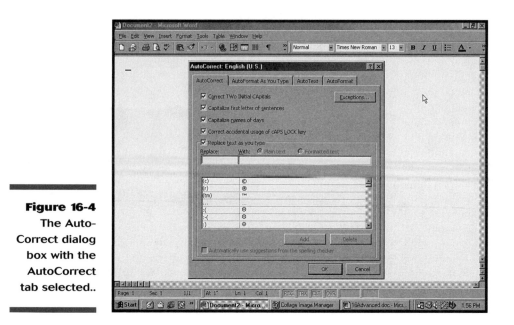

Figure 16-4
The Auto-
Correct dialog
box with the
AutoCorrect
tab selected..

- Select AutoCorrect.

Or . . .

- Hit Alt + T + A.

To turn AutoCorrect on or off:

- Open the AutoCorrect dialog box to the AutoCorrect tab.

- To turn it on, click in the "Replace text as you type" check box; to turn it off, clear the check box.

- While you're there, check any of the other boxes that seem appropriate for your typing peccadilloes. (I don't know how I ever managed without the "Capitalize first letter of a sentence" option.)

Checking the "Replace text as you type" check box tells Word to use the list below it to correct your typing errors as you go. If that list contains words you want the program to ignore, you can remove them.

To remove a word from the AutoCorrect list:

- Open the AutoCorrect dialog box to the AutoCorrect tab.

- In the "Replace" box, type the first few letters of the word you want to delete from AutoCorrect.

- **The list of words and replacements scrolls to show your word.**
- **Select your word.**
- **Click Delete.**
- **Click OK.**

Word's built in AutoCorrect replacement list is extensive, but you can add to it anytime you like. If the words you commonly mistype aren't on the list, or if you want to create a shorthand version of a word or short phrase, Word lets you do it.

To add a word or short phrase to the AutoCorrect list:

- **In your document, either type the word or phrase as you want it to appear and select it, or just select text that has already been typed.**
- **Open the AutoCorrect dialog box to the AutoCorrect tab.**
- **The selected word or phrase now appears in the "With" text box.**
- **In the "Replace" text box, type the incorrect word—in other words, the mistake you usually make—or type in a two- or three-letter shorthand code.**
- **Click OK.**
- **Now, whenever you type the letters you put in the "Replace" box and then you hit the spacebar, the word from the "With" box will replace it.**

Word's AutoCorrect feature allows you to specify exceptions to its AutoCorrection rules. Click on the Exceptions button to open the AutoCorrect Exceptions dialog box. Choose a tab to list your exceptions. For example, I write a lot about software companies, so I listed the name of a software development tool, JBuilder, as an exception under the "Correct Two Initial Caps" rule. (This feature was driving me nuts until I figured it out!)

TIP

AutoText

Another great tool for cutting down on your typing is AutoText. A coinhabitor of the AutoCorrect dialog box, AutoText is a little different from AutoCorrect. Like AutoCorrect, this feature lets you assign codes to frequently typed words and phrases. But when you type an AutoText code or abbreviation, a ScreenTip box

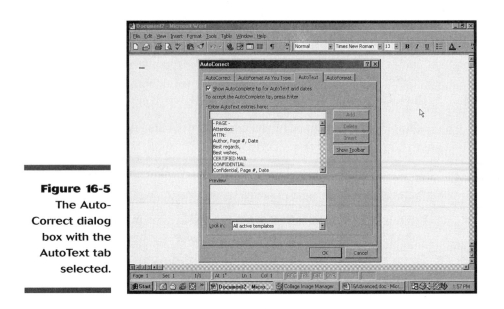

Figure 16-5
The Auto-
Correct dialog
box with the
AutoText tab
selected.

pops up in your document displaying your entry. If you continue typing, the ScreenTip box goes away and nothing happens; if you hit Enter, AutoText inserts the text into your document. (See Figure 16-5.)

Also AutoCorrect only allows for entries of up to 255 words; AutoText entries can be of any length, from a short sentence to an entire letter. And these things are a breeze to save and use.

To create an AutoText entry:

- In your document, type the text you want to include in your AutoText entry or select some existing text.
- While you're at it, apply the formatting you're going to want it to have. (For example, *Gone with the Wind*).
- Go to the Menu Bar.
- Open Insert.
- Select AutoText to open the submenu.
- Click New to open the Create AutoText dialog box.
- A few words from your selected text appear in the text box.
- If you don't want to use these words to identify your AutoText entry, type in the abbreviation you want to assign to your text entry.

Note: *Keep it short and memorable.*

> You can turn your AutoText entries on or off by opening the AutoCorrect dialog box at the AutoText tab and then checking or clearing the "Show AutoComplete tip for AutoText and dates" check box.
>
> **TIP**

- Click OK.
- The next time you type the abbreviation, the ScreenTip text box will appear with your entry.
- Hit Enter to insert the entry into your document.

Where the Action Is

AutoText entries are managed from the AutoCorrect dialog box. Here's how to open it with the AutoText tab already selected:

- **Go to the Menu Bar.**
- **Open Insert.**
- **Select AutoText to open the submenu.**
- **Click on AutoText.**

Or . . .

- **Hit Alt + I + A + Enter.**

To delete or insert an AutoText entry manually:

- **Open the AutoCorrect dialog box to the AutoText tab.**
- **Your and Word's AutoText categories are shown in a display window.**
- **Select the category you want.**

The entries are displayed in the window. If there's more than one, select the one you want to affect.

- **Click on the Delete or Insert button.**
- **Click OK.**

AutoText has its own toolbar, which makes accessing the commands even easier. To open it into your Program Window, Open the View menu, select Toolbars to open the submenu, and click on AutoText. From here you can use the "New" button to add new entries without going through the dialog boxes. (The "New" button is available only when some text has been selected.) To insert an entry from the toolbar, click the All Entries button to open a menu, select the entry category you want to open the submenu, and click on the entry you want to insert.

TIP

AutoSave

Word comes with an AutoSave feature that acts as a safety net for your documents. When turned on, AutoSave automatically saves the document you're working on to your hard disk at prescribed intervals, say, every five minutes.

But AutoSave and the Save button in your File menu are two very different animals. With AutoSave, Word creates and constantly updates a backup copy of your working document. If your computer were to shut down while you were working on any given document, a backup copy of the document would be there when the power came back on, even if you hadn't gotten around to saving it. (See Figure 16-6.)

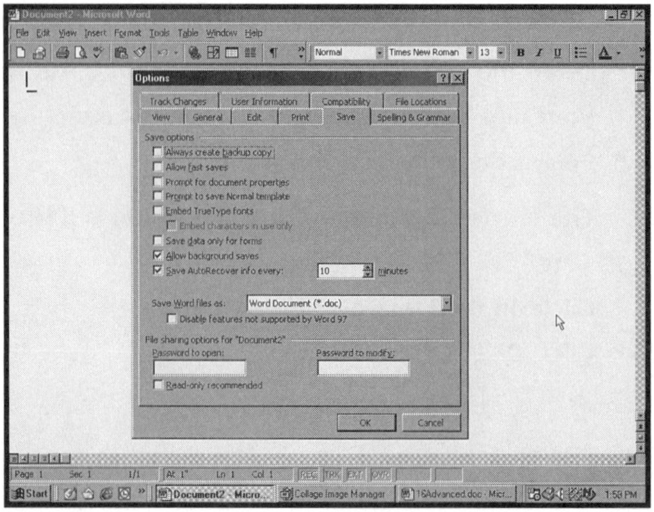

Figure 16-6
The Options dialog box with the Save tab selected.

But you've still got to save your documents! AutoSave only backs up the documents you're working on, while you're working on them. If you decide not to save the "recovery file" that Word gives you when you start up the program after a crash, it dumps the file. If you save the recovery file and you had ever saved the document to your hard disk, Word replaces the old version of the document with the recovery version. Or, you can save the recovery version as a new file with a new name.

To turn on AutoSave:

- **Go to the Menu Bar.**
- **Open Tools.**
- **Select Options to open the Options dialog box.**
- **Click on the Save tab.**
- **If a check isn't already in it, click in the Save AutoRecover Info Every check box.**
- **Now decide how often you want your work automatically saved. Every ten minutes is a common choice, but I've seen people with one minute selected. Use the arrow buttons to enter your choice in the "minutes" box.**
- **Click OK.**
- **AutoSave is now on and periodically backing up your working document.**

A word of caution: On older, slower machines, AutoSave can cause little pauses in the action while your computer grinds out a new backup copy. This can take a couple of seconds when it's a long document. If you're using a machine that does this, you'll have to decide whether the safety net is worth these momentary distractions.

Fast Saves

Simply put, when you enable Fast Saves, you tell Word not to waste time resaving your entire document but to just save the changes you make to it. To accomplish this, Word keeps a little index of your changes in a temporary file until you invoke a full save.

I'm not a fan of Fast Saves. They make me feel insecure. As fast as computers are nowadays, I see no reason to take a chance on losing my work in a bunch of temporary files, which just accumulate and take up space. My recommendation, and the recommendation of many well-informed Wordiacs, is to leave this feature off.

To turn off Fast Saves:

- **Go to the Menu Bar.**
- **Open Tools.**

- **Select Options to open the Options dialog box.**
- **Click on the Save tab.**
- **Make sure that the check box next to "Allow Fast Saves" is clear.**

TOCs and Indexes

Word comes with tools to help you build tables of contents—TOCs—and indexes for your documents. (See Figure 16-7.)

Building a TOC

In Word, a *table of contents* is a list of the headings in your document. To create one, you must have salted your document with standard headings (the ones in the Style list in your Formatting toolbar). You can go in and insert the headings at any time before you start building the TOC. Once you've laid this groundwork, the TOC is a piece of cake. (See Figure 16-8.)

To build a Table of Contents:

- **Go to the very beginning of your document.**
- **Before the first line of text, create a page or section break.**

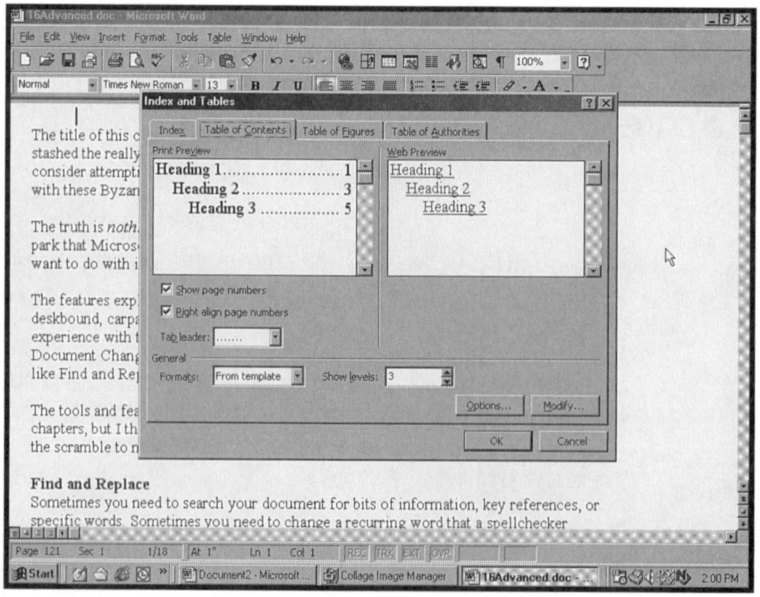

Figure 16-7
The Index and
Tables dialog
box with the
Table of
Contents tab
selected.

Note: *You could put your TOC anywhere, but they usually go up front.*

- **Position your cursor at the beginning of the new page or section.**
- **Go to the Menu Bar.**
- **Open Insert.**
- **Select Index and Tables to open the Index and Tables dialog box.**
- **Click on the Table of Contents tab.**
- **Word displays both Print and Web previews of how it plans to organize the headings in your document, as well as several formatting options.**
- **Select the formatting options you want to apply to your TOC.**
- **Click OK.**
- **Word sorts your headings and creates the TOC.**

Building an Index

Indexes are much more detailed reference lists than TOCs, and building them is a little more complicated. Indexes list specific terms and ideas that you used in your document and tells which page they're on. Word lets you create index entries for individual word, phrases, and even symbols. It also allows you to develop multilevel indexes, with entries grouped under subject headings. (See Figure 16-9.)

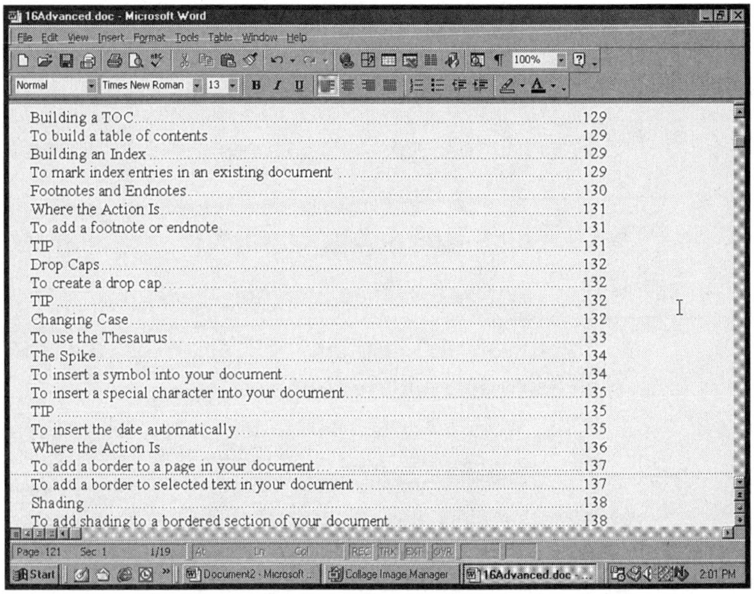

Figure 16-8
The Document
Window
displaying a
Table of
Contents.

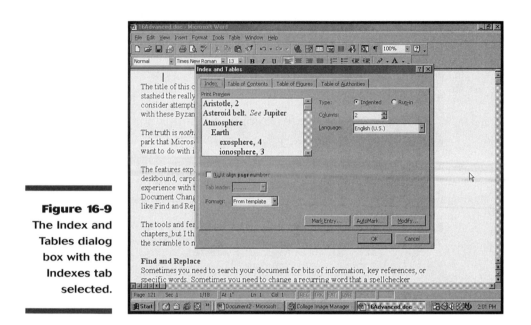

Figure 16-9
The Index and
Tables dialog
box with the
Indexes tab
selected.

Before you can create an index for your Word document, you have to do a little footwork: You have to mark the individual words and phrases you want to list. (See Figure 16-10.)

To mark index entries in an existing document:

- Select the text you want to mark. It can be a word, a phrase, or a symbol.
- Go to the Menu Bar.
- Open Insert.
- Select Index and Tables to open the Index and Tables dialog box.
- Click on the Index tab.
- Click on the Mark Entry button to open the Mark Index Entry dialog box.

Note: *The text you selected appears in the "Main entry" text box.*

- If you want to mark only this occurrence of the word or phrase in your text, click on the Mark button.
- If you want to create an index entry for every occurrence of this word or phrase, click the Mark All button.

Note: *Word lets you create a "subentry" to go with your main index entry. You can just type it into the text box. You can include a third-level entry in the same box by typing a colon after the first subentry.*

- When you click on one of the Mark keys, Word turns on the Show/Hide switch so your document is (temporarily) filled with paragraph, tab, and space symbols.
- The Mark Entry dialog box stays open as you cruise through the rest of your document, marking index entries.

Note: *Other options in the Mark Entry dialog box let you format your index entries as you mark them; for example, you can italicize book titles, and make the page numbers bold.*

- When you're finished, click on the Close button.

Note: *Click on the Show/Hide button in your Standard toolbar to hide the nonprinting symbols.*

To create the index:

- Go to the very end of your document.

Note: *You could put this thing anywhere, but traditionally, they go at the end.*

- Beyond the last line of text, insert a Section break.
- Go to the Menu Bar.
- Open Insert.
- Select Index and Tables to open the Index and Tables dialog box.
- Click on the Index tab.
- The Print Preview window shows your index.

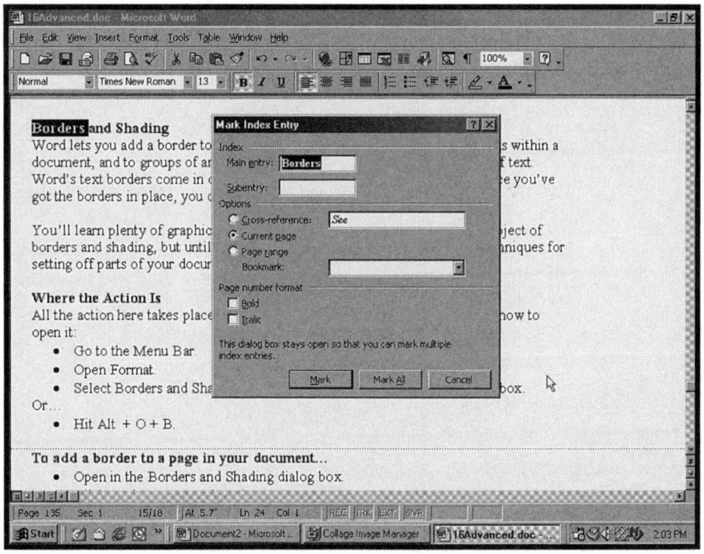

Figure 16-10
The Mark Entry
dialog box.

Note: *Experiment with the options in the "Format" drop–down list; your choices will be reflected in the Print Preview windows. Notice that the Columns box shows 2 by default, but you can change it if you like.*

- **Click OK.**
- **The index you designed appears at the end of your document.**

Footnotes and Endnotes

Working with footnotes on a typewriter in the bad old precomputer days was absolutely maddening—which is why I always opted for endnotes whenever possible. But sometimes it wasn't, and I would spend endless, hair-pulling hours trying to get those things to come out right. (See Figure 16-11.)

Footnotes and endnotes identify sources of information used in your documents. Footnotes appear at the bottom of each page, and endnotes appear at the end. And Word makes working with them a breeze (comparatively, anyway).

Where the Action Is

All the action here takes place in the Footnote and Endnote dialog box. (See Figure 16-12.) Here's how to open it:

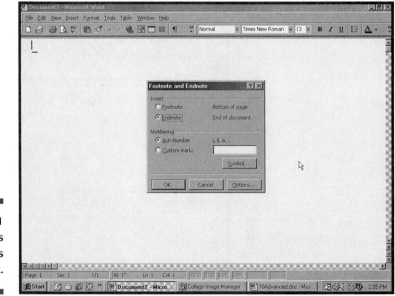

Figure 16-11
The Footnotes and Endnotes dialog box.

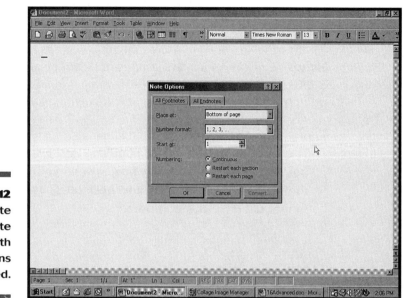

Figure 16-12
The Footnote
and Endnote
dialog box with
the Note Options
tab selected.

- Go to the Menu Bar.
- Open Insert.
- Select Footnote.

Or . . .

- Hit Alt + I + N.

To add a footnote or endnote:

- Position your cursor next to the text you want to reference. This is where the footnote or endnote number will appear.
- Open the Footnote and Endnote dialog box.
- Under the "Insert" area, select either Footnote or Endnote.
- Click OK to exit the dialog box and return to the document page.
- A superscript reference number has been added at the insertion point.
- If you're working in Normal view, your Document Window is now split, giving you access to the bottom of the page (for footnotes) or the end of your document (for endnotes).

Note: *In Print Layout and Web view, you have an actual footnote space at the bottom of your document.*

- Click inside the area and type in your reference.
- If you're using Normal view, click Close to exit the note pane.

Note: *Word automatically numbers the references for you by default. Each new note is assigned the next consecutive number. The Custom mark option in the Footnote and Endnote dialog box allows you to select another mark, such as a letter or symbol.*

> The Options button in the Footnote and Endnote dialog box opens another dialog box, where you can change the location of footnotes and endnotes, as well as the format used for the numbers.
>
> **TIP**

Counting Words and Characters

Sometimes you need to get an exact, to-the-word count of the length of your documents. Journalists "write to length" every day, but thanks to Word, they no longer have to go by old-fashioned 250-words-per-double-spaced page estimates. Word's Word Count dialog box is a treasure chest of intimate document statistics, including to-the-locution word counts, page counts, paragraph counts, lines counts, and even *character* counts. (See Figure 16-13.)

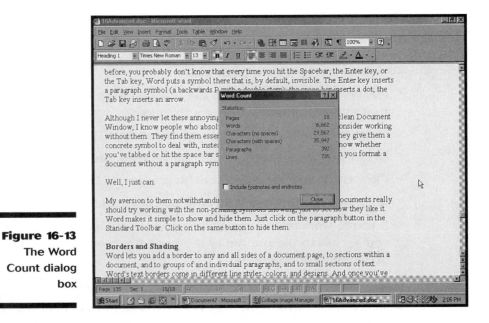

Figure 16-13
The Word
Count dialog
box

To get your hands on these statistics, open the document you want analyzed and hit Alt + T + W. Word's Word Count dialog box will have all the stats.

Drop Caps

Drop caps are large, capital letters, usually applied to the first letter of a paragraph and often in a font different from the rest of the text. A drop cap is a nice effect, a design element reminiscent of classic children's books, and they really liven up the look of a newsletter or brochure. You can only see them on the screen in Print Layout or Web view, but Word makes them easy to create. (See Figures 16-14 and 16-15.)

To create a drop cap:

- **Select the letter you want to change to a drop–cap character.**
- **Go to the Menu Bar.**
- **Open Format.**
- **Select Drop Cap to open the Drop Cap dialog box.**
- **Choose either to set the drop cap in with the rest of the text, or along the margin. (The third choice, "None," removes the drop-cap effect.)**
- **When you click on one of the options, the formatting options become available. Click to assign any formatting adjustments.**

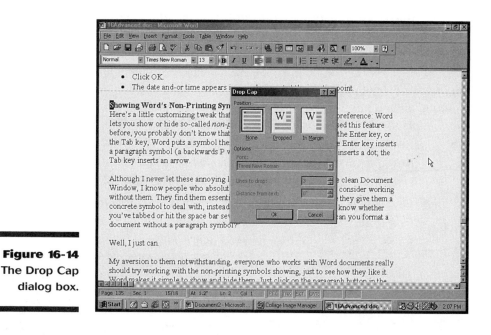

Figure 16-14
The Drop Cap dialog box.

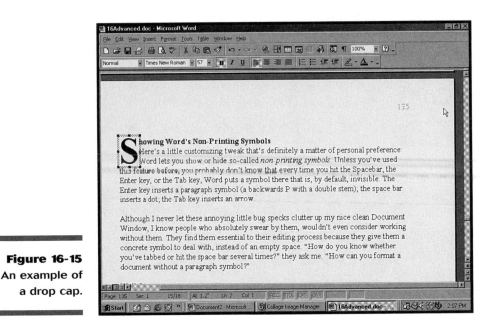

Figure 16-15
An example of
a drop cap.

- **Click OK.**
- **If you're not already in it, Word bumps you into Print Layout view. Your drop-cap choices appear in your document.**

Note: *Word thinks of your drop cap as an object. (You might have noticed the selection handles.)*

Changing Case

There are many reasons you might want to change the *case*—as in uppercase and lowercase—of some text in your document. Maybe you decided to create a title or put in a subhead, or maybe you just want to emphasize a phrase in a particular way.

Word gives you two ways to change the case of selected text in your documents. One way is to open the Format menu, select Change Case, and start futzing around in a dialog box. Here's an easier way: Select the text and hold down Shift and hit F3 to "toggle" your way to the case configuration you want. The first one gives you all caps, the next all lower case, and the third "title," which capitalizes each word in the text.

To quickly adjust the text wrap qualities and other formatting of your drop cap, select it to reveal its border, and then double-click on the border to open the a dialog box. From this box, you can tweak things like text wrapping. To remove the drop-cap effect, go back into the Drop Cap dialog box and click on the "None" option. For some reason, Word provides no preview of its drop-cap effects, so you'll have to experiment.

TIP

The Thesaurus

Word's Thesaurus isn't a great reference source—it's sometimes not even accurate—but I have to admit, I use it all the time (sometimes just to remind myself why I keep actual books nearby). Word's Thesaurus is a storehouse of synonyms (word with similar meanings) and antonyms (words with opposite meanings). You can use it to find replacements for overused words, to come up with *i' mot juste* on the fly, and to look up word meanings. Though this thing is unlikely to replace your dictionary, it's a handy, if lightweight, tool for punching up your writing. (See Figure 16-16.)

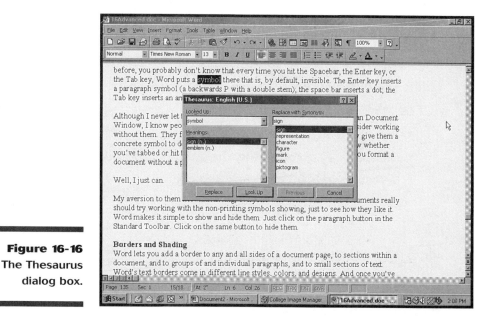

Figure 16-16
The Thesaurus
dialog box.

To use the Thesaurus:

- Select the word for which you need a synonym, antonym, or meaning.
- Go the Menu Bar.
- Open Tools.
- Select Language to open the submenu.
- Click on Thesaurus to open the Thesaurus dialog box.
- The dialog box displays the word you selected and a list of synonyms and sometimes antonyms.
- To look up a word's meanings, select it from the Synonym list box and click the Look Up button.
- The Thesaurus displays the word you selected along with its meanings and another synonym list.

Note: *To return to a previous word viewed, click the Previous button. You can continue looking up words and meanings this way until you find the replacement word you want.*

- Select the word.
- Click on the Replace button.
- The dialog box closes and the selected word is replaced.

Note: *If you find no word that works for you, you can click on the Cancel button to exit the Thesaurus without replacing the word in your document.*

Or . . .

- Right-click over the selected word to invoke a shortcut menu.
- Select Synonyms to display a list of possible synonyms.
- Click the word you want from the list to replace the selected word in your document.

Or . . .

- Select a word.
- Hit Shift + F7 to open the Thesaurus dialog box.
- Select a synonym and click Replace.

The Spike

The Spike is a place where you can keep several items you've cut from various documents until you're ready to drop them somewhere, as a group and in the order in which you collected them.

To use the Spike, select the item you want to move and then hit Ctrl F3. This cuts the text from the document and holds it in the Spike. To add more items, do the same thing. When you're ready to paste them into a new location, position your cursor in the document and hit Ctrl + Shift + F3. This key combination "empties" the Spike, but you can copy the items from the Spike without emptying it by going to the AutoText tab of the AutoCorrect dialog box. Scroll down the "Enter AutoText entries here" list box to find Spike. Select it and its content appear in the Preview window. Click the Insert button to copy the contents into your document.

The Spike might seem a bit anachronistic compared with the new Clipboard toolbar—you only use it to cut, not copy, and you can't insert the collected items individually—but the number of items you can add to the Spike is unlimited, and sometimes it's just quicker to scoop and run.

Special Characters and Symbols

No keyboard could possibly include all the different characters and symbols you might need to type into your documents from time to time. And if someone *did* design a "complete" keyboard, would you really want it taking up your whole desk. No. You wouldn't. (The people at the patent office already explained it to me.) (See Figure 16-17.)

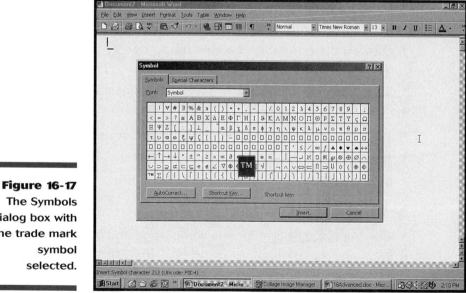

Figure 16-17
The Symbols dialog box with the trade mark symbol selected.

For this and, I'm sure, other reasons, Word comes with a boatload of non-standard characters, including copyright and trademark symbols, math signs, Greek stuff, and much more.

To insert a symbol into your document:

- Position your cursor in your document where you want the symbol inserted.
- Go to the Menu Bar.
- Open Insert.
- Select Symbol to open the Symbols dialog box.
- Click on the Symbols tab to open up a palette of symbols.

Note: *They're kind of hard to see, but each symbol you click is magnified.*

- Click on the symbol you want.
- Click the Insert button.
- The symbol appears in your document at the insertion point.
- The Symbol dialog box remains open to let you add another symbol.
- Click the Close button to exit the dialog box.

To insert a special character into your document:

- Position your cursor in your document where you want the symbol inserted.
- Go to the Menu Bar.
- Open Insert.
- Select Symbol to open the Symbols dialog box.
- Click on the Special Characters tab to open a list of characters and their shortcut keys.
- Select the special character you want to insert.
- Click on the Insert button.
- The character appears in your document at the insertion point.
- The Symbol dialog box remains open to let you add another special character.
- Click the Close button to exit the dialog box.

Other options in the Symbols dialog box are worth checking out:

- The "Font" drop-down list lets you change and preview symbols in different fonts.
- Selecting certain fonts activates the "Subset" drop-down list. From this list, you can access all kinds of additional symbols, including characters from the Greek, Cyrillic, and Hebrew alphabets.

- Both the Symbols tab and the Special Characters tab, include buttons that give you access to the AutoCorrect dialog box, where you can create and AutoCorrect entry using a symbol, and a Shortcut Key dialog box, where you can change the keyboard combinations that evoke these symbols.

Date and Time

Hey, who has time to mess with the time, let alone the date? You don't have to spend one more minute typing in "a.m." or . . . what's that other one? Oh yeah . . . "p.m.," or messing around with date styles. Word can insert the current date in a several different formats, it'll even update to the current date every time you open a document. (See Figure 16-18.)

To automatically insert the date in your document:

- Position your cursor at the insertion point in your document.
- Go to the Menu Bar.
- Open Insert.
- Select Date and Time to open the Date and Time dialog box.
- In the "Available formats" list box, select the format you want to use.
- If you want the date or time automatically updated every time you open the document, click the "Update automatically" check box.
- Click OK.
- The date and/or time appears in your document at the insertion point.

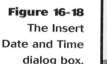

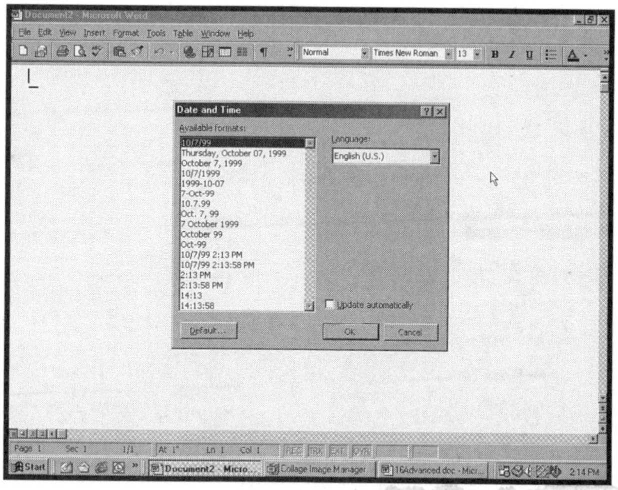

Figure 16-18
The Insert
Date and Time
dialog box.

Showing Word's Nonprinting Symbols

Here's a little customizing tweak that's definitely a matter of personal preference: Word lets you show or hide so-called *nonprinting symbols*. Unless you've used this feature before, you probably don't know that every time you hit the Spacebar, the Enter key, or the Tab key, Word puts a symbol there that is, by default, invisible. The Enter key inserts a paragraph symbol (a backwards P with a double stem); the space bar inserts a dot; the Tab key inserts an arrow. (See Figure 16-19.)

Although I never let these annoying little bug specks clutter up my nice clean Document Window, I know people who absolutely swear by them, wouldn't even consider working without them. They find them essential to their editing process because they give them a concrete symbol to deal with, instead of an empty space. "How do you know whether you've tabbed or hit the space bar several times?" they ask me. "How can you format a document without a paragraph symbol?"

Well, I just can.

My aversion to them notwithstanding, everyone who works with Word documents really should try working with the nonprinting symbols showing, just to see how they like it. Word makes it simple to show and hide them. Just click on the paragraph button in the Standard toolbar. Click on the same button to hide them.

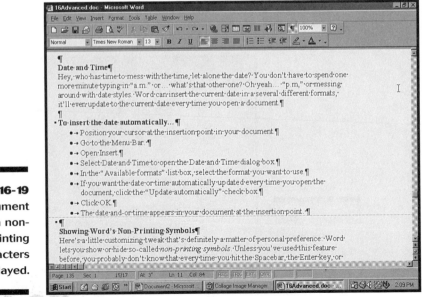

Figure 16-19
A document with non-printing characters displayed.

Borders and Shading

Word lets you add a border to any and all sides of a document page, to sections within a document, and to groups of paragraphs and individual paragraphs, and to small sections of text. Word's text borders come in different line styles, colors, and designs. And once you've got the borders in place, you can add shading effect. (See Figure 16-20.)

You'll learn plenty of graphics techniques in Chapter 18, including more on the subject of borders and shading, but until you get there, here are some quick and easy techniques for setting off parts of your documents graphically.

Where the Action Is

All the action here takes place in the Borders and Shading dialog box. Here's how to open it:

- **Go to the Menu Bar.**
- **Open Format.**
- **Select Borders and Shading to open in the Borders and Shading dialog box.**

Or . . .

- **Hit Alt + O + B.**

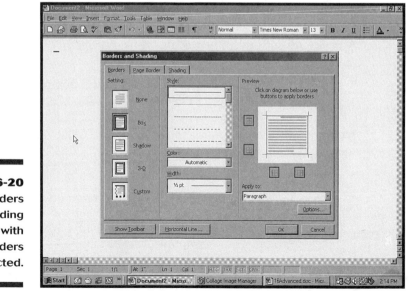

Figure 16-20
The Borders and Shading dialog box with the Borders tab selected.

To add a border to a page in your document:

• Open the Borders and Shading dialog box.

• Click on the Page Border tab.

• Select the border type you want, and then select the line style, color, and width of your border.

Note: *The "Art" drop-down list includes some figurative border choices.*

Note: *All of your formatting choices are reflected in the Preview window.*

• To specify a particular page or section for the border, click the down arrow next to the "Apply to" drop-down list and make a selection.

• To specify the exact position of the border on the page, click on the Options button to open the Borders and Shading Options dialog box. Here, you can adjust the margins and placement.

• To specify which sides get the border, click on the buttons inside the Preview window.

• Click OK.

• Word bumps you into Print Layout view.

• Your new border now encloses your page.

To add a Border to selected text in your document:

• Select the text you want set off by a border.

• Open the Borders and Shading dialog box.

• Click on the Borders tab.

• Select a border type.

• If you're putting a border around a paragraph, make sure that "Paragraph" is showing in the "Apply to" list box.

• If you're putting a border around a piece of text, make sure that "Text" is showing in the "Apply to" list box.

Note: *When "Paragraph" is showing in the "Apply to" list box, your border will go from margin to margin; when "Text" is showing, the border hugs the selected text.*

• Choose your formatting and margin options.

• To specify which sides get the border, click on the buttons inside the Preview window.

• Click OK.

• Word bumps you into Print Layout view.

• Your new border now encloses your text.

Shading

Word's shading effects fill in the bordered space with shades of gray and color to make them really stand out. Word also lets you add the shading without the borders—which is the same thing as the highlighting effect. (See Figure 16-21.)

To add shading to a bordered section of your document:

- Select the bordered section you want to fill.
- Open the Borders and Shading dialog box.
- Click the Shading tab.
- Check the "Apply to" list for the correct border type.
- Click on the shading and formatting options you want.

Note: *Your changes are reflected in the Preview window.*

- Click OK.
- Your shading appears in your bordered text.

Macros

The reaction I usually get when I start talking about creating macros in Word is either glazed disinterest or stark terror. I don't know what's going on here. Maybe

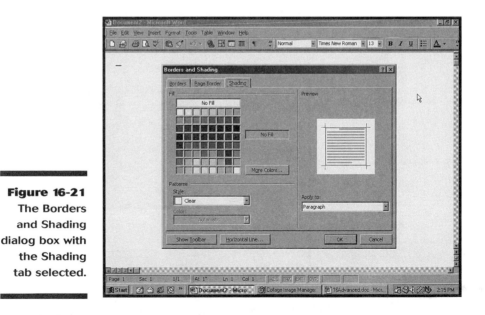

Figure 16-21
The Borders and Shading dialog box with the Shading tab selected.

it's because it sounds technical. The news is always bleating warnings about the latest "macro virus." (Bar the door and hide the women!) Maybe it's because creating a macro seems a little too much like actual programming. (Yikes!)

But in fact, macros are no big deal, they're easy to create and remove, and they can make your work a lot easier by automating some of your tasks.

What Is a Macro?

A *macro* is just a series of mouse and/or keyboard actions, recorded in Word, which you can execute all at once with a keyboard shortcut. All of your keyboard shortcuts are macros.

You can record macros for virtually anything you do in Word. For example, you could record a macro that opens the Format menu, selects the Font dialog box, and applies the small caps option to your selected text. In fact, let's do just that. (See Figure 16-22.)

To record a Macro:

- **Go to the Menu Bar.**
- **Open Tools.**
- **Select Macro to open the submenu.**
- **Click on Record New Macro.**

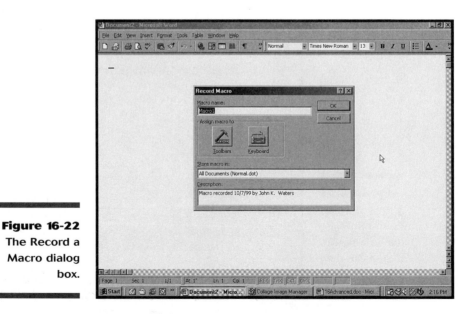

Figure 16-22
The Record a
Macro dialog
box.

- Click inside the "Macro name" text box and type in a one-word name for your macro.
- Click on the large Keyboard button to open a dialog box for defining a shortcut key combination to use to run the macro.
- Enter your shortcut.

Note: *Try using the Alt or Ctrl keys along with other keyboard characters. You'll probably have to try several combinations until you find one that isn't already assigned.*

- Click the Assign button.
- Click Close to exit the dialog box and start recording the macro.
- The Macro toolbar appears in your Document Window in record mode.

  The tricky part here is to take your steps very carefully. To record our macro:

  - Click on Format in the Menu Bar.
  - Click on Font.
  - In the Font dialog box, put a check next to Small Caps.
  - Click the OK button.

- Click the Stop button on the Macro toolbar to stop recording the macro.

  Now, select some text and hit your shortcut keys. Cool, huh? (See Figure 16-23.)

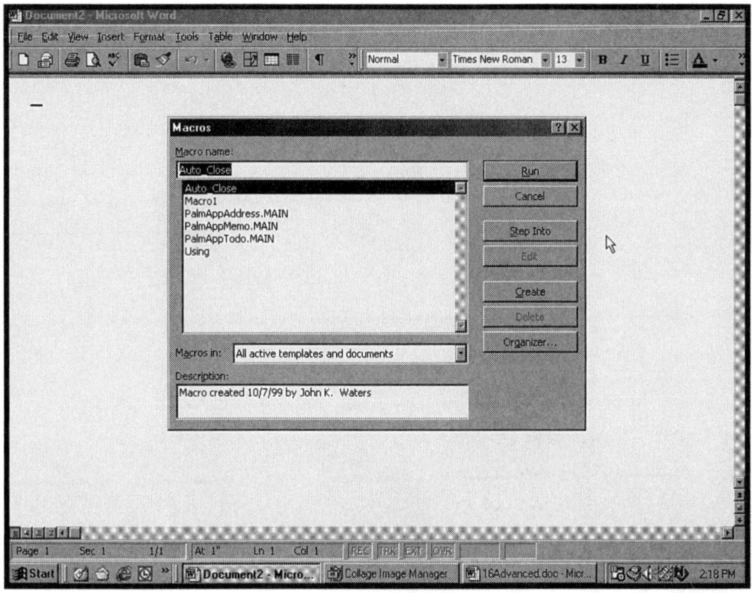

Figure 16-23
The Recording
Macro toolbar.

The real trick to recording a macro is to plan out your steps in advance. I recommend writing them down, so they're easy to follow. If you make a mistake, or if you no longer need a macro and want the keyboard shortcut for a new one, getting rid of them is easy.

To delete a Macro:

- Go to the Menu Bar.
- Open Tools.
- Select Macro to open the submenu.
- Click on Macros to open the Macros dialog box.
- A list of macros appears in the box.
- Click the name of the macro you want to delete.
- Click Delete.

17

Setting Your Table

Building and Working with Tables in Word

f you've ever tabbed your way through a fragile row of carefully constructed columns of text only to hit the wrong key and knock the whole thing askew, and then you couldn't visualize exactly where you needed to go to correct the problem, and everything you did just seemed to make things worse until you were ready to print the whole damned thing out and just put it all back together with scotch tape and an exacto knife . . . well then, you're going to *love* working with tables.

Sooner or later, we all find ourselves lining up text up in a document. If it's just a couple of items, the Tab key works fine. But once you start tabbing out long columns and wide rows, that's when the pain begins.

Word's Tables tools can make the pain go away (most of it anyway). Definitely file this group of tools and features under the heading "Making Life Easier for Harried Word Processors." Building and working with tables in Word is simple and straightforward. Heck, the tools even have their own Menu Bar heading. You do have to know a few tricks and understand a couple of table-specific concepts, but it's not rocket science, and it might be worth learning even if it were.

What Is a Table?

Tables are great for tidying up the information in your documents, for imposing order on lists, and for organizing groups of related material into visually meaningful structures. You can use tables to create charts, invoices, to-do lists, and employee rolls. But how exactly does Word define "table?" (See Figure 17-1.)

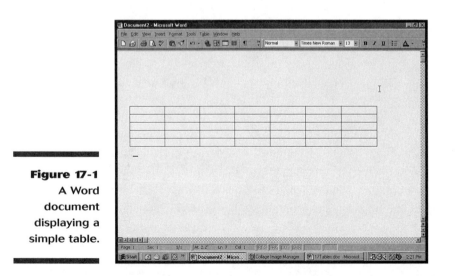

Figure 17-1
A Word
document
displaying a
simple table.

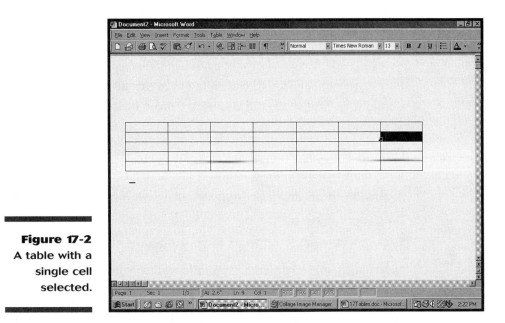

Figure 17-2
A table with a
single cell
selected.

In Word, a *table* is simple a group of rows and columns, organized roughly into a grid, and probably containing text (maybe graphics). Those rows and columns can be equally spaced and inflexible, or customized and fluid. Word lets you define exactly how the columns and rows in your table are placed. You can set up a table anywhere in your document. You can build the table and then add the text, or type the text and then shove it all into a table. You can fancy up your table with borders and shading. You can even build *invisible* tables.

What Is a Cell?

Before we go on, you need to understand one bit of table nomenclature: A *cell* in a table is the intersection of a column and a row. Cells can be resized and rearranged within the table. You move from cell to cell with the Tab key. (Tab moves you forward to the right; Shift + Tab moves you to the left). (See Figure 17-2.)

Once you've created a table, you click inside the cell to type in your text. Inside a cell, text behaves fairly normally: it warps at the edge of the cell; hitting the Enter key starts a new paragraph; all the formatting buttons work.

The Quickest Way to Put a Table into Your Documents

Let's cut to the chase: The single quickest way to build a basic table in your documents is by clicking on the Insert Table button in the Standard toolbar. Here's how you do it:

- **Position your cursor where you want the table inserted in your document.**
- **Click on the Insert Table button.**
- **A grid-like drop-down list appears displaying five columns and four rows.**
- **Drag your mouse pointer over the rows and columns to select the size of your table.**
- **Click, and the table appears in your document.**

Now you just click inside a cell and start typing. (See Figure 17-3.)

Adding Rows and Columns to Your Table

So now you've got your table up and running, and you've started entering text into the cells, when suddenly you look up and realize you need another row. No sweat.

To add a row to your table:

- **Click inside a row to position your cursor above or below where you want the new one inserted.**

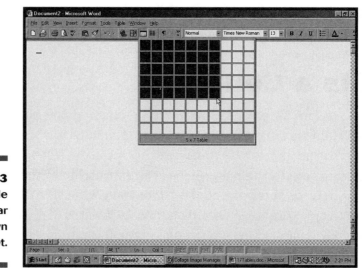

Figure 17-3
The Table toolbar drop-down menu/pallet.

- Open the Table Menu.
- Select Insert to open the submenu.
- Select "Rows Above" or "Rows Below," depending on whether you want it relative to your cursor.
- The menus close up, and your table has a new row.

Or...

- Position your cursor in the last cell of your table.
- Hit the Tab key.
- Another row appears.

As you might have guessed, adding columns (if you looked up and realized you needed more of them) works exactly the same way.

To add a column to your table:

- Click inside a column to position your cursor to the right or left of where you want the new one inserted.
- Open the Table Menu.
- Select Insert to open the submenu.
- Select "Columns to the Left" or "Columns to the Right."
- The menus close up, and your table has a new column.

If what you suddenly realized when you looked up was that you had too many rows or columns, here's how you snip them off:

To delete a row or column:

- Click in the row or column you want to cut.
- Open Table.
- Select "Delete."

You can select individual columns and rows with your mouse pointer. To do this, hover your I-beam pointer either above the column or beside the row you want to select. You'll have to squiggle around until you find the sweet spot that turns it into a black arrow. Click, and you've selected the column or row

TIP

- Select "Rows" to cut out a row or "Columns" to chop off a column.
- The menus close up, and your table is now shy one column or row.

Adding Borders and Shading to Tables

To add a border and/or shading to your table:

- Click inside your table.
- Open the Table menu.
- Click on Select to open the submenu.
- Click on Table, Column, Row, or Cell.
- Open the Format Menu.
- Select Borders and Shading to display the Borders and Shading dialog box.
- Click the Borders tab, if you're adding a border.
- Under "Setting," click on a border type.
- Under "Style," scroll through the line styles and select one or leave the default style.
- Click on the arrow keys next to the "Color" and "Width" drop-down lists to further modify the line style.
- Click on the Shading tab, if you're adding shading.
- Click on the shading or color you want in the "Fill" palette.

Note: *The name of the color or shade you select appears in the text box next to the palette.*

- To add a pattern, click the Style drop-down arrow and select a pattern.

Note: *All of your choices are reflected in the Preview window. The Preview window is surrounded by buttons that allow you to apply your border formatting changes to individual sections of your table's border, as well as interior dividing lines.*

- Click OK.
- The dialog box closes, and your new setting(s) appear in your table.

Draw Your Own Custom Table

Until now, we've been working with what you might call a standard table. But Word also makes it possible for you to create or "draw" a decidedly nonstandard table,

MOVING TABLES

The hard way really isn't so hard: Select your table, then click on it with your mouse pointer, and drag and drop it to a new spot. While you're dragging, your pointer carries a ghost box, and along the way a ghost cursor flashes at the left side of the document indicating the insertion point. I call this the hard way, because whenever I do it, I always "drop" the table a couple of times before I get to where I'm going.

an asymmetrical beast with random column widths and odd row depths to accommodate virtually any kind of text or graphics. Word's Tables and Borders toolbar helps you to create tables in which you control the size, placement, and style of each row and every column. (See Figure 17-4.)

To draw your own customized table:

- Make sure you've spaced out a little open spot in your document to accommodate your new table.
- Click the Tables and Borders button on the Standard toolbar. Or . . .
- Open the Table menu.
- Select Draw Table.

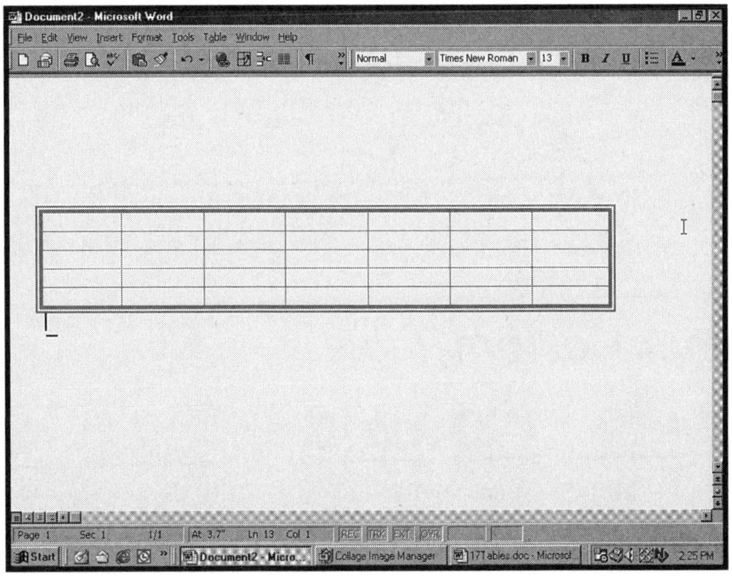

Figure 17-4
The Table
menu.

When you do either one, three things happen:

- **The Tables and Borders toolbar appears in the Document Window.**
- **If you're not in it already, Word bumps you into Print Layout view.**
- **Your mouse pointer turns into a little pencil.**
- **Click on the arrow next to the Line Style drop-down list.**
- **Select a line style.**
- **Click on the arrow next to the Line Weight drop-down list.**
- **Select a line weight.**
- **Click on the Border Color button to open a palette.**
- **Select a color.**
- **Make sure your pointer still looks like a pencil.**

Note: *If it doesn't, click on the Draw Table button.*

Draw the outside border of your table like this:
- **Make sure the Draw Table button is selected (your pointer still looks like a pencil).**
- **Click on what will be the upper left corner of your table.**
- **Click and drag the mouse down toward what would be the lower-right corner.**
- **Doing this creates a rectangle based on the style selections you made.**
- **Release the mouse button.**
- **Use your pencil-like mouse pointer to "draw" the column and row lines inside the border you just created (drag and drop, like you did before).**

Note: *As you drag, a dashed line shows you where the line will be inserted.*

- **When you release the mouse button, the lines appear in the same style as the border.**
- **Your table is ready for you to add or edit text.**
- **Click the Close button to turn off the Tables and Borders toolbar.**

Edit Your Custom Table

The Tables and Borders toolbar gives you a number of tools to refine the design of your new table. You can add more column lines, erase some of them, even out rows and columns, combine cells and merge text, and split cells. (See Figure 17-5.)

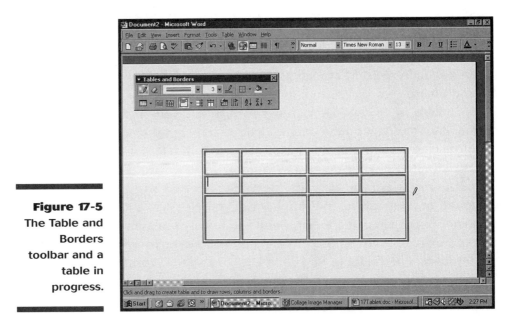

Figure 17-5
The Table and
Borders
toolbar and a
table in
progress.

If you want some of the text in your custom box to read sideways, click inside the cell and then click the Change Text Direction button on the Tables and Borders toolbar. Keep clicking until the text is repositioned in the direction you want it to read.

Add more rows and columns to your custom table the same way you added them to the standard table. You can even use the Tab key to create additional rows.

To make your rows even, click the Distribute Rows Evenly button.

To make your columns even, click on the Distribute Columns Evenly button.

To add shading, click on the Shading Color button and select from the palette.

To remove unwanted lines within the border, click on the Eraser button. Your mouse pointer becomes an eraser. Erase lines by clicking on them or by dragging the pointer over them. You can even erase the whole table, border and all. You can always go back and redraw lines you erase or add new ones. You can erase lines before or after you type in text. When you do it after, the text in the adjoining cells will merge.

To merge an entire column or row, select it, and then click the Merge Cells button on the toolbar. The individual cells become a single column or row.

To split a single column or row into multiple cells, select the column or row, and then click the Split Cells button to the Split Cells dialog box. Enter the number of columns or rows you want (or use the spin arrows). Click OK and the cells split.

RESIZING YOUR TABLES

You can do some resizing of your tables in any view, but when you're in Print Layout view, you can do more.

When you're in Normal view, you can position your mouse pointer over the column separator lines to summon the double-headed arrow that lets you widen or narrow individual columns by clicking and dragging the separators to the left or right. When you do this, a Ruler appears at the top of your Document Window showing the column widths.

In Print Layout view, you also get the double-headed arrow on the row separators, so you can expand or contract the individual rows. You also get a little box just outside the lower right corner of the table. It appears when you hover your curser there. Clicking and dragging that little box resizes the entire table. When you hover your mouse pointer just outside the upper left corner of the table, you get a little box with a cross in it. Clicking and dragging this little box moves the table around in the Document Window.

18

When Word's Words Fail You

Working with Word's Graphics Tools

n Chapter 7 I made the comment that the main purpose of this program is word processing and that everything else you could do with it was really just a bunch of bells and whistles. Well, I'm not changing my mind here, but *boy*, does Word have some cool bells and whistles! In particular, the program makes it easy to add graphical images to your documents.

Pictures can do more than just dress up your documents—although they can certainly do that. Thoughtfully applied images can liven up letters, add visual clarity to reports, and brighten otherwise humdrum pages. Because Word lets you mix text and graphics, you can use it to create whole new categories of documents, such as brochures, product letters, and even catalogs. Pictures just make your documents more *interesting*.

And the thing is, Word makes it easy. Word lets you add images that come with the program, pictures that you scan into your computer, art from other program files, and simple pictures you draw yourself, right in the Document Window.

If you're learning to use the program for the first time, don't let this stuff intimidate you. With a few basic concepts and a couple of menu commands, you'll be ready to rock 'n' roll. If you've been using Word for a while and have never bothered with the graphics stuff (which pretty much describes me until recently), all I can say is, you just *gotta* try it.

But first, a couple of definitions:

Picture. In Word, *picture* refers to graphical elements that you bring into your document from other sources—in other words, everything but drawing objects. These include clip art, bitmaps, and scanned pictures and photographs. You tweak pictures in Word primarily through the Picture toolbar, but also to a lesser extent through the Drawing toolbar.

Clip Art. Word comes packed with little cartoons and photos called *Clip Art*, which it keeps in the *Clip Art Gallery*. They come in color and black and white. Word lets you grab any of these little nuggets 'o art and pop them into your document. Additional Clip Art is available on the Web and on disks you can buy at most computer stores.

Clip Art Gallery. This is the file in which Word keeps all its Clip Art. (Well, *duh!*) But it's also where you'll find sound and video clips. Word comes with hundreds of pieces of clip art, and you can add more.

Object Whatever it might mean in the computer-programming world, in the context of this chapter, an *object* is any nontext element you're adding to your document. Usually, that means something like a piece of clip art, a shape you've drawn, or a photo you've scanned in, but it can also refer to a sound or video clip. (That's why I used "nontext element.") An object can be moved around on the page, and it usually can be resized.

Drawing Object. A *drawing object* is the simple art that you draw yourself inside the document using the Drawing toolbar. Because a drawing object doesn't come from another file (such as the Clip Art Gallery), it is *part of the document*, just like the text. The Drawing toolbar lets you enhance drawing objects with colors, patterns, borders, and other effects. The types of drawing objects you'll be seeing in Word include AutoShapes, curves, lines, and WordArt drawing objects.

AutoShapes. *AutoShapes* are a type of drawing object, groups of basic, ready-made shapes, like rectangles, circles, lines, connectors, block arrows, flowchart symbols, stars and banners, and callouts. AutoShapes are considered to be drawing objects, and you summon them from the Drawing toolbar.

WordArt. *WordArt* is another kind of drawing object. Think of it as "text art" or "picture words" that you can bend and twist and rotate, and to which you can assign special effects. The WordArt tools let you turn any ordinary text in your document into these graphic objects.

Inserting Pictures

The quickest and easiest way to start working with graphics in your Word documents is by inserting a picture from the Clip Art Gallery. (See Figure 18-1.)

Where the Action Is

The action in this next section takes place in the ClipArt dialog box.

To open the ClipArt dialog box:

- **Go to the Menu Bar.**
- **Open Insert.**
- **Select Picture to open the submenu.**
- **Click on Clip Art to open the Insert Clip Art dialog box.**

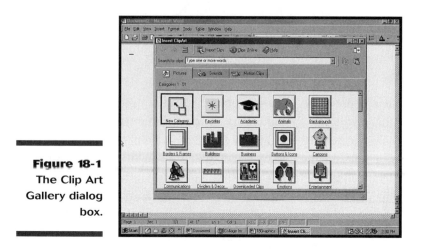

Figure 18-1
The Clip Art
Gallery dialog
box.

To insert a piece of clip art into your document:

* Position your cursor at the place in your document where you want to insert to the clip art.
* Open the Insert Clip Art dialog box.
* Click on the Pictures tab.
* Scroll through the Categories display window.
* Click on a category, and the window displays a selection of clip art.

Note: *If you want to switch categories, use the Back arrow at the top of the dialog box to return to the Categories display window. (You can use the Forward button to return to a previous display window.)*

* Find the picture you want to insert and click on it.

Note: *A "Keep Looking" icon at the bottom of the picture list means there's more. Click on it to see another group of pictures in the same category. Use the Back arrow at the top of the dialog box to return to an earlier list.*

* Clicking on a picture opens a balloon menu.
* Click on the "Insert Clip" button on the balloon menu.

Note: *To preview the picture before adding it to your file, click the Preview Clip button.*

* Click the Close button to exit the dialog box.
* The clip art you selected appears in your document accompanied by the Picture toolbar.

Note: *You might have to click on the picture to see the toolbar.*

ClipArt Search

You don't have to scroll through pages of cartoons or to rely on unclear categories to find the clip art you want. You can track down your pix using the ClipArt Gallery's search tool. Here's how:

- **Open the ClipArt Gallery dialog box.**
- **Click inside the "Search for Clips" text box.**
- **Type in a key word (cats, guitars, San Francisco).**
- **Hit Enter and the list box displays any matches.**

Clip Art on the Web

You don't have to settle for the selection of clip art Word includes with the program (though it's huge). You can reach out from your Program Window and directly access the virtually limitless capacities of the Word Wide Web or at least Microsoft's Word Web site. Here's how you do it:

- **Open the ClipArt Gallery dialog box.**
- **Click on the Clips Online button.**
- **Click OK.**
- **Word launches your Web browser, which takes you to the Microsoft Web site and a page full of clip art.**

Inserting a Picture from Another File

Word lets you insert pictures from all kinds of other files, including Clip Art-like collections, scanned images, Excel worksheets, and bunches of others. Once inserted into your document, these images can be manipulated just like a piece of clip art. (See Figure 18-2.)

Where the Action Is

The action in this next section takes place in the Object dialog box.

To open the Object dialog box:

- **Go to the Menu Bar.**

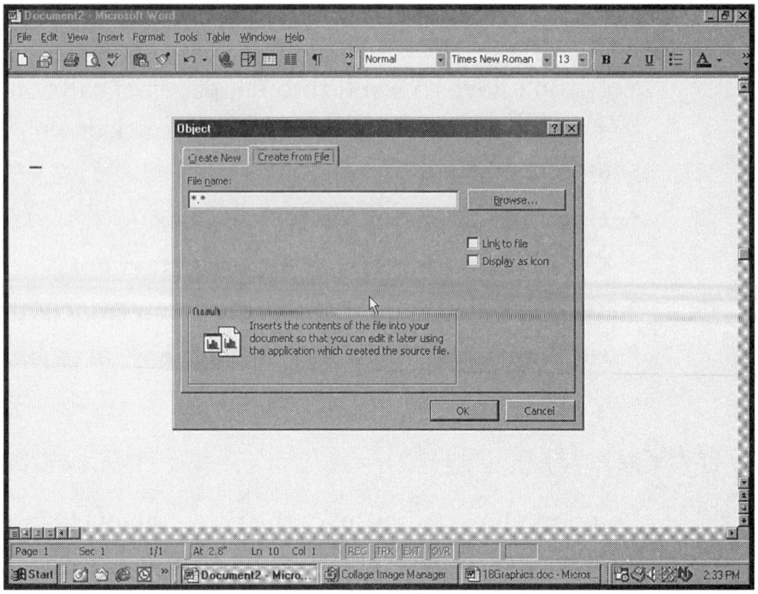

Figure 18-2
The Object
dialog box with
the Create
from File
dialog box
selected

- Open Insert.
- Select Object to open the Object dialog box.

To insert a picture from another file:

- Open the Object dialog box.

Note: *Remember, an "object" is any nontext item you insert in your document.*

- Click on the "Create from File" tab.
- Click on the Browse button to open the Browse dialog box and access the files in your computer.
- Click through the folders on your computer to find the file (the picture) you want to insert.
- Click on the Insert button to return to the Insert Object dialog box.
- Click OK.
- The new picture appears in your document.

Here's a very cool trick: Word lets you put pictures into its AutoCorrect collection, so that you can add them to your documents just by typing a key word. This is a great way to deal with things like company logos. Here's how you add a picture to the file:

> The Browse dialog box lets you preview the object/
> picture/file you want to insert into your document.
> Here's how:
>
> 🗁 Click on the drop-down arrow next to the "Views"
>   icon on the Browse toolbar.
> 🗁 Select Preview.
> 🗁 Click the file you want to see.
> 🗁 A preview window opens in the dialog box with your
>   picture displayed in it.
>
> **TIP**

- Open a document with the picture already inserted (or insert it into the one you have open).

- Select it.

- Open the Tools menu.

- Select AutoCorrect to open the AutoCorrect dialog box.

- In the "Replace" text box, type a name for the picture.

Note: *Pick a name that's easy to remember, simple to type, and most important, made up (copix, mypix, deeble); you don't want the company logo popping up in your document every time you type the word "work."*

- Click the Add button to add it to the list.

- Click OK.

- Now, whenever you type that keyword, the picture will automatically replace the text.

Graphics File Formats

Word lets you insert lots of different types of pictures into your documents. It utilizes *filters* to convert many common graphics file formats so that just about anything will fit. If something doesn't, Word might have the converter on the disk (it'll let you know that you need to install it), or the converter might be available on the Microsoft® Word Web site (not all of them are free).

Here's a list of the graphics file formats you can use in Word. You don't really need to know anything about them, except maybe their file extensions, which are listed here next to format name.

Computer Graphics Metafile (.cgm)

CorelDRAW (.cdr) file

Encapsulated PostScript (.eps) file

Enhanced Metafile (.emf)

FlashPix graphics filter (.fpx)

Graphics Interchange Format (.gif) file

Hanako graphics filter (.jsh, .jah, and .jbh)

JPEG File Interchange Format (.jpg) file

Kodak Photo CD (.pcd) file

Macintosh PICT (.pct) file

PC Paintbrush (.pcx) file

Portable Network Graphics (.png) file

Tagged Image File Format (.tif) file

Windows Bitmap (.bmp, .rle, .dib) file

Windows Metafile (.wmf)

WordPerfect Graphics (.wpg) file

Word's WordArt Objects

WordArt is like text made out of Play Dough®. You can squish it, stretch it, bend it, pull it, and turn it upside down. As WordArt, ordinary text becomes graphical objects that are, well, just plain fun. But they're also very practical *and* great for creating newsletter banners, company logos, and flyer headlines. (See Figures 18-3 and 18-4.)

Where the Action Is

The action in this next section takes place in the WordArt Gallery dialog box.

To open the WordArt Gallery dialog box:

• **Go to the Insert Menu.**

• **Select Picture to open the submenu.**

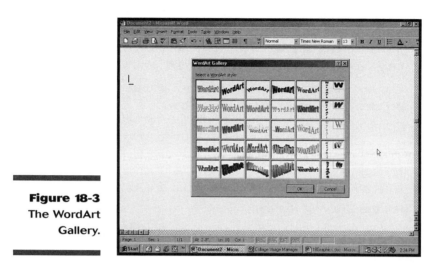

Figure 18-3
The WordArt
Gallery.

- Click on WordArt to open the WordArt Gallery dialog box.

Or . . .

- Click on the WordArt button in the Drawing toolbar.

To insert WordArt into your document:

- Open the WordArt Gallery dialog box.
- Click on the WordArt you want.

Note: *The WordArt samples in the dialog box are tweaked and yanked to illustrate the effect of the style.*

- Click OK to open the Edit WordArt Text dialog box.
- Type the words you want to appear as WordArt into the "Text" window where you see "Your Text Here."

Note: *You can reformat the text here by using the "Font" drop-down list to select another font style. You can click the buttons for bold and italics, and you can change the size by clicking on the down arrow next to the "Size" list box and selecting a point size. (But you can also resize on the desktop.)*

- Click OK.

You can delete objects in your document by selecting them and hitting the Delete key.

TIP

Two things happen:

- **If you weren't already in it, Word bumps you into Print Layout view. (You can only view WordArt in Print Layout and Web views.)**
- **The text you typed appears in your document in the style you selected, accompanied by the WordArt toolbar.**

Expanding the ClipArt Gallery

Word has a hefty selection of ClipArt, but you can always add to it. Here's how.

- **Open the Drawing toolbar.**
- **Click the Insert Clip Art button to open the Insert Clip Art dialog box. (It's the button with the little cartoon portrait.)**
- **Click on the tab for the type of clip you want to add.**
- **Select a category to store the clip in.**
- **Click Import Clips.**
- **Locate the folder that contains the clip you want to add.**
- **Select the clip.**
- **Under Clip import option, select the option you want.**
- **Click Import.**
- **In the Clip Properties dialog box, type a description of the clip and choose the options you want.**

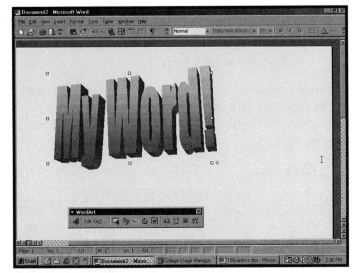

Figure 18-4
A WordArt
object
displayed in a
document.

You can also add a Drawing object of your own creation to the ClipArt Gallery:

- **Select the Drawing object.**
- **Copy it the way you would text.**
- **On the Edit menu, click Copy.**
- **Click Insert Clip Art on the Drawing toolbar.**
- **Select a category in the Clip Art Gallery.**
- **Paste the copied Drawing object on the Clip Art Gallery toolbar.**
- **When prompted, give the object a name.**

Editing Your WordArt Object

Once you've created a WordArt object, you can edit it in one of several ways. (See Figure 18-5.)

1. **Double-click on the WordArt to reopen the Edit WordArt Text dialog box and adjust the formatting as you did when you first created it.**
2. **Use the tools on the WordArt toolbar to format the object.**
3. **Select the WordArt object and then click on the WordArt Gallery button on the toolbar to open the dialog box, then choose a new style to apply.**

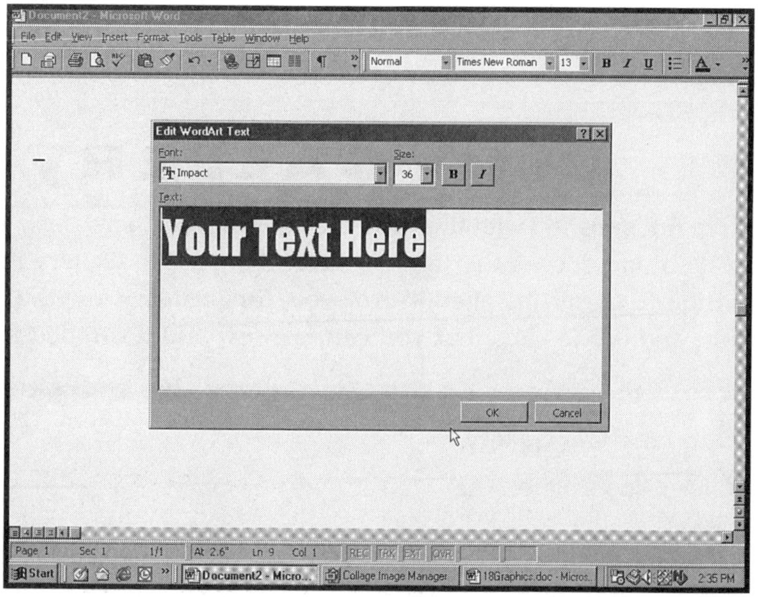

Figure 18-5
The Edit
WordArt text
dialog box.

> Word lets you reverse the formatting changes you impose on your WordArt with the Undo command. Just hit Ctrl + Z to reverse the change.
>
> **TIP**

Where the Action Is

The action in this next section takes place on the Drawing Toolbar.

To open the Drawing toolbar:

- Go to the View Menu.
- Select Toolbars to open the submenu.
- Click on Drawing to open the Drawing toolbar.

Note: *This toolbar appears at the bottom of your Document Window by default, but you can move it around just like the other toolbars.*

Drawing It Yourself

Word is not a full-on graphics program, but it does let you "draw" some basic shapes—rectangles, ovals, and other polygons—called AutoShapes. Word also lets you draw straight lines of various styles and thickness, arcs, and simple freeform shapes and squiggly lines. (See Figure 18-6.)

CLIP GALLERY LIVE

If you're not satisfied with the clips that live on your hard disk, you can reach out to the World Wide Web and access Clip Gallery Live. Word's Clip Gallery must be installed. (If you didn't install it when you installed Word, you can install it now.) Clip Gallery Live lists pictures, sounds, and movie clips that you can preview and download to your computer.

To access the objects on the Clip Gallery Live Web site:

- Open the Clip Gallery.
- Click Clips Online.
- You're computer fires up your browser, dials up, and opens the site on your screen.

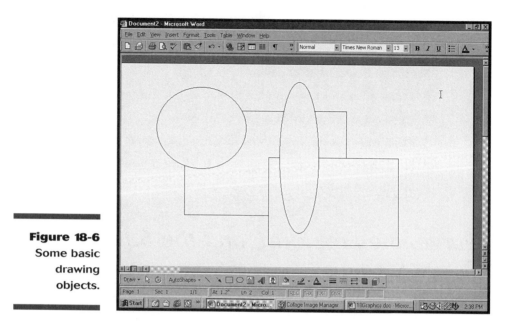

Figure 18-6
Some basic
drawing
objects.

When you click on an AutoShape button in the Drawing toolbar, your cursor becomes a pair of crosshairs; the center of the crosshairs is your insertion point, the place where you start drawing your shape or line. Once you've created a drawing object, Word treats it just like any other object.

The most basic drawable AutoShapes are the rectangle and the oval—think of them as square shapes and round shapes, because you can resize them into squares and circles; they are so commonly used that they have their own buttons on the Drawing toolbar.

To draw rectangles and ovals:

* **Make sure the Drawing toolbar is visible on your Program Window.**
* **Click on the rectangle or the oval button.**
* **Find an empty spot on your document.**
* **Click the crosshairs mouse pointer to create an insertion point.**
* **Hold down the button and drag out a shape from that point.**

Note: *When you make this dragging move, you actually want to go at an angle, so your shape will have both height and width. As you drag, the shape sort of blooms on the page.*

* **Release the button when you've got the size shape you want.**

The Drawing toolbar also has buttons to facilitate line drawing and an arrow button for, well . . . lines with little arrowheads on them.

To draw lines and arrows:

- Make sure the Drawing toolbar is visible on your Program Window.
- Click on the button of a line or arrow.
- Click the crosshairs pointer in your document to create an insertion point.
- Hold down the button and drag to draw a line out from that point.
- When the line is the size you want, release the mouse button.

The Curve, the Freeform, and the Squiggle

The AutoShapes button in the Drawing toolbar opens a menu of other basic shapes you can draw. Click on it, and you can chose from palettes of additional basic polygons, freeform shapes and lines, block arrows, banners, flowcharts, and callouts. A button at the bottom of the menu allows you to open the Clip Art Gallery. (See Figure 18-7.)

Most of the AutoShapes listed in the menu are drawn just as you drew the rectangle, the oval, the lines, and the arrows from the main tool. But in the "Lines" submenu, you'll find three options that work a little differently.

Drawing both the Curve and the Freeform shape involve the use of "anchor" points.

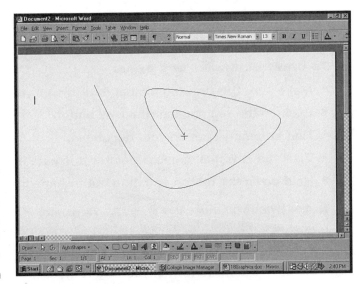

Figure 18-7

A manually drawn spiral basic drawing object.

To draw a curved line:

- Select the Curve option from the AutoShapes "Lines" submenu.
- Click your crosshairs to establish your insertion point, but you don't have to hold down the mouse button.
- Drag out the line.
- Click again to establish your anchor.
- Now, as you continue to drag out the line, the anchor acts like a fence post around which you bend your line; the closer you wrap around the fence post, the tighter the curve.
- Click to establish more anchor points and continue dragging and bending until you have the curved line or shape you want.
- To establish the end point of your line, double-click.

Selecting either the Freeform shape or the Squiggle turns your mouse pointer into a pencil with which you draw completely unstructured lines on your document. Like the Curve, the Freeform shape option lets you establish anchor points, but instead of acting like a fence post, the anchor points act like new insertion points from which you draw out the line; what you create here look more like corners.

Connecting the ends of curved or squiggly lines creates a shape. Once you've drawn any of the AutoShapes, you can change the thickness of their lines by clicking on the Line Style or Dash Line buttons in the Drawing toolbar and selecting an option from the pop-up menu. To modify arrows you've drawn, click on the Arrow Style button.

Moving, Copying, Resizing, and Rotating

Whatever the type of graphic object—ClipArt, drawing objects, AutoShapes, or pictures from other files—you move and resize them the same way.

If what you want is an AutoShape that is exactly as wide as it is tall, here's a trick that'll keep those two dimension in exact proportion as you draw: hold down the Shift key while you drag. This trick doesn't work with the freeform shapes.

TIP

To resize an object:

- Click on the object to select it.
- Eight tiny boxes pop up all around it. These are its "selection handles."
- To make the object wider or narrower, hover your mouse pointer over the center square on the right or left side until you hit the sweet spot and it changes to a double-headed arrow. Now, you just click and drag.
- To make the object taller or shorter, hover your mouse pointer over the center square on the top or bottom until you hit the sweet spot, and it changes to a double-headed arrow. Now, you just click and drag.
- To adjust both the height and the width at the same time, hover your mouse pointer over any corner square until you hit the sweet spot, and it changes to a double-headed arrow. Now, you just click and drag.

You can resize an object in all directions at once by selecting it, holding down the Ctrl key, and then clicking and dragging a corner box.

To move an object:

- Click on the object you want to move.
- Hover your mouse pointer over the selected object until it becomes a four-headed arrow.
- Click and drag the object to its new location.
- The mouse pointer carries a ghost box, and a ghost cursor appears at the left edge of the document to indicate the insertion point.
- When you get it where you want it, release the button.

Or . . .

- Cut and paste the object exactly as you would text.

To copy objects:

- Cut, copy, and paste just as you would text.

Or . . .

- Click on the object to select it.
- Place the mouse pointer on the object.
- Hold down either the Shift or the Ctrl key.
- Click on the object and drag.
- A copy of the object comes with you while the original stays in place.
- Drag the copy to a new location and release the mouse button.

Rotating WordArt

WordArt objects are moved, resized, and copied in the same way as other objects, but WordArt comes with a couple of additional tricks.

To rotate a piece of WordArt:

- Select the WordArt.
- The WordArt toolbar appears.
- Click on the Free Rotate button in the toolbar.
- The boxes are replaced by four green circles, and your mouse pointer becomes a looped arrow.
- Click on any of the green circles to rotate the WordArt around a center axis.
- Hold down the Ctrl key when you click on a circle to rotate around the opposite circle. (That circle becomes the axis.)

To knock your WordArt askew:

- Click on the WordArt to select it.
- A yellow diamond appears with the boxes.
- Click and drag the diamond to change the object's angle.

Wrapping Text Around Objects

You might have noticed that the objects you've been placing in your document up to now have been sitting more or less on a line, just like text. Word lets you move your objects off the text line and "wrap" text around it. Word's text–wrap controls let you define exactly how the text wraps around the object. You can let it go right up to the edge of the picture or leave some extra space around it. (See Figure 18-8.)

To define how text will wrap around an object:

- Select the object you want the text to wrap.
- Open the Picture toolbar.
- Click the Text Wrapping button to open a drop-down menu.
- Select a wrap option from the menu.
- If you're not already in it, Word bumps you into Print Layout view and wraps the text per your selection.

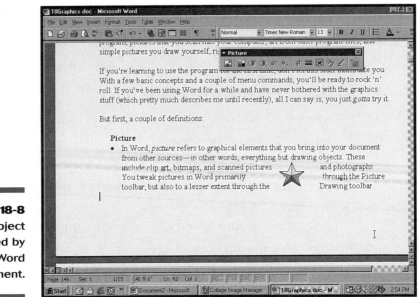

Figure 18-8
An object
wrapped by
text in a Word
document.

Callouts and Text Boxes

Sometimes your picture needs a caption—a cartoon balloon with just the right pithy saying. Or maybe your diagram needs an explanatory box, or your report needs some extra information set off in a box. Word lets you add these kinds of text-carrying elements to your documents in the form of callouts and text boxes. (See Figure 18-9.)

Callouts can look like a dialog balloon from the Sunday comics or a box with a dangling line. You use them to direct the text in them to specific parts of another object or text.

If you want text to wrap around an object in your document, but you don't like the way any of the text wrap options look, clicking on the Edit Wrap Points button in the Text Wrapping submenu lets you do it your way.

TIP

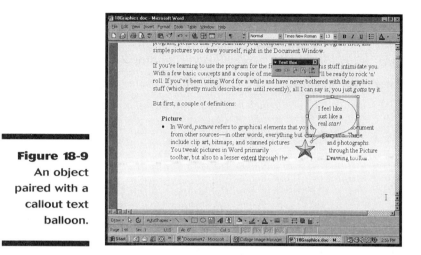

Figure 18-9
An object paired with a callout text balloon.

To add a callout to an object in your document:

- Make sure the object in question is showing.
- Click on the AutoShapes button in the Drawing toolbar to open the AutoShapes menu.
- Click Callouts.
- Select a callout style from the palette.
- Your mouse pointer becomes a crosshair icon.
- Click next to the object to insert the callout.
- To adjust the callout's position, click on the yellow diamond; this is the callout's anchor point.
- Click and drag to shape and size the callout.
- When you have inserted the callout, a Text Box toolbar appeared in the Document Window.
- Click inside the callout text box and type.

Text boxes are objects that hold text. They behave just like any other object—you can resize them, reshape them, and move them around your document just like a piece of ClipArt or a Drawing object—but you can also put text in them.

To create a text box:

- Click on the TextBox tool in the Drawing toolbar.
- Your mouse pointer becomes crosshairs.
- Click, draw, and size the text box just as you would an AutoShape.

- Click inside the text box to insert text; edit and format it just as you would text in the main document.
- Click outside the text box when you've finished typing.
- To edit the text inside the box or to resize or move the box itself, select it again.

Formatting Objects

Almost all of the art you've been adding to your document can be formatted: Drawing objects can have shadows; ClipArt can fade into the background; squiggly lines can be made into thicker squiggly lines.

To format an object:
- Select the object you want to format.
- Right-click the object to display a shortcut menu.
- Select the Format option to open a Format dialog box.
- Use the commands in the dialog box to format the object. Or . . .
- Open the Drawing toolbar.
- Select the object you want to format.
- Use the options in the toolbar to format the object.

Layering and Grouping Objects

Inserting objects individually into your documents can enhance them considerably, but it's when you get your objects to work together that things really get interesting. Word lets you "stack" objects on top of each another, float objects over the top of your text or tuck it in behind, and group objects together so you can treat them as a single object. Getting your objects together makes them easier to move, resize, and format. Here's how you do it:

To layer objects, just drag and drop them on top of each other.

To shuffle the order of your layered objects:
- Right-click on the object you want to move to bring up the shortcut menu.
- Select Order to open the submenu.
- Click on the action you want:

Bring to Front: brings the object to the front of the stack.

Send to Back: sends the object to the back of the stack.

Bring Forward: brings the object forward one layer at a time

Send Backward: sends the object backward one layer at a time.

Bring in Front of Text: sets the object on top of the document text.

Send behind Text: slips the object behind the document text.

To group objects together:

- Select each object by clicking while you hold down the Shift key.

Note: *You'll know they've each been selected by the presence of the selection handles.*

- Right-click any of the selected objects to open the shortcut menu.
- Select Grouping to open the submenu.
- Click on Group.
- The objects are now recognized as one.

Note: *To ungroup these objects, just follow the above steps until you get to the submenu, and then select Ungroup.*

Creating a Watermark

A *watermark* is a logo or design pressed into fine quality paper by the manufacturer during the manufacturing process. It's a faint mark, usually visible only when you hold the paper up to the light. It's the mark of pretty good paper. It's also one of the coolest effects you can produce with Word's graphics tools.

I use a watermark to dress up my personal correspondence and to make my business stationery look like it came from a print shop. You can "watermark" any object in a Word document. Here's how you do it with a piece of ClipArt.

- Make sure you're in Print Layout view. (It's just easier when you can see the effect.) Right-click on the ClipArt to open the formatting shortcut menu.
- Select Format Picture to open the Format Picture dialog box.
- Click on the Picture tab.
- Click on the down arrow next to the "Colors" list box to open the drop-down list.
- Select Watermark.

- **Your object now appears faded.**
- **Click on the Layout tab.**
- **Select Behind Text.**
- **Click OK.**
- **Your ClipArt has become a watermark.**

Note: *If your new watermark interferes with the legibility of the text, go back to the Format Picture dialog box, click on the Picture tab, and adjust the contrast and brightness values (increase brightness and reduce the contrast).*

To remove the watermark, select it and hit the Delete key.

Shadow and 3-D Effects

Finally, if you want to make your images look more dramatic, try out Word's shadow and 3-D effects. Word lets you apply shadow effects to any box (including text boxes), shape, line, piece of ClipArt picture, and WordArt designs in your document. Using the Shadow buttons on the Drawing toolbar and the Shadow Settings toolbar, you can add and arrange shadows. And the 3-D button will give you access to affects that will have your Drawing objects popping off the page. (See Figure 18-10.)

Figure 18-10
Shadowed 3-D objects in a Word document.

To add a shadow effect to any object:

- Select the image to which you want to add a shadow effect.
- On the Drawing toolbar, click the Shadow button to open a palette of shadow effects.
- Select an effect.
- The shadow effect you selected is immediately applied to the object.
- Now, click on the Shadow button again to bring up the shadow effects palette.
- Click on "Shadow Settings" to bring up the Shadow Settings toolbar.
- You can use this little toolbar to "nudge" your shadow slightly in any direction, make it darker or lighter, and turn it off and on. It also lets you change the shadow's color. (Click on the down arrow next to the Shadow Color button to open a palette of color options.)

To add a 3-D effect to Drawing objects:

- Select the object.
- On the Drawing toolbar, click on the 3-D button to open a palette of 3-D effects.
- Select an effect.
- The 3-D effect you selected is immediately applied to the object.
- Now, click on the 3-D button again to open the effects palette.
- Click 3-D Settings to open the 3-D Settings toolbar.
- This little toolbar lets you "tilt" your now 3-D object up, down, right, and left; make it deeper, change its direction, change its "lighting source" to manipulate which sides of the shape are shadowed, and apply several surface effects and color.

If you're having trouble tracking down the pictures, music, sound, video clips, and animations you want, make sure to look in the Windows Media folder. Windows keeps extra sounds and music in that folder, which you can insert into a document. Just point to Object on the Insert menu, and then click Create from File. Locate and open the Media folder (in the Windows folder) and then select the sound you want.

TIP

19

Satisfying the Urge to Merge
Working with Word's Mail Merge Features

One of the most complicated things you'll ever do in Word is the mail merge. I know, *not* a promising beginning to a chapter, but better you hear from me than on the street. It's not like laser eye surgery or programming your VCR, but it's darned close. The concept is simple enough: Create a single document, leave some blanks, copy information from an address book into the document to fill in the blanks, and customize each letter—write one letter; send it out to lots of people. But somehow, between concept and execution, things got tricky.

Still, for those who take the time to master the mail merge, the rewards are great—especially if you do a lot of mass mailings. But even if you only plan to use it for the family Christmas letter, mail merge can, once you *get* it, make your life a lot easier. (But just in case, keep this book nearby during the holidays.)

The best way I can think of to explain the process of a mail merge is to walk you through a simple one, step by step. (I'll be sitting; you'll be walking.) Once you get through one of these things, I think it'll all make sense.

But first, some definitions:

Mail Merge. In a nutshell, a mail merge is the process of combining a form letter with an address book to create a stack of duplicate documents, each one of which has been uniquely customized. Word copies addresses (records) from the address book (the data source) and pastes them into specific spots (fields) in the form letter (main document).

Main Document. The form letter—this is the file *to which* the addresses are going to be sent.

Data Source. The address book—this is the file *from which* the addresses are going to be taken.

Fields. The blanks in the form letter—these are the specific locations *that will receive* the individual addresses (or the parts of them).

Records. The addresses—these are the individual addresses that will be taken apart and *sent to* the form letter to fill in the blanks.

Executing a mail merge involves four big steps—create the main document, specify the data source, prepare the main document, and merge the two files—as well as many small ones along the way. You can start the process from an existing document or just plunge in and make one as you go. For the purposes of this exercise, let's just start from scratch.

Where the Action Is

Most of the action in this chapter takes place in the Mail Merge Helper dialog box. Here's how to open it:

- **Go to the Menu Bar.**
- **Open Tools.**
- **Select Mail Merge to open the Mail Merge Helper dialog box.**

Or . . .

- **Hit Alt + T + R**

Step 1: Create the Main Document

The first step is to create the Main Document, the form letter, into which you'll be copying addresses from the data source. (See Figures 19-1 and 19-2.)

To create the main document:

- **Open the Mail Merge Helper dialog box.**
- **Click on the Create button to open a drop-down list.**
- **Select Form Letter.**
- **Word pops up a query window. If you already had a form letter open and ready to go, you would click on the Active Window button. But since we're creating a new form letter, click on New Main Document.**

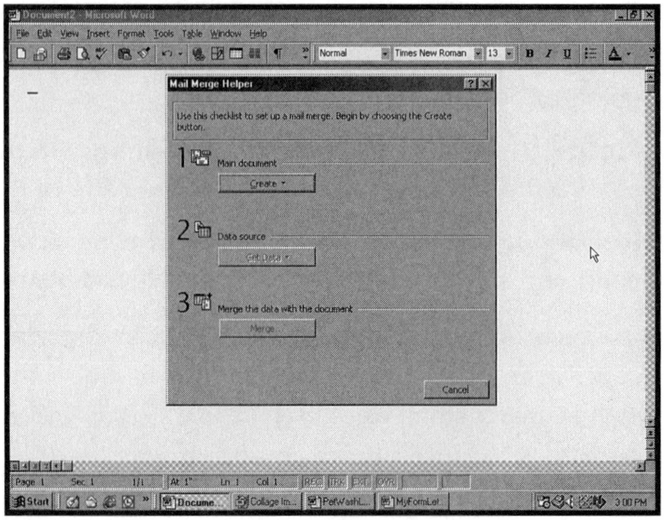

Figure 19-1
The Mail
Merge Helper
dialog box,
step one.

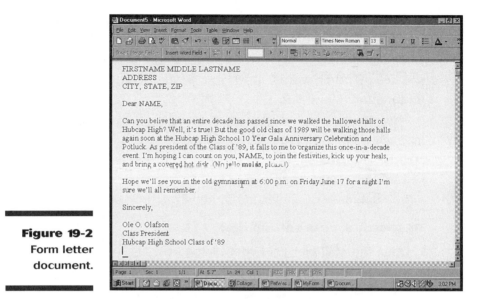

Figure 19-2
Form letter
document.

- Doing this opens a new, blank document behind the Mail Merge Helper dialog box.

- In the dialog box, a new button has appeared: Edit.

- Click Edit to open a drop-down list.

- Select Form Letters (it's the only option). Notice that it bears the name of your working document.

- When you click on this button, the Mail Merge Helper dialog box goes away, and you're ready to go to work in the new document.

Note: *Compose your letter exactly as you would any new document in Word—type in the text, apply your formatting preferences, etc.—but leave out the information you'll be inserting from the data source, things like names and addresses.*

When I'm creating a main document, I just type in everything that would be included in one of the finished letters. When you get to the step in which you set up the letter to receive data from the source file, you'll just select the name, address, and other variables and replace them with field codes. Some people type in generic placeholders, like NAME, to help them keep things straight.

TIP

Step 2: Specify the Data Source

Once the form letter is written and ready to go, the next step is to specify the data source. In other words, now you have to tell Word where to get the merge information.

The source file for your mail merge can be a PIM (personal information manager), such as Outlook or Schedule+, or an address book database you've created in a program like Access, or you can create a special source file in Word just for this merge. In this exercise, we're going to be creating a special source file, a little database of names and addresses, in Word. (See Figure 19-3 and 19-4.)

To specify a data source file:

- **Open the Mail Merge Helper dialog box.**
- **Click the Get Data Button to open a drop-down list.**
- **Select Create Data Source to open the Create Data Source dialog box. (See Figures 19-4.)**

Note: *Clicking on Use Address Book would have opened a list of address book options, from which you could have chosen something like Outlook.*

Note: *If you were using an Access database, you would choose Open Data Source.*

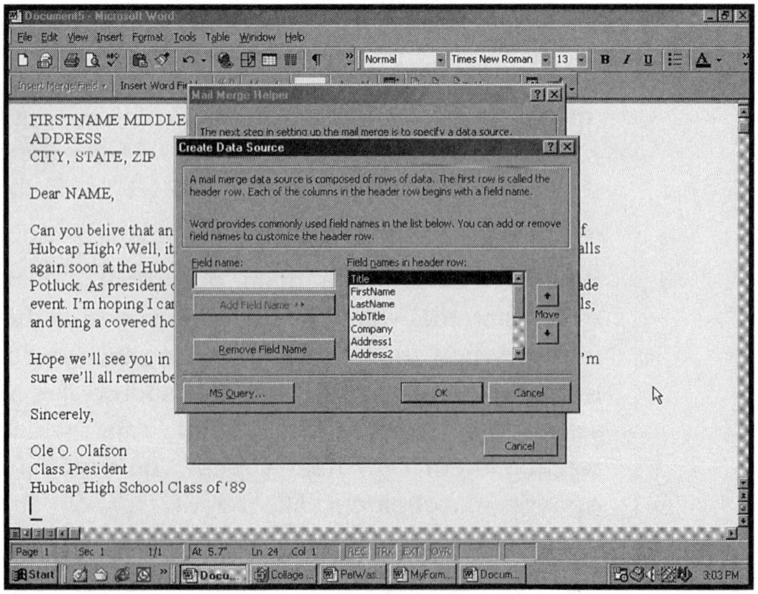

Figure 19-3
The Mail Merge Helper dialog box with the Create Data Source dialog box open.

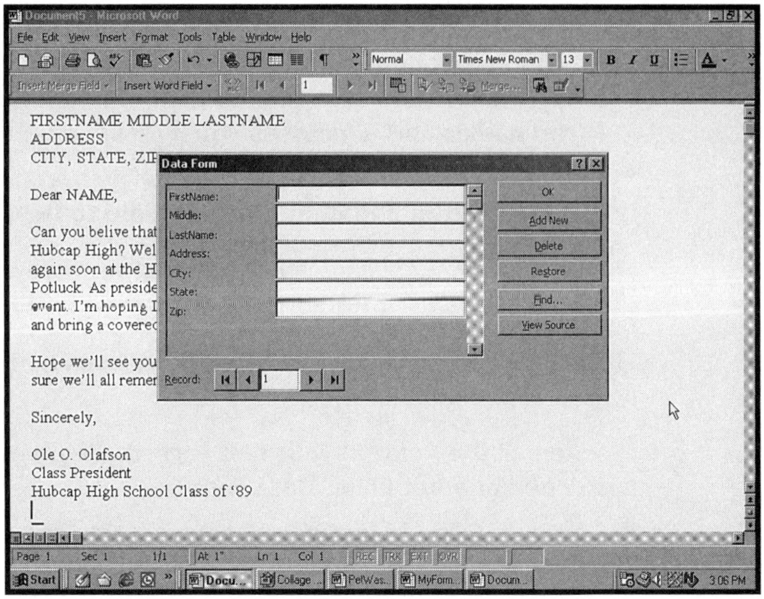

Figure 19-4
A blank data
form.

To create the data source file in Word:

- In the Create Data Source dialog box, Word displays a list of common field names—name, city, state, etc.

- You can use these fields, or you can change them, but you want to end up with only the fields you will be using in the list.

- To add a field, type it in the "Field name" text box and click the Add Field Name button.

- To remove a field, select it and then click the Remove Field Name button.

- To rearrange the fields (you probably want to keep **firstname** with **lastname**, and **state** with **zip**), select the field you want to move and click on the big up and down arrows.

- When you've got things the way you want them, click OK.

- The Save As dialog box opens.

- Name your data source file and save it. (In this example, I've created a new folder called MyData and then saved my new data source file there.)

- When you click on the Save button, Word prompts you that there are no records in your file—duh!

- Click the Edit Data Source button to open a Data Form and begin adding records.

- A Data Form opens on your screen. Notice that your field names are listed along the left side next to a column of blank text boxes. This is where you type in the names and addresses you'll be sending to the main document.

- Enter the name and address for your first record into the text boxes. (You can just start typing and then tab from field to field.)

Note: *This is where things really slow down, while you enter all your new records; things go much faster when you're using an existing address book.*

Note: *You can add a space to the end of each name in the record or include the spaces on the form letter.*

- When all the fields in your first record are typed in, click the Add New button to open another blank Data Form.

- Continue filling in forms until you've completed your mailing list. For this example, let's stop at four.

Note: *You can edit and re-edit your data forms a much as you like during this step. Use the arrow buttons at the bottom of the form to move back and forth between them. The forward arrow with the line takes you to the last record; the backward arrow with the line takes you to the first record. To dump the changes you've made to an existing record, hit the Restore button.*

- When all your records have been entered, click OK.

As Word explains it, a mail merge data source is composed of rows of data. The first row is the header row. Each column in the header row begins with a field name.

Here are some things to keep in mind while you're typing in the field names for that header row:

Field names must start with a letter, but they can include numbers.

No spaces in a field name, but you can put a space on the end.

The names may be no longer than 20 characters.

No two fields may have the same name.

Try to name your fields something relevant to what they represent: last name, date, that kind of thing.

Separate the parts of addresses: city, state, and zip code.

Adding more records to your data source file after you've closed it is relatively easy:

📁 Open the Mail Merge Helper dialog box.

📁 Under Data Sources, click on the Edit button to open the drop-down list.

📁 Select your data source from the list to reopen the Data Forms in your file.

Or . . .

📁 Click on the Edit Data Source button on the Mail Merge toolbar.

TIP

Step 3: Prepare the Main Document

Now that you've created your main document and your data source, the only thing left to set up is where in the document the data from the file is going to land. To do this, you just insert a few field codes. (See Figures 19-5 and 19-6.)

To insert field codes into the main document:

• Open the Mail Merge Helper dialog box.

• Under Main Document, click the Edit button to open a drop-down list.

• Your saved form letter is listed there by name.

• Select your form letter.

• The Mail Merge toolbar appears onscreen along with your form letter.

To insert a data field in your form letter:

• Position your cursor where you want a field inserted into your document.

• Click the Insert Merge Field button on the Mail Merge toolbar to open a drop-down list of your field names.

• Select a field name, and a field code appears at the insertion point in your document. The field code is double-bracketed.

Note: *This is where those placeholders come in handy. Just select the placeholder and then click on the field name to replace it.*

Enter the rest of the field codes you want in your main document. (See Figure 19-7.)

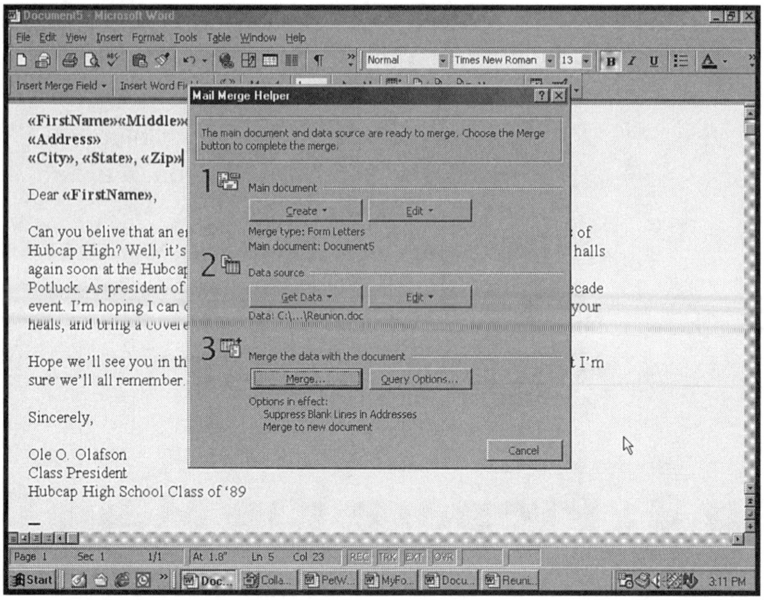

Figure 19-5
The Mail
Merge Helper
dialog box,
step three.

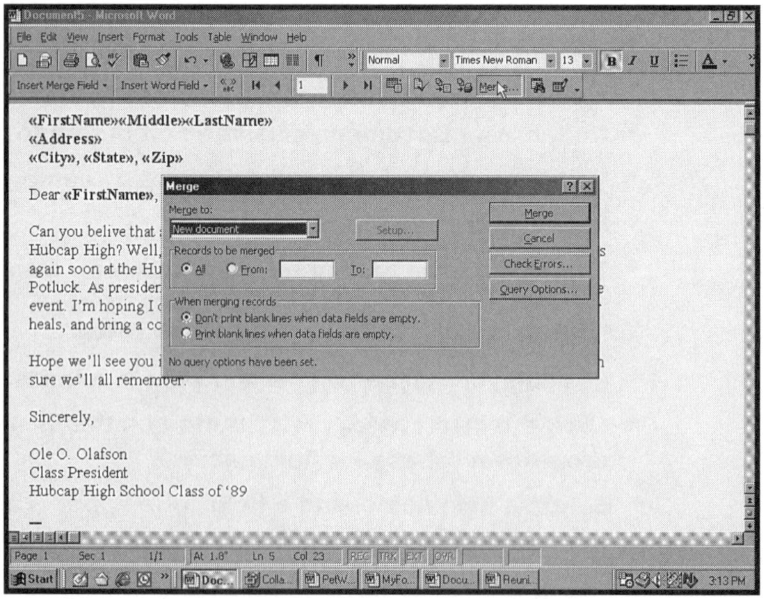

Figure 19-6
The Mail
Merge toolbar.

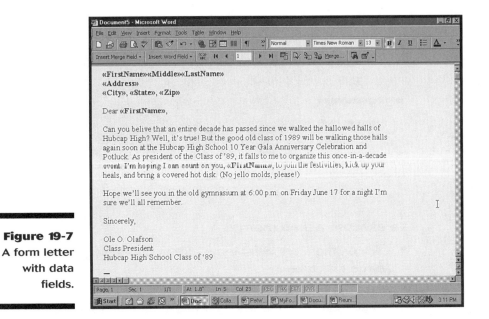

Note: *Check to see that you have proper spacing and punctuation relative to the code.*

Note: *To remove a field code from your document, select the code along with its brackets and delete as you would any other characters in a Word document.*

Note: *When you click on the View Merged Data button on the Mail Merge toolbar, Word gives you a preview of all your form letters with the merged data inserted. Forward and back arrows appear next to the button when you click it. You can use these buttons to flip through and check all the letters in this merge session. As you check over the letters, Word lets you add individual touches—say, to add a little note to Aunt Bertha's letter, thanking her for the nice, chewy fruitcake. Click the button again to turn off the preview.*

Step 4: Merge the Files

Finally! You've composed your form letter, created a data source, and seasoned your letter liberally with field codes. You've been patient. You've been careful. Now it's time to execute the merge. (Has a nice ring to it, doesn't it?) (See Figure 19-8.)

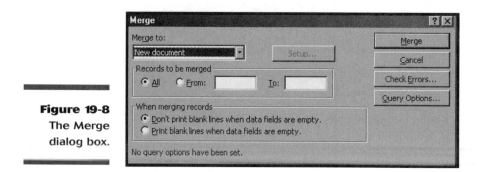

Figure 19-8
The Merge
dialog box.

To execute a mail merge:

- Click on the Start Mail-Merge button on the Mail-merge toolbar to open the Merge dialog box.

- Click on the down arrow next to the "Merge to" list box to open a list of destinations for your merge—in other words, **where** the two files are going to meet to form the new documents. You can send them to a document file, from where you can edit, save, and print them; to an e-mail program, from where you can send them out electronically; or directly to your printer. For this example, select New Document.

- Notice the "Records to be merged" options. This option lets you designate how much of your data source you want included in this merge session. You can specify a range or choose to merge all the records. For this example, click the "All" radio button.

- Notice the "When merging records" options. For most situations, it's best to click on the "Don't print blank lines when data fields are empty" radio button.

- Now, cross your fingers, spit over your left shoulder three times, rub your brass Buddha's belly, make sure you're facing Mecca, drape a rosary blessed by the Pope over your CPU . . . and click "Merge."

- If there is a God, Word creates four versions of your form letter, each with its fields filled with the information from one data source record. (If this didn't happen, you must be prepared to sacrifice a rooster, maybe a goat . . . probably nothing bigger than a goat.)

- You now have a batch of letters you can print, save, or both, as you would any other new document.

Clearly the key to a successful mail merge is patience and a careful setup. Once you get the steps down, this thing is really no big deal, and you'll want to use Word's mail merge tools in other ways. For example:

Addressing Envelopes and Creating Mailing Labels

The procedures for creating mail merge envelope addresses and mailing labels are basically same. And you can use any of the data sources available for form letters. (See Figure 19-9.)

To complete an envelope or label mail merge:

- Open the Mail Merge Helper dialog box.
- Click on the Create button to open a drop-down list.
- Select either Envelopes or Labels from the list. (For this example, click on Envelopes.)
- Word pops up a prompt box, asking which document you want to use. For this example, click on New Main Document. Doing this opens a new, blank document behind the Mail Merge Helper dialog box.

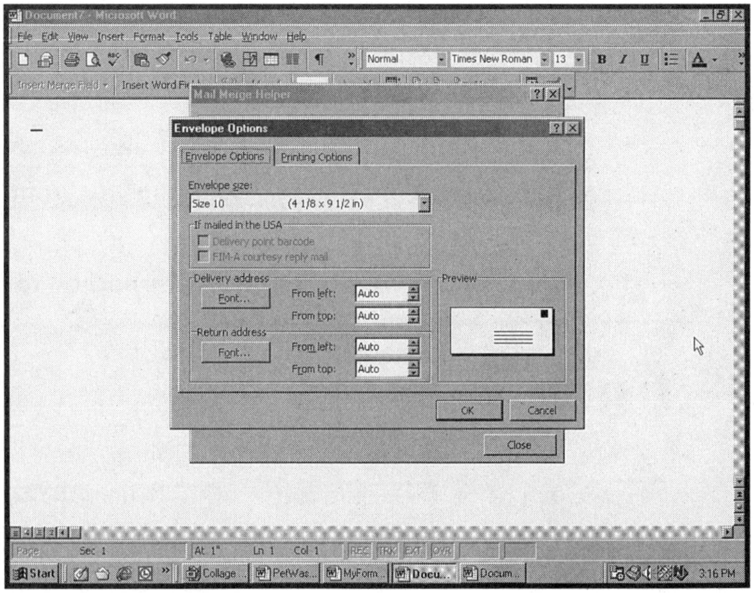

Figure 19-9
The Envelope Options dialog box.

- Click the Get Data button and choose a data source from the drop-down list. For this example, select Open Data Source to open the Open Data Source dialog box.
- Select the data source file we created in the first exercise and open it.
- Another prompt box pops up to tell you to set up your main document.
- Click Set Up Main Document to open the Envelope Options dialog box.
- You could click on the "Envelope size" drop–down arrow to open a list of standard envelope sizes, but for now, let's go with the default Number 10 envelope.
- Click OK to open the Envelope Address dialog box.
- Click the "Insert Merge Field" button to open a drop–down list.
- Select the field codes you want to include on each envelope in the merge.
- Click the fields to add them to the "Sample envelope address" display window.
- Click inside the display window to position the fields and to add spaces and punctuation.

Note: *If you didn't include a space at the end of the name fields in your records, make sure to put a space between parts of the names here.*

- Click OK.
- Open the Mail Merge Helper dialog box.
- Click the Merge button.
- Click the "Merge to" drop-down arrow to select the merge destination. (For this exercise, select New Document.)
- Click the "All" radio button to include all the records in the data source.
- Click the Merge button. (See, it's already so easy it's boring.)
- Word creates a file with all the addresses from your data source.
- Save the file.
- Load up your printer with envelopes and go to town.

Catalogs

There's one more very cool application of Word's mail merge feature: You can use mail merge to collect records from your data source into a single directory-like configuration that Word calls a "catalog." You can use this strategy to create master lists of all kinds, membership directories, parts lists, and even real catalogs.

To create a catalog using mail merge:

- Open the Mail Merge Helper dialog box.

- Click on the Create button to open a drop—down list.

- Select Catalog.

- In the prompt box, click on New Main Document.

- In the Mail Merge Helper dialog box, click on Edit.

- Compose your catalog page just as you did your form letter. In this exercise, type "Membership Information" at the top of the page and then type a column that includes "Name:," "Address:," and "Company:"

- Click on the button in the toolbar to open the Mail Merge Helper dialog box.

- Click on Open Data Source.

- Follow the steps to open the data source file we created in the first exercise.

- In the new prompt box, click Edit Main Document.

- Click the "Insert Merge Field" button in the toolbar to open a drop-down list.

- Select and insert the field codes in the list under the document heading and beside the appropriate text in the document.

- Open the Mail Merge Helper dialog box.

- Click on the Merge button.

- Select the merge destination. (For this exercise, select New Document.)

- Click the "All" radio button.

- Click the Merge button.

- Word creates a file with all the addresses from your data source formatted as a membership list.

- Save the file.

You are now a Merge Master! (I bow to your awesome power!)

20

Working Well with Others

Working with Word's Collaboration Tools

you can use Word to write your memoirs, keep a journal, compose pithy observations on life and love and the perfect chilidog, and never *ever* share those documents with anyone. (And frankly, that's probably best.) But just about everything else you write with this program is going to be looked at, commented on, and/or corrected by other people. And if you ever manage to find a publisher for those memoirs, you can expect an editor or two to provide you with a few notes, suggest changes, and maybe even insert a correction or two.

I don't mean to present this situation as a bad thing (necessarily). You're probably going to *want* a little feedback on that annual report copy before it goes to the printer to be turned into thousands of expensive, four-color booklets. Legal documents are poured over by dozens of people . . . I mean lawyers . . . who tweak and tweak and *tweak* until they fairly scream. And what writer doesn't secretly rely on his publisher's intrepid, underpaid, and overworked copy editors to keep him from looking like a moron in print. (Um, did I ever say thanks?)

Catalogs, sales letters, business reports, proposals, resumes, news stories, book manuscripts—all routinely pass through many hands on their way to a final draft.

With all that juggling and rewriting, how does one keep track of who did what to which version? With the help of some very cool tools, Word makes tracking the lifecycle of your documents fairly simple.

Tracking Document Changes

Word lets you keep track of all changes made to a document, as well as who made them, from start to finish. (Microsoft bills this as a collaboration feature, but I think of it as more of a CYA tool.) (See Figure 20-1.)

After the document is returned to you, you can review each person's comments and revision marks and choose to incorporate them into the final document or not.

To track changes in a document:

- **Open the document in which you want to keep track of changes.**
- **Go to the Menu Bar.**
- **Open Tools menu.**
- **Select Track Changes to open the submenu.**
- **Select Highlight Changes to open the Highlight Changes dialog box.**
- **Click the "Track changes while editing" check box to turn on the tracking feature.**

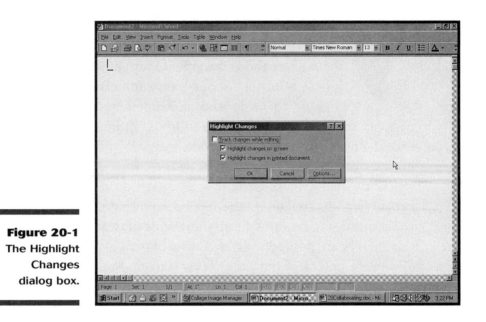

Figure 20-1
The Highlight
Changes
dialog box.

- Click OK.

- Click on the Options button to open the Track Changes dialog box. This box gives you a preview of how all the revision marks will look in your document— new text, deleted text, reformatted text, and borders.

Note: *The default setting in this box are probably good enough, but you can change them if you want to by clicking the "Mark" drop-down arrow in each category and choosing a different option.*

- Click OK.

- Click OK again to exit the Highlight Changes dialog box.

- Now any changes made to the document by you or another user will appear marked in a different color.

Even with the Track Changes feature turned off, you can still compare changes made to the document against the original file. When you get the revised document back, open the Tools menu, select Track Changes, and then select Compare Documents. Word's Compare Documents command lets you open and view each file and track down differences between them.

TIP

- With the Color options set to "By author" and "Auto" in the Track Changes dialog box, Word can keep track of each new editor by applying a new color to his or her changes. (See Figure 20-2.)

Reviewing and Accepting Changes

Your document has finally made the rounds, and you've got it back, and it's open in your Document Window, with all the changes showing red and green. (It's very Christmassy.) Now you have to make some decisions: which changes do I keep; which do I reject. (See Figure 20-3.)

To review and accept changes:

- Go to the Menu Bar.
- Open Tools.
- Select Track Changes to open the submenu.
- Make sure the "Highlight changes onscreen" box is checked; if it is not, click it on now.
- Click on Accept or Reject Changes to open the Accept or Reject Changes dialog box.
- Click the "Find" button to go to the first change in the document. The change is highlighted.

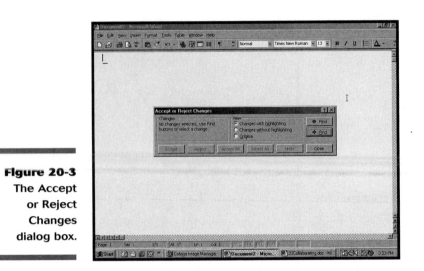

Figure 20-3
The Accept
or Reject
Changes
dialog box.

- To accept the change, click the Accept button; to reject the change and keep the original text intact, click the Reject button.
- After you click one of these buttons, Word takes you to the next change and on through the rest of the document, one change at a time.
- When you've accepted or rejected all the edits in the document, Word lets you know and prompts whether you want to "continue searching . . ." and/or that it found no additional "tracked changes." Click OK to the prompt(s).
- Click Close to exit the Accept or Reject Changes dialog box.
- The red and greed are gone, and your document is finished.

If you just want to accept or reject all of the changes in the document at once, you can do that too. In the Accept or Reject Changes dialog box, just click the Accept All or the Reject All button. Word prompts you to ask whether you've lost your mind. Click Yes, and the deed is done.

You can also accept or reject changes within blocks of selected text, or even within a single sentence. Just select the text before you open the Accept or Reject Changes dialog box, and the commands you activate will apply to that text.

TIP

User Comments

While your document is making the rounds, you might want to give people a chance to offer feedback. Word's User Comments are the electronic equivalent of Post-it® notes for your documents. (See Figure 20-4.)

To insert a user comment:

- Position your cursor at an insertion point in your document near the text you want to comment on and click.
- Go to the Menu Bar.
- Open Insert.
- Select Comment.
- A separate Comment Pane opens at the bottom of your screen.
- Type your comments into the Comment Pane.
- Click the Close button.
- The word to the left of your insertion point is now highlighted in yellow.
- Hover your mouse pointer over the highlighted word and a comment box appears with the text you just typed into the Comment Pane as well as the name of the person who wrote it.

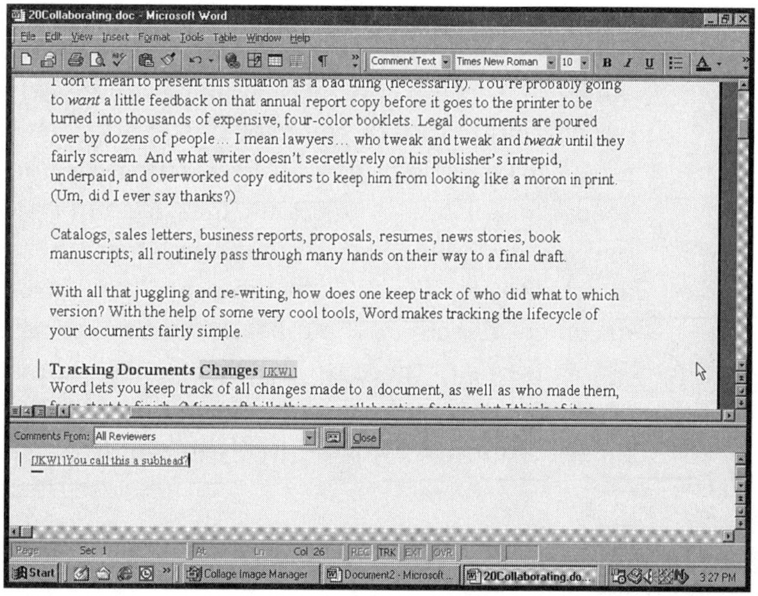

Figure 20-4
A split document screen showing user comments.

To edit a comment:

- Right-click on the highlighted word to open a shortcut menu.
- Select Edit Comment to reopen the comment pane.
- Make your changes.

To delete a comment:

- Right-click on the highlighted area.
- Select Delete Comment from the shortcut menu.
- To print comments in a document:
- Go to the Menu Bar.
- Open File.
- Select Print to open the Print dialog box.
- Click the "Print What" drop-down arrow.
- Select Comments.
- Click OK.

E-mailing with Word

Nowadays, you don't even have to see the people you collaborate with. Thanks to the Internet and e-mail, you can have "virtual" relationships with coworkers and colleagues literally a world away.

Among what you might call Word's Internet-facing new features is the program's ability to e-mail a copy of a document directly from the Program Window. For all intents and purposes, the copy of the document *is* the e-mail. You can create an e-mail from scratch or send an existing document as an e-mail message. Word sends these kinds of electronic messages in HTML file format, so just about any-one who is "online" can read it. And when you send an e-mail like this, there's no attachment for the folks at the other end to futz around with. You can edit the document directly, without having to open or save an extra file.

This is one of those techie features that can make your life faster, if not exactly easier. Depending on how much virtual collaboration you do, this might be one of those features you wonder how you ever lived without.

To e-mail a Word document:

- Open or create the document you want to send as an e-mail.
- Go to the Standard toolbar.
- Click on the E-mail button. (It's the one that looks like an envelope.)
- Word displays an e-mail header, docked at the top of your Document Window.

Note: *This header should be familiar to anyone who has done much e-mailing. It includes the standard text boxes: To, Cc, and Subject. (You can add a Bcc line by clicking on the Bcc button.)*

Note: *If working from an existing document, Word enters the first line of text in the Subject line.*

- Type in your recipient's e-mail address in the "To" text box or use the Address Book key to access your Outlook address book.
- Add a subject line, if Word hasn't done it for you.
- Click on the Options button to open the Messages Options dialog box. From here you can select some standard e-mail options.
- Now just click on "Send a Copy."

Note: *To remove the e-mail header, click on the e-mail button again.*

Word fires up your modem, dials into your ISP, and e-mails a copy of the document; the original document remains open so that you can keep right on working. When you save the document, the e-mail information (recipient list, e-mail options, and any file attachments) is saved with it. The next time you e-mail a copy of the document, the e-mail information appears in the e-mail header, which makes it simple to send updates of the document to the same people.

The idea here is to avoid attachments, but if you need to include one, Word gives you that option as well.

Routing Slips

All this collaborating can get pretty confusing. Word's Track Changes options can help you keep track of who *worked* on the document. But if you want to keep track of everyone who gets the document via e-mail, you'd better route it.

Word's routing slip feature lets you send out a document as an e-mail message to your collaborators, but to spell out the order in which they get it—you *route* it through the recipients and track its progress. It's a good way to make sure that each person along the route sees the changes and comments of the person who had it last. Or you can send it out to everyone at once. You can track a routed document's status, and when everyone has reviewed it, it automatically comes back to you.

Routed documents are sent in Word format (.doc) as attachments to an e-mail messages.

To create a routing slip and start routing a document:

- Open or create the document you want to route.
- Go to the Menu Bar.
- Click on File.
- Select Send To.
- Click on Routing Recipient to open the Routing Slip dialog box.
- Click on the Address button to select the recipients through whom you want to route the document.
- Type the first recipient's name in the "Type name or select from list" text box or select it from the list.
- Click the To button to add the name to the display window or double-click it.
- Repeat until you've entered all the people who will be receiving the document.
- Click OK to return to the Routing Slip dialog box.
- Select among the other routing options.

Note: *If you select the "One at a time" option under "Route to recipients," the order of the names in the list in this dialog box determines the order in which your recipients will receive the document. You can change the order by selecting the names you want to move and clicking on the up and down arrows.*

- If you plan to route the document right away, click on the Route button. Or . . .
- If you intend to route the document later, click on the Add Slip button. When you're ready to route that document, open it, open File/Send To, and then click on the Next Routing Recipient.

21

Dubya–dubya–dubya–dot Word

Word 2000 and the Web

odern word-processing programs have put sophisticated print shops right on our desktops, allowing average Joes like thee and me to create professional—even beautiful—documents with a few keystrokes and a couple of clicks of the mouse. With the inclusion in Word 2000 of a new set of Web publishing tools, Microsoft has begun taking the concept of word processing to a new level.

This is very big stuff, and I'm appalled at those jaded technophiles who pooh-pooh it. It's true that Word's Web tools aren't made for much heavy lifting—this is no FrontPage or Adobe PageMill—but, jeez, that's not really the point. With the addition of this set of Web publishing tools, Word 2000 has begun to create a seamless connection between our desktops and the Internet. Notice I said "begun;" the connection is there, but it's hardly seamless. But it is developments like this (lightweight as this one may be) that are changing the definition of "document."

(Okay, I feel better now.)

This version of Word was designed to interact with the World Wide Web, and it includes features that allow you to access the Web from within the program itself. In this chapter, you'll learn how to build Web pages using templates and themes, and how to build them from scratch. You'll see how easy it is to insert hyperlinks, and . . .

Before we start, let's go over some definitions:

The Internet. The Internet is a worldwide network of computer networks. It links thousands of smaller computer networks, which in turn link millions of individuals with computers, PDAs, pagers, and even cell phones. It's the Information Superhighway, it's where the World Wide Web lives and breathes, it's where you go when you "log on." It's cyberspace.

The World Wide Web. The Web is an aspect of the Internet, a system characterized by colorful and often animated "pages" that live on "servers" (high–powered computers), which are connected to other pages through *hyperlinks*. You navigate the Web with a Web *browser*, with which you "surf" from page to page. Web *sites* are collections of Web pages. In recent years, the Web has become a multi-media maelstrom of text, pictures, sounds, and digital movies.

Browser. A browser is a piece of software with which you surf the Web. Browsers can speak HTML, the "language" with which most Web pages are built. Some browsers also let you read, send, and receive e-mail, read newsgroups, and play sound or video files that are embedded in Web documents. The two most popular ones are Microsoft's Internet Explorer and Netscape's Navigator.

ISP. Stands for Internet Service Provider. This is the company that provides you with Internet access, sometimes called a dial-up service. When you "log on" you connect to their server, and it connects you to the rest of the Net.

HTML. The Hypertext Markup Language is a system of text "tags" that describes the contents and appearance of Web pages. Browsers interpret HTML and display the Web pages.

URL. Think of Uniform Resource Locators as Web addresses. This is that dubya–dubya–dubya–dot thing that identifies an object, document, page, or other destination on the Internet.

Hyperlink. Hyperlinks take you directly to another page, file, object, document, Web page, or whatever it's linked to. They are "hotspots" you click on to go to a file, a location in a file, an HTML page on the World Wide Web, or an HTML page on an intranet. (Of course, you don't really "go" anywhere; the page comes to you.) In a Word document, hyperlinks appear as colored and underlined text or graphics.

Frame. Frames are used to help organize information on a Web page. Each frame in a page can display other pages. Frames can make information easier to access, and they can show the contents of a Web site made up of more than one page.

Building Web Pages in Word

Let's jump right into the good stuff: building Web pages. You can build simple Web pages in Word with a wizard or from scratch. Both approaches are easy and fairly straightforward, but if you've never build a Web page before, you can't go wrong starting with the wizard.

The Web Page Wizard

Word's Web Page Wizard walks you through the process of building, not just a single Web page (although it will let you do that), but also a multipage Web *site*. Like all Word wizards, it uses preset layouts in a variety of styles, and it lets you access Themes for a lively design blueprint. Once your generic Web page is set up, all you have to do is fill in the blanks. You learned all about working with wizards and themes in Chapter 15, so this should be a snap. (See Figure 21-1.)

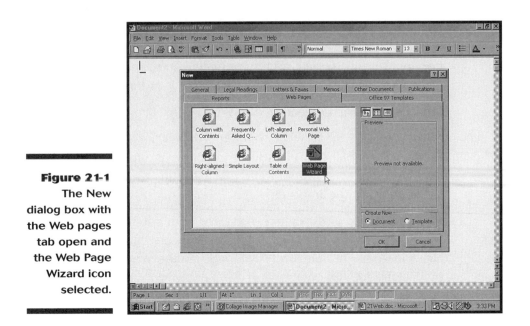

Figure 21-1
The New
dialog box with
the Web pages
tab open and
the Web Page
Wizard icon
selected.

To build a Web page using Word's Web Page Wizard:

- Go to the Menu Bar.
- Open File.
- Select New to open the New dialog box.
- Click on the Web Pages tab.
- Double-click on the Web Page Wizard icon to open the wizard.

Note: *Word bumps you into Web Layout view.*

- Click on the Next button to start the wizard.
- Click inside the "Web site title" text box and type a name for your Web site.
- Notice the "Web site location" text box.
- If this is where you want to save your Web page, click Next; if you want to save it somewhere else, click Browse to access another location.
- Click Next to continue.
- Now the wizard wants to know which type of navigation you want to use on your Web site. For this exercise, click in the "Vertical frame" radio button.

Note: *See the definition of Frames at the beginning of this chapter.*

- Click Next to continue.

- Remember, you're not just building a page here, but a whole site. By default, the wizard is setting up a three-page site, with a Personal Page (home page) and two blanks. You can add more by clicking on the "Add New Blank Page" button, but for this exercise, let's leave it at three.
- Click Next to continue.

Note: *For now, don't worry about the other options.*

- Now the wizard wants to know how you want your pages organized. You can change the order of the pages by clicking on the Move Up and Move Down buttons, but for this exercise, the default order is fine.
- Click Next to continue.
- Click on the Browse Themes button to open the Theme dialog box.
- Click on a theme in the "Choose a Theme" list box to see a preview in the displayed window. For this exercise, select the Blends theme and put a checkmark next to all the options below the list.
- Click OK to return to the Wizard dialog box.
- Click Next to continue to the final Wizard dialog box.
- Click Finish.
- **Ta-daaaaa!** Your Web page opens in your Document Window, along with the Frames toolbar.

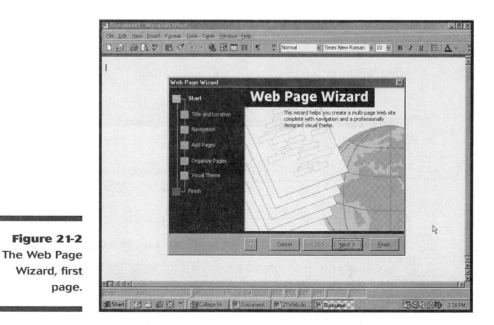

Figure 21-2
The Web Page Wizard, first page.

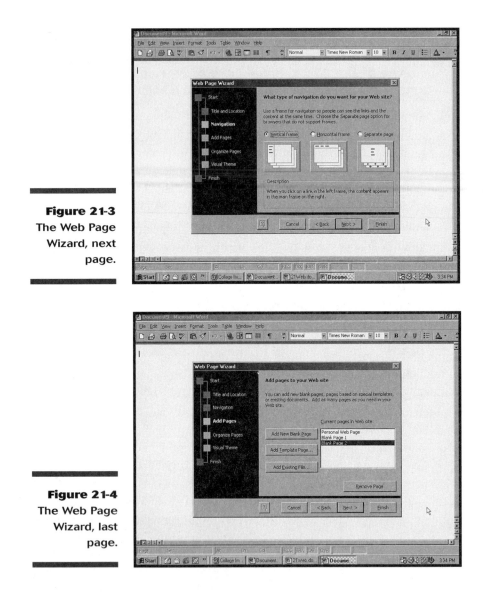

Figure 21-3
The Web Page
Wizard, next
page.

Figure 21-4
The Web Page
Wizard, last
page.

Now you've got yourself a generic Home Page, complete with a frame, extra pages, and a jazzy layout. But you still have to put something into it.

To insert text in your generic Web page:

* Select any block of "placeholder" text on the page and start typing.

* The placeholder text disappears, and your text, automatically formatted, replaces it.

* Hit Ctrl + S to save your changes. (See Figure 21-5.)

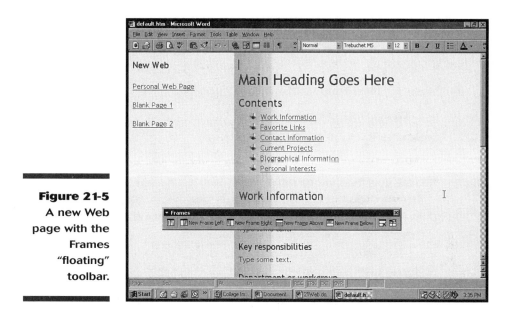

Figure 21-5
A new Web
page with the
Frames
"floating"
toolbar.

Custom Web Pages

Wizards are great, but you don't *have* to use one to build a nice Web page with Word. You can use Word's standard formatting tools to layout your page and then save it in a Web page format. (See Figure 21-6.)

Figure 21-6
The New Web
Page dialog
box.

To build a custom Web page in Word:

- Go to the Menu Bar.
- Open File.
- Select New to open the New dialog box.
- Click on the General tab.
- Double-click on the Web Page icon.
- Word opens a new, blank document and bumps you into Web Layout view.
- Now you can put together your page any way you like. Type in the text content; format the text; assign headings; add links, graphics, tables, borders, shading—everything you've learned to do to design a dynamic Word document. Insert hyperlinks as described in this chapter.
- When you've got everything set the way you want, hit F12 to open the Save As dialog box.
- Open the folder in which you plan to save the document.
- Enter a name in the "File name" text box.
- The "Save as type" text box lists the file type as a Web page.
- Click on the Change Title button to open the Set Page Title dialog box.
- Type in the title you want visitors to see in their browser Title Bars.
- Click OK to return to the Save As dialog box.
- Click Save.
- Your page can now be displayed in a Web browser, and posted on the Web.

Whether you build your new Web page using a wizard or cobble it together from scratch, you can use Microsoft's Web Publishing Wizard to post it on the Web. Many ISPs include free space on their servers for personal pages just like the one you just created, but before you try to post it, call your service provider and ask. When you're ready to post your pages, click on the Start button in the Task Bar, select Programs, Accessories, Internet Tools, Web Publishing Wizard. Run through the wizard once, noting the questions it asks, and then call your ISP to get the answers.

TIP

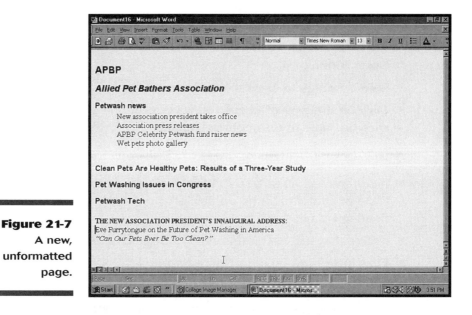

Figure 21-7
A new,
unformatted
page.

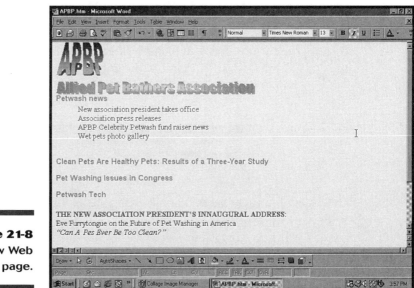

Figure 21-8
A new Web
page.

Frames

Frames are an important part of Web-page design. Because each frame in your Web document behaves like a separate page, you can layer information into the page and manage how people access your site.

To add a frame to your Web page:

- Go to the Menu Bar.
- Open Format.
- Select Frames to open the submenu.
- Click on the type of frame you want to add to your document. (For this example, click on Table of Contents in Frames.)

Note: *Click on New Frames Page to create a blank frame.*

- If you weren't already in it, Word kicks you into Web Layout view and opens a table of contents frame on the left side of the Document Window, and a floating Frames toolbar appears.
- Notice that the TOC frame has it's own scroll bar.
- Click inside the Table of Contents frame to edit the contents.
- The Frames toolbar allows you to add additional blank frames to your Web page.
- Each frame in your Web page is like a separate document. You can add text, graphics and effects, assign backgrounds, and insert hyperlinks without affecting the others. (See Figure 21-9.)

To remove a frame from your Web page click inside the frame and then click the Delete frame button on the Frames toolbar.

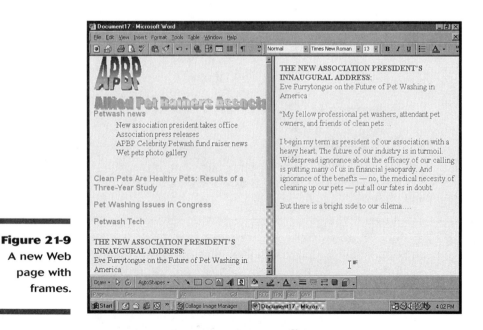

Figure 21-9
A new Web
page with
frames.

Hyperlinks

Clicking on a hyperlink is like opening a worm hole to another location, and that location can be virtually anywhere: the Web, an Excel spread sheet, a Power Point presentation, an e-mail address, and even another document right there on your hard drive. You can use hyperlinks to add an incredible amount of associative depth to a Word document, by linking it with related information sources virtually anywhere in the world.

Hyperlinks live quite comfortably on any Word 2000 document. They can be created by typing a URL into a document or by using commands in the Insert menu to turn text or objects into hyperlinks.

Hyperlinks to URLs

Inserting hyperlinks to URLs—that is, to Web page addresses—into your Word documents is easy. All you do is type them in. As soon as you hit the space bar at the end of the text, Word recognizes it as a link and reformats it as blue, underlined text. Then, whenever you hover your mouse pointer over the text, it turns into a little pointing hand.

Here are some examples of the different forms URLs can take from Word's own Help database:

http://www.someones.homepage/default.htm

ftp://ftp.server.somewhere/ftp.file

news:alt.hypertext

gopher://gopher.someones.homepage/default.htm

file:///\\server\share

file:///c:\

But you can also type **www.sitename.whatever**, and Word will recognize it as a hyperlink. (See Figure 21-10.)

Note: *Word recognizes any text you type in standard URL forms as a link, and Word will fire up your browser and dial into your ISP when you click on it, but if you got the address wrong, you won't end up where you expect.*

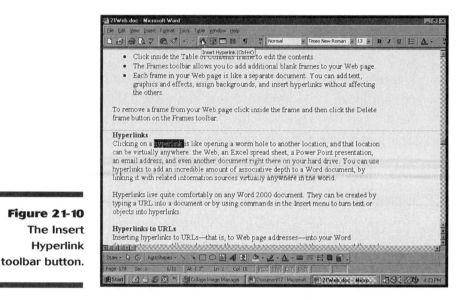

Figure 21-10

The Insert Hyperlink toolbar button.

To turn text and objects into URL hyperlinks:

- Select the text or object you want to designate as the hyperlink.
- Go to the Menu Bar.
- Open Insert.
- Select Hyperlink to open the Insert Hyperlink dialog box.

Or . . .

- Click on the Insert Hyperlink button on the Standard toolbar.
- Type the URL of the Web page you are linking to in the "Type the file or Web page name" text box.
- Click OK to close the dialog box.
- The text you selected is now blue and underlined; clicking on it takes you to the URL you entered.

Internal Hyperlinks

We think of hyperlinks primarily as Web elements, the hotspots on Web pages that shoot us instantaneously from Web site to Web site. But hyperlinks can also link you to other files on your computer—even to other locations within the same document. (See Figure 21-11.)

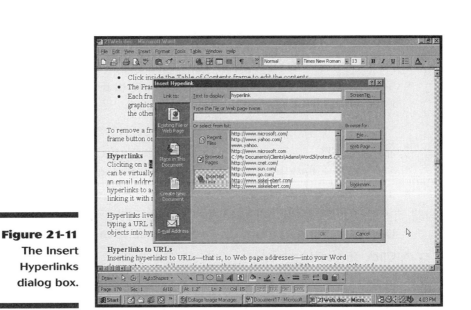

Figure 21-11
The Insert
Hyperlinks
dialog box.

Word establishes these kinds of internal hyperlinks through the use of bookmarks. A *bookmark* is a specific location or selection of text that you identify by name for future reference. Though they weren't identified as such, you used bookmarks to set your index entries in Chapter 16. (See Figure 21-12.)

To see just how easy it is to create a hyperlink, take a minute to create one from one spot in a Word document to another.

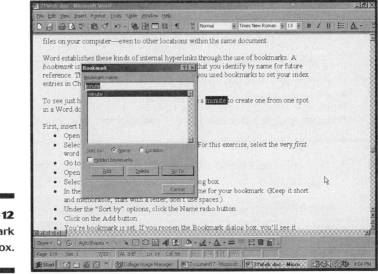

Figure 21-12
The Bookmark
dialog box.

First, insert the bookmark:

- Open an existing Word document.
- Select the text or object to be bookmarked. (For this exercise, select the very **first** word of the document.)
- Go to the Menu Bar.
- Open Insert.
- Select Bookmark to open the Bookmark dialog box.
- In the "Bookmark name" text box, type a name for your bookmark. (Keep it short and memorable; start with a letter; don't use spaces.)
- Under the "Sort by" options, click the Name radio button.
- Click on the Add button.
- You're bookmark is set. If you reopen the Bookmark dialog box, you'll see it listed.

Second, insert the hyperlink:

- Select the text or object you want to designate as the hyperlink. (For this exercise, select the very **last** word of the document.)
- Go to the Menu Bar.
- Open Insert.
- Select Hyperlink to open the Insert Hyperlink dialog box.
- In the "Link to" bar, click Existing File or Web Page.
- Click on the File button to access your file folders.
- Locate the file in which you inserted the bookmark (the file you're currently working in).
- Double-click on the file icon to return to the Insert Hyperlink dialog box.
- Notice that the file name and location now appear in the "Type the file or Web page name" box.
- Click on the Bookmark button.
- Find your bookmark in the display list and click on it.
- Click OK to exit the dialog box.
- The selected word now appears in blue and underlined, and your hyperlink is established.

Try it out: Scroll to the end of your document and click on the last word. The hyperlink will send you instantly to the beginning of the document.

You can use this method to turn any text or object in your Word documents into a hyperlink. Check out Word's Help files for more on this subject.

> Word's Web toolbar allows you to type in URLs or to click on your bookmarked favorites to launch your Web browser without ever leaving your program window.
>
> The buttons on the Web toolbar are very similar to the toolbar buttons in Internet Explorer. They let you stop a page from downloading, move backward and forward between Web pages, and even refresh a page.
>
> In order for it to work, though, you must have a Web browser installed on your computer, and you must be signed up with an Internet Service Provider, **and** your dial-up connection has to be working.
>
> **TIP**

Special Web-Page Effects

Word lets you apply all of its standard text, paragraph, and page formatting, as well as all of its graphics effects to your Web page designs. But Word also provides some Special Web-page effects. You access most of these effects through the floating Web Tools toolbar (which should not to be confused with the Web Toolbar, which primarily provides browser commands). From this toolbar you can sounds, video clips, and animation effects.

Scrolling Text

One of Word's coolest Web-page effects is scrolling text. When you add this effect to your Word-spawned Web page, it really *looks* like a Web page. (See Figure 21-13.)

To create scrolling text:

* Make certain the Web-page document to which you want to apply this effect is open.

* Set the insertion point with your cursor.

* Open the Web Tools toolbar. (Right-click on any toolbar and select it from the submenu.)

* Click on the Scrolling Text button on the toolbar to open the Scrolling Text dialog box.

* Click inside the "Type the scrolling text here" box and type in the text you want to scroll.

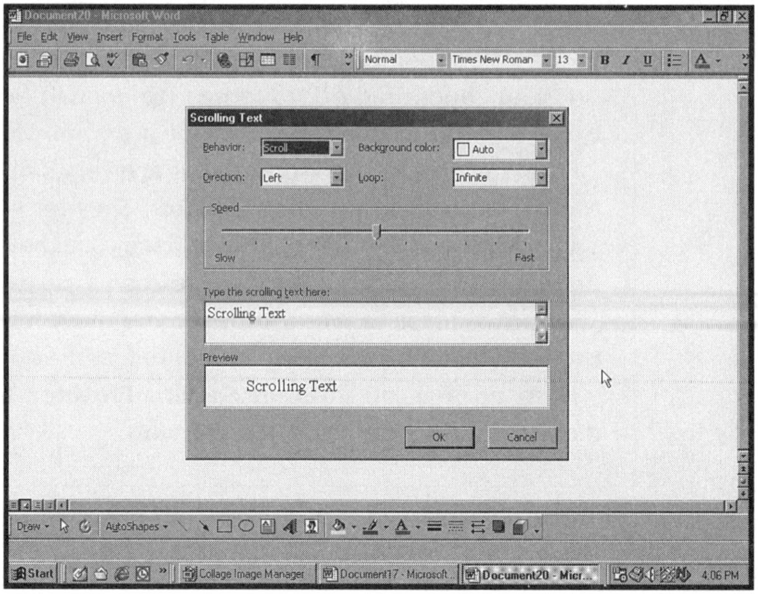

Figure 21-13
The Scrolling
Text dialog
box.

- Now you can adjust the way your text looks and behaves. Open the Behavior drop-down list and select a behavior: Scroll, Slide, or Alternate.
- Use the slider bar to set the scrolling speed.
- Open the Direction drop-down list to set the scrolling direction.
- Open the Loop drop-down list to set how often the text loops around.
- Add a color to the background from the color palette.
- All of your choices are reflected in the Preview window.
- Click OK.
- Your scrolling text appears in your document at the insertion point.

This is one of the few cool effects you can see in Normal view. But in Web Layout view, you can right click on the scrolling text to open a shortcut menu that lets you start and stop it, and reopen the dialog box.

Sounds

Word also lets you add background sounds to your Web pages. These are sounds that play automatically in the background when a Web browser opens your page, like the sounds Windows makes when it starts on your computer.

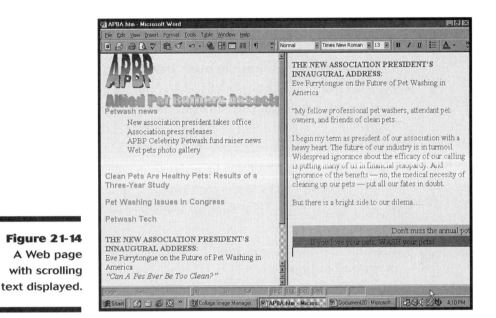

Figure 21-14
A Web page
with scrolling
text displayed.

To add a sound to your Web page:

- Open the Web Tools toolbar.
- Click on the Sounds button to open the Background Sound dialog box.
- Click on the Browse button to access the sound files that came with Word.
- Click on a sound file to return to the dialog box.
- Click on the down arrow next to the Loop drop-down list to set the number of times the sound repeats.
- Click OK.
- The sound will play each time your Web page is opened.

Video

Video clips take a long time to download, and not every visitor to your site will have the browser features they need to view them, but they sure look great on a Web page. Word lets you insert short video clips into your Web pages from the Web Tools toolbar.

To insert a video clip into your Web page:

- Open the Web Tools toolbar.

- Click on the Movie button to open the Movie Clip dialog box.

- Click on the Browse button to access your video clip files. (Word doesn't come with anything you can use here, so these have to be clips you've collected yourself.)

- Click on a file to return to the dialog box.

- Click on the Alternate Image button to provide a graphic for Web surfers whose browsers can't play video clips.

- Type in some Alternative Text for browsers with no movie or graphics capabilities available.

- Click on the down arrow next to Start to preview how the video will be prompted to play.

- Click on the down arrow next to the Loop drop-down list to set the number of times the clip repeats.

- Click OK.

- The video clip is now part of your Web site.

22

The Geek-Speak Dictionary

The word "geek" is no longer a pejorative. It's true! Neither is "nerd," "propeller-head," or "techno-weenie." The members of the pocket-protector brigade now hold the distinction of simultaneously being both counter culture icons and symbols of entrepreneurial capitalism. Where I live, in Silicon Valley, they're treated like rock stars. Ted Turner is turning their life stories into TV movies. A computer geek in Redmond, Washington, is the richest man on Earth. They even have their own cartoon character. Someday, they'll take over the world. And when they do, most of us won't understand a word they say.

Tech talk can be as incomprehensible to average humans as the clicks and squeals of dolphins, and as far as I'm concerned, it's ruining the language (which, now that I think of it, is exactly what my parents said about rock 'n' roll). Fully half of all the sentence mangling, acronym spewing, and unrestrained verbizing that goes on in the computer world is not only unnecessary, but counterproductive; the other half we should all just shut up and learn.

And what better place to learn a few new words than a Word book. Undoubtedly many of the terms listed here will be familiar to readers, and some were defined in the chapters. But just in case you don't speak geek, here's a list of all the tech terms used in this book with their English translations.

Active Document The document currently open in your program window.

Active Window In a multiple-window environment, the window that you are currently using or that is currently selected. Only one window can be active at a time, and keystrokes and commands affect the active window.

Alignment The way text lines up against the margins of a page, within the width of a *column*, or against tab stops.

Alternative text Descriptive text that appears instead of a graphic or movie on a Web page. Alternative text is used by Web browsers to display text during image downloads, for users who have graphics turned off, and for users who rely on screen-reading software to convert graphics on the screen to spoken words.

Animated GIF A file that contains a series of GIF (Graphics Interchange Format) images that are displayed in rapid sequence by some Web browsers to produce an animated effect.

AutoCorrect A *Word* feature that corrects text or changes a string of characters to a word or phrase automatically.

AutoText A formatted block of boilerplate text that you can insert wherever you need it.

Bitmap A picture made from a series of small dots that form shapes and lines. Bitmaps are created by using paint programs (for example, Microsoft Paint) or by scanning an image. Bitmaps can't be converted to drawing objects, although they can be scaled, cropped, and recolored by using the tools on the Picture toolbar.

Browser A browser is a piece of software with which you surf the Web. Browsers can speak *HTML*, the "language" with which most Web pages are built. Some browsers also let you read, send, and receive e-mail, read newsgroups, and play sound or video files that are embedded in Web documents. The two most popular ones are Microsoft's Internet Explorer and Netscape's Navigator.

Cell The intersection of a *column* and a *row* in a table; the box they make.

Click and Type A new feature in Word 2000 that lets you double-click anywhere on the document page and start typing. You can use this feature only in Print Layout or Web Layout view.

Click To hover the mouse pointer over something on your screen and press the left mouse button once.

Clip Art A pre-drawn illustration or graphics object you can insert into a Word file. Microsoft® Word comes with a collection of clip art files you can use to illustrate your documents.

Clipboard,   Clipboard toolbar A feature that's new to Word 2000, the Clipboard toolbar lets you paste multiple items in random order. The Clipboard can hold up to 12 cut or copied items.

Close Box A small box with an X in it that's located in the upper-right corner of every Windows window and many dialog boxes; click it to close the program file, dialog box, or floating toolbar.

Command An instruction that tells the computer to carry out a task or perform an action.

Comment Extra information you can insert regarding your *Word* text. A comment can be a note to yourself or someone else who will read the file. The comment remains hidden until you point to the Comment indicator symbol.

Cool Indefinable by mere words, but dude, you know it when you see it.

Cursor The flashing vertical line that shows where text is entered. Also referred to as the insertion point.

Data Source In a mail-merge procedure, the data source is the database list containing all the records you want to use with the mail-merge file.

Database A computer program that specializes in organizing, storing, and retrieving data. The term also describes a collection of data.

Dialog box The big window that opens up when you invoke a command. It's filled with the options that go with that command, which you choose by clicking on buttons and inserting checkmarks. (See, it's asking you what you want, and you're answering, so it's kind of like a dialog. Kind of.)

Docked Toolbar A toolbar that is attached to one edge of the program window. You can dock a toolbar below the program title bar or to the left, right, or bottom edge of the program window. When you drag a toolbar to the edge of the program window, the toolbar outline snaps into place along the length of the program window edge.

Document Window A rectangular portion of the screen in which you view and edit a document. A document window is typically located inside a program window.

Document A file you create with a program such as *Word*. A document can be saved with a unique file name by which it can be retrieved.

Double-click To click twice.

Download To transfer a file from the *Internet* to your computer through telephone lines and a modem.

Drag and Drop A technique for moving or copying data from one location to another. Select the item to move or copy, hold down the left mouse button, drag the item to a new location, and release the mouse button to drop it in place.

E-mail Electronic mail; a system that uses the *Internet* to send messages electronically over telephone wires instead of on paper.

Export The process of converting and saving a file to be used in another program. See also *import*.

Field In a mail-merge document, a field indicates a piece of data from a data source that contains a particular type of information, such as Last Name, Phone Number, or Quantity.

File Format When you save a file, it's saved in a format that tells the program how to display the file. To open the file in another program, you must convert the file into a format the other program can read. With Word, you can save your document files in different file formats so other users can read the files. For example, you can save a Word document as a WordPerfect file.

File A document you create and save in Word.

Floating Palette A *palette* that can be dragged away from its *toolbar*.

Floating Toolbar A toolbar that is not docked at the edges of the application window. A floating toolbar stays on top of other windows within the application window.

Font A typeface, such as Arial or Times New Roman, distinguished by a set of similarly styled characters.

Footer Text that appears at the bottom of every printed page. See also *header*.

Footprint The size in bytes of a file or program, which determines how much room it will take up on your hard disk.

Formatting Characteristics you can apply to text, paragraphs, or pages to change the way the data looks; formatting commands include bold, italic, color, fonts, and alignment.

Frame A container that you can resize and position anywhere on the page. When you move the frame to a new location, Microsoft® Word automatically makes room for the frame at the new location. When you position framed items in Page Layout view, you can see exactly how they will look on the page. Frames are used to help organize information on a Web page. Each frame in a page can display other pages. Frames can make information easier to access, and they can show the contents of a Web site made up of more than one page.

Graphics Object A picture you paste into a file or a line or shape (text box, rectangle, arc, picture) that you draw by using the tools on the Drawing toolbar.

Handles Small black squares located around the perimeter of selected *graphics objects*. By dragging the handles, you can move, copy, or size the selected object.

Header Text that appears at the top of every printed page.

Home Page The main page of a World Wide Web site. A home page is generated by a Web site owner and usually has hyperlinks to other pages, both within and outside the site. There are many different home pages on the Web, and one Web site can contain many home pages. For example, the Microsoft home page (**http://www.microsoft.com/**) also contains a Products home page, which in turn contains other home pages such as the Windows 95 home page and the Office home page.

HTML The Hypertext Markup Language is a system of text "tags" that describes the contents and appearance of Web pages. Browsers interpret HTML and display the Web pages.

Hyperlink Hyperlinks take you directly to another page, file, object, document, Web page, or whatever it's linked to. They are "hotspots" you click on to go to a file, a location in a file, an HTML page on the World Wide Web, or an HTML page on an intranet. (Of course, you don't really "go" anywhere; the page comes to you.) In a Word document, hyperlinks appear as colored and underlined text or graphics.

Icon The little pictures on the toolbar buttons and next to commands in the menus. Icons are always clickable.

Import The process of converting and opening a file that was stored or created in another program.

Insertion Point A flashing vertical line that shows the text entry point. Also referred to as the *cursor*.

Interface The stuff you see on the screen that lets you interact with your computer. The program window, the toolbars, the scrollbars, the mouse pointer, the icons, the Office Assistant: all of them together make up the computer interface.

Internet A worldwide network of computer networks. It links thousands of smaller computer networks, which in turn link millions of individuals with computers, PDAs, pagers, and even cell phones. It's the Information Superhighway, it's where the World Wide Web lives and breathes, it's where you go when you "log on." It's cyberspace.

Intranet A miniature Internet that operates within a company or organization.

Invoke To issue a command or summon a toolbar.

ISP Internet Service Provider. This is the company that provides you with Internet access, sometimes called a dial-up service. When you "log on" you connect to their server, and it connects you to the rest of the Net.

Landscape The horizontal orientation of a page; opposite of *portrait*, or vertical, orientation.

Launch Another way of saying "start," as in, launch the program.

Link Used to insert a copy of information created in Microsoft® Word or another program into another Word document while maintaining a connection between the two files. When the information changes in the source file, the changes are reflected in the destination document. You can choose to update linked information manually or automatically. When you link a Word document to another file, Word stores the link in the form of a field code.

Linked Object Information (the object) that is created in one file (the source file) and inserted into another file (the destination file) while maintaining a connection between the two files. The linked object in the destination file can be updated when the source file is updated. A linked object does not become part of the destination file.

Mail Merge The process of creating several identical *documents* (such as form letters or mailing labels) that each pull a different set of information (such as addresses) out of a *database* (also called a data source).

Master Document A "container" for a set of separate files (or subdocuments). You can use a master document to set up and manage a multipart document, such as a book with several chapters. For example, you can view, reorganize, format, proof, print, and create a table of contents for multiple documents as a whole.

Merge Fields The placeholder text in a mail-merge document, where database information is inserted in each finished, or merged, copy of the document.

Nested In Word, refers to "nested" tables, which are tables within tables.

Object A table, chart, or graphic you create and edit. An object can be inserted, pasted, or copied into any file.

Office Assistant Animated Office help system that provides interactive help, tips, and other online assistance.

Palette A box containing choices for color and other special effects that you use when working with objects and text. A palette appears when you click a *toolbar* button, such as Border or Fill Color.

Paste To insert text or graphics into a document that you've cut or copied from somewhere else in the document, or some other document.

Plug-in Additional features for Web browsers, like sound-interpreting software, that you usually find on the Web and download.

Portrait The vertical orientation of a page; opposite of landscape, or horizontal, orientation.

Preview A view that displays your document as it will appear when you print it. Items such as text and graphics appear in their actual positions.

Print Layout View A view of a document as it will appear when you print it. For example, items such as headers, footnotes, columns, and text boxes appear in their actual positions. You can edit and format text in print layout view; for example, you can drag a text box to a new position. To switch to print layout view, click Print Layout on the View menu. Or click the Print Layout View button on the horizontal scroll bar.

Read–Only Describes a document that you can open and view but cannot save any changes you make to it. If you change a read-only document, you can save your changes only if you give the document a new name.

Record A single row in a *database* or list. The first row of a database usually contains *field* names, and each additional row in the database is a record.

Right-click To click with the right mouse button. Often it invokes a shortcut menu.

ScreenTips Helpful notes that appear on your screen to explain a function or feature.

Server A computer used on the *Internet* or a network environment that stores e-mail messages, *Web* pages, and other data.

Split Bar The horizontal or vertical line dividing a split *document*. You can change the position of the split bar by dragging it, or you can remove the split bar by double-clicking it.

Style A collection of formatting settings you can apply to text.

Submenu The menus that drop down when you select some menu items. Usually, there's an arrow next to the item; when you move your mouse cursor over the arrow, the submenu drops down. But you can also invoke many submenus called "shortcut menus" by right-clicking on some screen component, like a toolbar to summon a list of toolbars.

Suite A group of software programs bundled together under one title. Microsoft Office 2000 Standard Edition is a suite comprising the programs Word, Excel, Front Page, Outlook, and Power Point. Typically, the programs in a suite compliment each other and interact well.

Table A bunch of vertical and horizontal lines arranged into a grid pattern to create cells. You put text and data in the cells. Or cool graphics.

Taskbar The horizontal bar across the bottom of the Windows desktop; it includes the Start button and buttons for any programs, documents, or items that are open.

Template Available in all Office programs, including *Word*, templates provide pre-designed patterns on which files can be based.

Text Wrapping When you insert a picture into a bunch of text, you can use a word-wrapping option to get the text to hug the picture close along its outer edges.

Toolbar A row of shortcut buttons, usually docked at the top of Word's Document Window, but occasionally "floating" over the document itself. Clicking on the buttons in a toolbar executes a command. For example, clicking on the Bold button in the Formatting Toolbar changes the selected text to bold.

URL Think of Uniform Resource Locators as Web addresses. This is that dubya–dubya–dubya–dot thing that identifies an object, document, page, or other destination on the Internet.

Views The onscreen layout of the document. Word 2000 comes with several view modes, including Normal, Web Layout, Outline, Print Layout, Print Preview, Document Map, and Master Document.

Windows Clipboard A temporary holding area in computer memory that stores information that was cut or copied (such as text or graphics). You transfer data from the Clipboard by using the Paste *command*.

World Wide Web The Web is an aspect of the Internet, a system characterized by colorful and often animated "pages" that live on "servers" (high-powered computers), which are connected to other pages through *hyperlinks*. You navigate the Web with a Web *browser*, with which you "surf" from page to page. Web "sites" are collections of Web pages. In recent years, the Web has become a multi-media maelstrom of text, pictures, sounds, and digital movies.

Index

We Have EVERYTHING

More bestselling Everything titles available from your local bookseller:

Everything **After College Book**
Everything **Astrology Book**
Everything **Baby Names Book**
Everything **Baby Shower Book**
Everything **Barbeque Cookbook**
Everything® **Bartender's Book**
Everything **Bedtime Story Book**
Everything **Beer Book**
Everything **Bicycle Book**
Everything **Bird Book**
Everything **Build Your Own**
       Home Page Book
Everything **Casino Gambling Book**
Everything **Cat Book**
Everything® **Christmas Book**
Everything **College Survival Book**
Everything **Cover Letter Book**
Everything **Crossword and Puzzle Book**
Everything **Dating Book**
Everything **Dessert Book**
Everything **Dog Book**
Everything **Dreams Book**
Everything **Etiquette Book**
Everything **Family Tree Book**

Everything **Fly-Fishing Book**
Everything **Games Book**
Everything **Get-a-Job Book**
Everything **Get Published Book**
Everything **Get Ready For Baby Book**
Everything **Golf Book**
Everything **Guide to New York City**
Everything **Guide to Walt Disney World®,**
       Universal Studios®, and
       Greater Orlando
Everything **Guide to Washington D.C.**
Everything **Herbal Remedies Book**
Everything **Homeselling Book**
Everything **Homebuying Book**
Everything **Home Improvement Book**
Everything **Internet Book**
Everything **Investing Book**
Everything **Jewish Wedding Book**
Everything **Kids' Money Book**
Everything **Kids' Nature Book**
Everything **Kids' Puzzle Book**
Everything **Low-Fat High-Flavor**
       Cookbook
Everything **Microsoft® Word 2000 Book**

Everything **Money Book**
Everything **One-Pot Cookbook**
Everything **Online Business Book**
Everything **Online Investing Book**
Everything **Online Shopping Book**
Everything **Pasta Book**
Everything **Pregnancy Book**
Everything **Pregnancy Organizer**
Everything **Resume Book**
Everything **Sailing Book**
Everything **Selling Book**
Everything **Study Book**
Everything **Tarot Book**
Everything **Toasts Book**
Everything **Total Fitness Book**
Everything **Trivia Book**
Everything **Tropical Fish Book**
Everything® **Wedding Book, 2nd Edition**
Everything® **Wedding Checklist**
Everything® **Wedding Etiquette Book**
Everything® **Wedding Organizer**
Everything® **Wedding Shower Book**
Everything® **Wedding Vows Book**
Everything **Wine Book**